Clavering at War

An Essex Village 1939-1945

Jacqueline Cooper

DEDICATED TO THE MEN & WOMEN OF CLAVERING WHO SERVED IN THE SECOND WORLD WAR, IN MILITARY AND CIVIL WARTIME WORK, AND PARTICULARLY THOSE WHO GAVE THEIR LIVES.

By the same author
Country Walks in Clavering (1987, out of print)
Discover Clavering: Walks in the District (1991, out of print)
Discover Walden: Saffron Walden Countryside History & Wildlife Walks (1996, out of print)
The Well-ordered Town: a story of Saffron Walden 1792-1862 (2000, available from author)
History Walks in Clavering: a journey in time through an Essex village (2003, available from author)
Bishop's Stortford: a History (Phillimore, 2005)
Hertford: a History (Phillimore, 2007)

Edited by the author
Saffron Walden Historical Journal (Saffron Walden Historical Society, 2001-12 ongoing)
Breaking New Ground: 19th century Allotments from local sources (Pub. FACHRS, Co-ed. with J. Burchardt, 2009)
Land, Agriculture & Industry: spotlights on a land remembered by Geoffrey Ball (SWHS Publications, 2009)
Clavering Remembered Series – various authors (Clavering History Group, 2010-2012 ongoing)
The Place Names of Saffron Walden by Malcolm White (SWHS Publications, 2011)
Discover Uttlesford: circular walks along the Uttlesford Way in Essex by Peter Cooper (2011, available from author)

Clavering at War © Jacqueline Cooper 2012

Designed & Published by Jacqueline Cooper
24 Pelham Road, Clavering, Saffron Walden, Essex CB11 4PQ, England

ISBN 978-1-873669-07-5

COVER IMAGE CREDITS

FRONT COVER: Empire Day Parade June 1944 at Bury Meadow. *Photograph by courtesy of John Barwood*
TITLE PAGE: Troops on The Bridges during WW2. *Photograph by courtesy of Ann Banks*
BACK COVER: Welcome Home Card designed by Allen Mold. *Image from Clavering Local History Collection*

Contents

Acknowledgements, Sources, Illustrations
Introduction
Clavering Map

**NOTE: The titles of the chapters are taken from the letters to his parishioners by Rev. Ernest Stone, Vicar of
Clavering, in the wartime church magazine.**

ACKNOWLEDGEMENTS

I owe a huge debt to a great many people who have helped with research for this book, particularly to Joy Barrow and Jane Laing for their work on the Clavering Oral History Project, to Dick Law for identifying photographs, to Gordon Ridgewell for design help on the book cover – and of course to the late Eileen Ludgate, local historian of Clavering. Others whose memories, archives, images, information or transcriptions are much appreciated include: Des, Eggie & Stuart Abrahams, Simon Baddeley and his mother Barbara, Marian Balaam, Ann Banks, Michael Barton, John Barwood, Colin Bazley, Gillian Blomley, John & Margaret Bowles, Judith Bridger, Sheila Cairns, Nancy Caton, Richard Carter, Patrick Casey, Len Clark, Lillian Clarke, Elsie Darlow, Fred Davies, Ethelwyn Dennison, Jill Duff, Martyn Everett, Ken Gill, Kate Good, Barbara Green, Martin Gruselle, Tina Hancock, June Holland, Gillian Holman, Rod Homer, Brenda Kegel, Molly Law, Sid & Audrey Law, Jack Livings, Ann Monk, David Monk, Connie Mowbray, Bill Newland, Roger Petchey, Angela Phillips, Robert Pike, Mike Preisig, Cynthia Priest, Geoffrey Rice, John Richards, Douglas Savill, Janice Sharpe, Malcolm Smither, Eileen Summers, Philippa Thurlow, Joan Trower, Peter Upson, Hamish Walker, Joan White, Fred Whyman & son Gerald, Barry Wilson, Jean Wilson, Jenny Wyatt, Jill Young; and the late Evelyn Aberneithie, George Barker, Isobel Beckwith, Jean Rous, Fred Sampford, Alf Smither and Harold Walford. Many others have been generous in sharing material, and I apologise for any omissions from this list. *Every effort has been made to check and verify the text but further additions can be notified to the author as Local History Recorder for the Clavering Local History Collection. Please write to 24 Pelham Road, Clavering, Essex CB11 4PQ or email jacqueline.cooper@virgin.net See the history pages on the village website www.claveringonline.org.uk for future updates.*

SOURCES OF INFORMATION

Church Magazine of Clavering with Langley, Essex 1937-46; *Clavering Remembered* Vols 1-6 (Clavering Landscape History Group); Clavering Parish Council Minutes 1939-45; ARP Incident Files 1940-44 (ERO C/W 1//2/61-62); Clavering School archives: Logbook 1922-49 (ERO E/ML 253/2); Managers' Minutes 1941-53 (ERO E/MM 276/1); School Registers 1939-45; Saffron Walden District Advisory Committee for Agriculture: Minutes 1941-44 (SWTL); *Herts & Essex Observer* and *Saffron Walden Weekly News* 1938-46; A. Calder, *The People's War: Britain 1939-45* (1969); Dorling Kingsley, *Chronicle of the 20th Century* (1995); E.M. Ludgate, *Clavering & Langley 1783-1983* (1983); D. E. Johnson, *East Anglia at War 1939-45* (1992); J. Cooper, *History Walks in Clavering* (2003); J.A. Garrard & N. Wade, *1824 (Saffron Walden) Squadron Air Training Corps 1941 to 1998*; M. Barton, *Newport News* Summer 2007; *Saffron Walden Historical Journal* Autumn 2011; W. Ramsey (Ed.), *The Blitz Then and Now* (1988); The War Resisters' International, *Down on the Farm: The Lansbury Gate Farm* (1942). Also the Australian War Memorial Archive for the scans of the Hooper Diary. Various websites including: www.cwgc.org; www.bbc.co.uk/ww2peopleswar; WW2talk.com; www.wikipedia.org

ILLUSTRATIONS

Images are from the Clavering Local History Collection apart from those on pages as below, with grateful acknowledgement to the following: Des Abrahams 42, 49, 60, 71, 125, 136, 137, 168; Stuart Abrahams 128, 137; Simon Baddeley 44, 45, 149; Ann Banks 43, 54, 69, 103, 138, 139; George Barker 36, 127, 140; John Barwood 68, 76 ,134; Clavering School 143; Michael Barton 32; Colin Bazley 47; Margaret Bowles 59, 86, 87, 89, 142, 146, 162; Judy Bridger 2, 29, 119, 133, 173; Richard Carter 63, 66, 145; Nancy Caton 54, 98; Lillian Clarke 147; Richard Davidson 10; Ann English 74; Fred Davies 24, 30, 31, 75, 81, 105, 114, 178; Ethelwyn Dennison 23; Martyn Everett 94, 95, 98, 118; June Holland 18, 19, 28, 145; Brenda Kegel 21; Elsie Kemp 51; Dick Law 6, 43, 71, 101, 122, 123; Molly Law 123, 145; Sid Law 123, 157 ; Jack Livings 23, 165, 167; Ann Monk 100, 127, 145; David Monk 157; Bill Newland 144; Robert Pike 63, 144, 155; Mike Preisig 33, 65; Joan Ringmore 47; Fred Sampford 4, 17, 34, 43, 54, 61, 111, 117, 121, 134, 147. 154, 158; Malcolm Smither 109; Eileen Summers 19, 115; Philippa Thurlow 127, 129, 145, 153; Joan Trower 21, 58, 85, 121, 123; Peter Upson 58, 135; Harold Walford 78; Joan White 79; Fred Whyman 8, 41, 108; Jean Wilson 11, 37, 77, 87, 103; Betty Woodall 96, 114. Also by courtesy of Saffron Walden Museum images on pp 27, 31, 81; and of the Trustees of Saffron Walden Town Library images on pp 6, 9, 15, 67, 97.

Introduction

Like most of the 'baby-boom' generation I have, thankfully, no direct experience of wartime, but my family were much affected by the Second World War. An uncle perished at Tobruk, with no known grave, just a name on the El Alamein Memorial; another uncle was 'never the same' after Dunkirk; an aunt married a member of the Free Polish Forces who had escaped from war-torn Europe. After their road was bombed, my parents escaped the Blitz to the relative safety of outer North London. My father was not allowed to join the Navy, because his metalworking skills were too useful to the war, which he spent building Halifax bombers for Handley Page at Cricklewood. Here he worked 12-hour shifts by day or night, sometimes seven days in a row, commuting amid the blackout and bombs, and working in factories targeted by air raids. Having been made homeless by the Blitz, his family qualified for one of the prefabs erected in great numbers post-war. It was here in Muswell Hill that I was born, into a world made safe by others, whose lives had been turned upside down by it all. It was my generation which benefited the most from the post-war movement for reform in education and social services, in the explosion of leisure and the digital revolution. It remains important not to forget the sacrifices which that generation made, and which prevented this country from becoming a Nazi dictatorship. As one of those who helped me with this book put it: 'I've been so fortunate to be waging peace, never exposed to the horrors and dangers my parents and grandparents faced in their lives. It is so easy to take this difference between generations for granted, to be unaware of having lived almost 70 years of peace.'

It seems that innumerable books, articles, TV programmes and films have come and gone, exploring the seemingly endless topics of wartime history. But every community played its part, and each has a story that should be told. This book, rather belatedly, aims to gather together the evidence which remains of what happened to the people of my village, Clavering, NW Essex during the Second World War. Little attempt has been made to filter the material through a more critical modern perspective, but to try to look at events as they seemed at the time by quoting the words of those who lived through it all. The book is broadly chronological and is structured as a series of features, with continuity through edited extracts from the Vicar's letters published in the parish magazine from 1938 to 1946. This was a very small publication compared to today, reducing over time to just four pages on thin wartime paper, but the progress of the war can be followed here. The wartime vicar, Rev. Ernest Stone, who came to Clavering as his first living in 1937 and stayed until 1946, emerges as a remarkable man and his wife Doris the ideal vicar's wife, shouldering many extra jobs for the war effort. His writings were always pertinent, well-written, principled and often Churchillian in tone - although some of his views belong in their time, much of what he wrote still strikes a chord. The Church then was not afraid to stand up and be counted and played an important role in society both locally and nationally. Again and again, the Vicar returned to the same theme – that it was not enough to win a war against an evil enemy, the war must also be won in the hearts and minds of the people, with a desire for change to set their lives back on a Christian path. Importantly for the historian, he related the Home Front to the wider world, and this enables us to follow almost month by month how the war was impacting on Clavering. In later life, Rev. Stone generously donated his collection of parish magazines to the Clavering Local History Collection. This central source has been expanded with documents, local newspapers, photographs and reminiscences. Few people here remember wartime Clavering, so cross-checking is difficult, but I have tried to relate memories to actual events. No doubt much information still awaits discovery, but I hope that this book, a record of a very important period in Clavering's history, may offer a tribute to the wartime generation of villagers who went through those extraordinary times, and afterwards helped to build a new world so that future generations could have the opportunity to live more creatively free from the deep anxieties of total war.

Jacqueline Cooper, Clavering, August 2012

KEY TO MAP

1 Arkesden Road - Wood Hall, Peacock butchers
2 Bridges - Blacksmiths Corner, Druce, Wayletts
3 Butts Green
4 Church End - Lower School, Old House, Church
5 Cock Lane - Dam meadows
6 Deers Green - Grange Farm, Marshalls Well, Watery Stones
7 Ford End
8 Further Ford End - Lansbury Gate Farm
9 High Street - Brooklands, Fairbanks/ Taylors shop, Fox & Hounds, The Swan
10 Hill Green - Chesham cottage, Chipperfield House, Horse Pond, Princess of Wales, Village Hall, Hill Green Farm
11 Langley roads: a.Lower Road – Brocking, Chequers; b. Upper Road - Thurrocks, Valance
12 Middle Street - Danceys, Lower Way, Bury Meadow
13 Mill End - Dairy Farm, Mills, Black Lodge, Catons Store
14 Moat Farm
15 Pelham Road - Piercewebbs, Baileys/Kells shop, Curles, Parsonage Farm, Upper School, Vicarage
16 Rickling Road
17 Roast Green - Waggon & Horses, R.Gn. Farm
18 Sheepcote Green - Sheepcote Gn. Farm
19 Starlings Green - Honey Lane, White Horse pub
20 Stickling Green - Clavering Court, Court Cottage, Place Farm
21 Stortford Road - Chapel Cottage, Appletree Cottage, Clavering Hall, Congregational, Danson, Searchlight Camp, War Memorial
22 Wicken Road - Blackbird Cottage, Stevens Farm

MAP OF CLAVERING SHOWING PRINCIPAL PLACES IN TEXT

LANGLEY

ARKESDEN

WICKEN BONHUNT

BERDEN

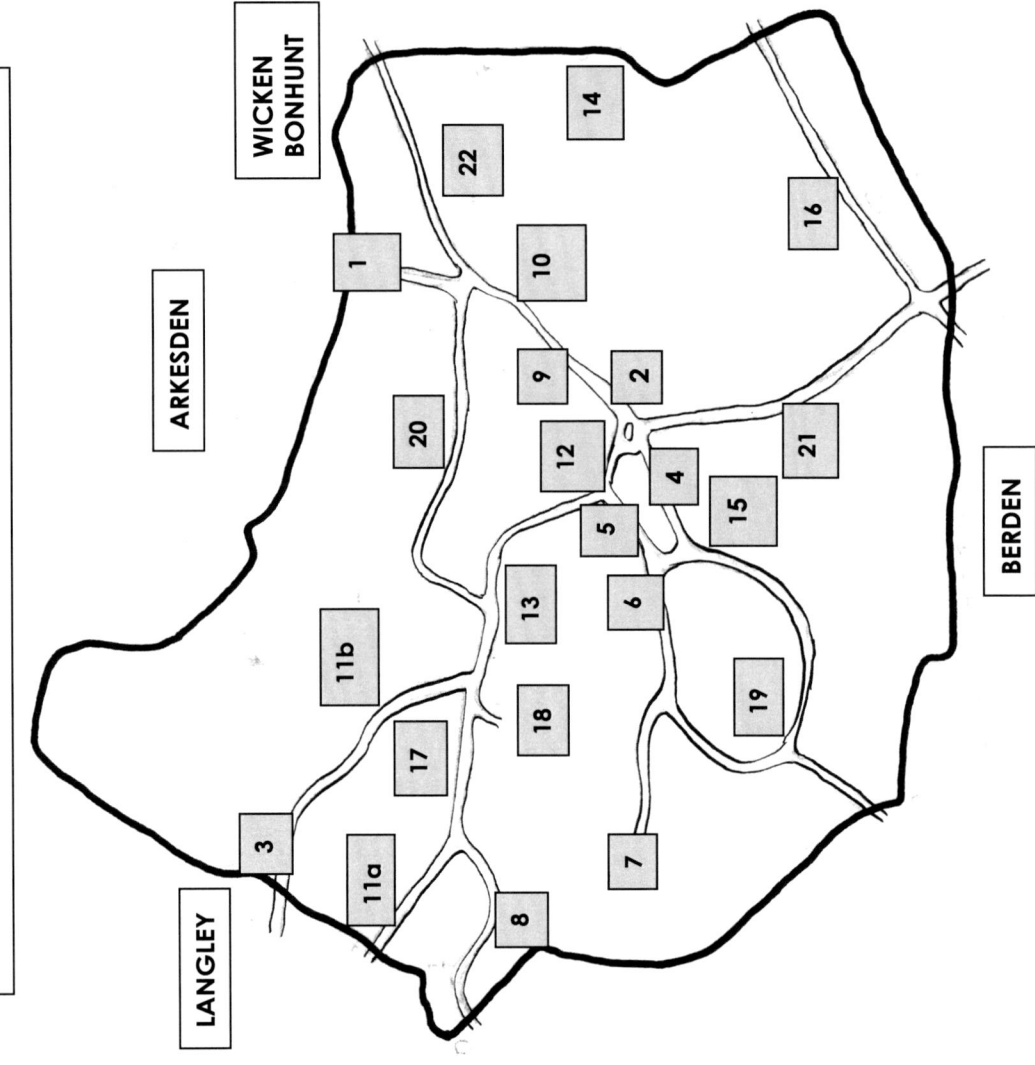

Chapter One
'The nations steadily arming'

Honey Lane at Starlings Green in earlier times.

While the build-up to war was going on in 1930s Europe, villages in England like Clavering still existed in something of a time warp, an agricultural world that was about to change forever. The population in 1931 had been its lowest ever - only 764 with just 222 households, so the village was only about half the size it is today. Most people still worked on the land – the wages were low and the hours long, typically from 6 a.m. to 5 pm or later at harvest time. Land was cheap and there were no combines and only a few tractors, so much of the work was still done by horse-power and manual labour. Children helped on the farm and with gleaning and spent much time doing errands for their parents, when not at school. Clavering had a school split between two buildings, one in the churchyard, the other in Pelham Road. Most children learned their three R's successfully, although discipline was quite harsh for those who stepped out of line. When they left school girls often went into service and boys on the land but they would supplement with road work and anything they could get. For leisure there were activities at the three churches - Sunday school, Band of Hope, choir, bellringers; whist drives and other meetings at the Church End clubroom or churchyard school; billiards, darts, dominoes and shove ha'penny at the pubs. Church or chapel going was more common though far from universal, but Sundays were quiet days. There were only a few cars in the village, but bikes were popular and Wilson's Bus would take you to the cinema or market. Clavering was quite self-sufficient with grocer, butcher, baker, post office, sweetshop, newsagent, wheelwright, blacksmith, saddler, cobbler, builder and undertaker, coal merchant and had its own District Nurse and village policeman. There were five pubs – the *Fox, Princess of Wales, Waggon & Horses, White Horse* and *The Swan* – in the latter the visiting doctor held a surgery and dispensed medicine. Life was no rural idyll as most people were poor, living in humble cottages with few amenities, yet they managed. People grew vegetables, kept chickens and shot rabbits to eke out food supplies. Water came from pumps or wells, milk from local farms and it was largely a case of make do and mend. The Slate Club encouraged a little temporary saving. The occasional suicide, court case or scandal suggests underlying tensions could break through at times, and there were a few troublesome youths. There was no lord of the manor, but a few of the larger houses were owned by people who helped out the community in various ways. There were occasional red-letter days – the Coronation of 1937, and the opening of the village hall that year, visits of the fair and circus. People who were here at that time, feel that the biggest change from then to now is that everyone knew everyone, you saw people all the time, there was no class feeling and it was a very close community. The war disrupted this old village community, irrevocably.

Rev Ernest and Doris Stone 1937

NEW VICAR OF CLAVERING 9/7/1937

Rev. E. A. Stone of Walden Appointed

On the recommendation of the Bishop of Chelmsford, the governors of Christ's Hospital, at their meeting on Wednesday, appointed Rev. E. A. Stone, A.K.C., curate of Saffron Walden, to the benefice of Clavering with Langley, vacant by the death of Rev. C. H. Malden.

An Essex man, born at Leytonstone, Mr. Stone has spent all his life in the county and has been curate at Saffron Walden since 1934. In addition to work at the Parish Church he has held the position of curate-in-charge at Sewards End.

Very interested in religious education, Mr. Stone was in 1935 appointed a Diocesan Inspector, and in that capacity visits a number of schools in the neighbourhood.

At the request of the local Education Sub-Committee, he also visits the Council Schools in the district.

Mr. Stone will take up his new duties in September.

Clavering and Langley were very fortunate to have Rev Ernest and Mrs Doris Stone at the helm during a critical time. As well as being Vicar of two parishes, and a schools inspector, he was very hands-on in the life of the village. Having been a curate for three years at Saffron Walden, he came to Clavering at the age of 28 in 1937 soon after his marriage to Doris Rogers. As war threatened in 1938, he took on initial responsibility for getting ARP going, and also the major task of Billeting Officer for evacuees. In addition, he was a salvage warden, assistant food organiser on the Invasion Committee, ran book recovery schemes, sorted out milk permits for small children, acted as treasurer to the Nursing Association and was a school manager. On the village hall committee, he was chairman one year and president another year. It was Mr Stone who inspired the creation of one of the first youth centres in Essex, and helped to run it. He served for a time on both district and parish councils. At the end of the war he was treasurer for the Victory celebrations. Every month he wrote most of the parish magazine, and throughout the war maintained a list of villagers serving with the King's Forces, writing a letter to every one of them at Christmas, even when away from the parish for long periods on chaplaincy duties. His wife Doris was also a great asset to Clavering. Formerly head of a large infants school, she met Ernest who was a teacher but training for the ministry. He became Curate at Saffron Walden Church but clergymen had to do three years' service before marriage. They finally married in 1937 and came to Clavering, where Mrs Stone also took on community and wartime tasks - billeting, savings, salvage, the Nursing Association, village hall, Youth Centre, Sunday School.

She was a wizard at needlework and made many items for the church. She would turn her hand to anything - fixing up a wartime cookery demo, organising a jam-making drive, sending magazines off to the troops in Burma. When the new Land Army hostel was about to open in Langley minus a warden, Mrs Stone agreed to go off with little daughter Judith and their home-help to run it for a few weeks until a warden was appointed, and she remained a sort of mother to the young women there. When the vicar wanted to start a Girl Guide troop, his wife took that on too. When he went away to become a Forces Chaplain, Mrs Stone shouldered even more. They had two daughters, Judith born in 1938, and Clare in 1946, shortly before leaving for another parish in Sussex after nine very full years here.

Signs of War 1938

The war news in 1938 was mostly grim, as Hitler annexed Austria in spring, then headed for Czechoslovakia, which was abandoned to its fate when, at Munich on 30 September, Prime Minister Neville Chamberlain agreed on appeasement with Hitler. The persecution of Jews was increasing in many countries. At home, the country was gearing up for war with gas drills, rationing schemes, air raid precautions well in hand. Planes, battleships and weapons were being produced in vast numbers, shelters constructed, trenches dug, barrage balloons flown, evacuation planned. The famous piece of paper and the fateful words, *'peace in our time'* were widely publicised, but nevertheless people started hoarding food and fixing hasty marriages. In Essex, the new airfield at Debden had been constructed, and men were already signing up. The changing mood was reflected in the Vicar's letters to his parishioners over the course of the year, starting with his January message.

> My dear Friends,
>   "A Happy New Year!" So we are wishing each other just now : but many of us are wondering as we give this time-honoured greeting whether the propects for 1938 are really happy. The signs of the time are bound to create anxiety in the minds of all thoughtful men. We see the nations steadily arming, watching one another across the frontiers with angry fear and suspicion : we watch the wars being raged in different parts of the world ; and everywhere there seems to be profound anxiety and bewilderment. Our

In March 1938 Hitler took over Austria, greeted by enthusiastic crowds and immediately began persecuting Austrian Jews – this was also happening in Italy. The tension was too much to bear, as the Vicar wrote in April:

'We are living in a world full of problems and very few of us are finding life easy. With trembling hands we open our daily newspaper only to learn of the latest outburst of savage violence committed in some part of the world that we thought was civilised. We listen to the broadcast news half expecting to hear that the nations of Europe are once again engaged in the cruelties of war.'

Then came the threat to Czechoslovakia, and the writing was on the wall - Britain was re-arming on a massive scale, doubling anti- aircraft forces, building battleships and ordering a thousand Spitfires. The Vicar reflected everyone's feelings in his October letter:

'As I write these words we seem to be at the very height of the European crisis and probably by the time you read them they will be out of date and our worse expectations may have been fulfilled... It does seem an intolerable absurdity that despite all our progress, happiness, peace and prosperity are so difficult for the nations to obtain and that once again we seem to be faced with misery, ruin and despair. There is no nation in all the world that wants war and probably every civilised nation dreads the very thought of it; but yet it is possible for a state of affairs to arise which may compel us to fly at one another's throats in a war which will wreck the world.'

In response to the Munich agreement of 30th September 1938, the Vicar expressed great relief but underlined with caution, in his November letter.

'What a contrast between these last few days of October and the corresponding days of September. What a weight of anxiety and care has been lifted from us; what a sense of thankfulness and relief we are able to experience now that the tension has been relaxed. One hardly had time to think clearly amid all the emergency regulations and plans that came to us so rapidly in those days of crisis, but yet throughout it all, the people of Clavering and Langley showed such a calmness and readiness to co-operate in the plans that had been made, that the task of those entrusted with the carrying out these instructions was made much easier... There is indeed reason to fear that Herr Hitler will soon be asking for more. Greater sacrifices will be asked of us in the future than we have made in the past... We must be ready to learn something of the measures that are being taken in the village in which we live, to ensure our safety in an Air Raid. It may be a real sacrifice for some to leave their own fireside on a cold evening, in order to attend a First-Aid Class or a Gas Lecture, but the Christian must be prepared to make the necessary sacrifice – it must be part of our thanksgiving for the preservation of peace...'

In Berlin on 9th November came the appalling '*Kristallnacht*', and the Vicar echoed everyone's feelings: 'We have all been horrified by the ferocious outburst of hate which has been shown in the shameful and brutal treatment of the Jews in central Europe'.

Meanwhile, day-to-day village life must go on against this background of rising anxiety. Christmas 1938 was a snowy one, as shown in this photo of *The Swan* pub with icicles hanging from the roof. On a sunnier day earlier in the year the pub darts team is pictured opposite the pub with their darts board, among them the Swan landlord (the man with a moustache), Bernard Law (with cigarette), his three-year-old son Hugh and kneeling next to him Hugh's uncle Hubert who joined up later.

Soon there would be so many able-bodied men and women engaged in war work or service of one sort or another, that it would be hard to find enough people to keep such village clubs going. But for now the normal gentle pace of village life continued.

Air Raid Wardens 1938

War was anticipated long before war came, and serious preparations were taking place, particularly over air raid precautions. This 'most important matter' was discussed in Clavering as

Air Raid Warning System
Now in Full Operation

early as April 1938 at the Annual Parish Meeting, and a committee set up to collect the names of volunteers: 'Very soon a meeting will be held at which we shall learn more about these precautionary measures but in the meantime Please Fill up a Form'. Clavering's size meant that it was supposed to have 86 wardens, which was quite a lot to find among the depleted number of able-bodied men left in the village, particularly as it was time-consuming voluntary work, requiring attendance at training classes. Both sexes could apply, and by September 1938 women's ARP classes were taking place on Wednesday evenings while male wardens met on Friday evenings.

As the shortage of volunteers continued into the autumn, the Vicar underlined the importance of ARP work, saying that every man aged 50 to 70 should 'consider very seriously his responsibility to the community and whether he ought not to enrol as a volunteer and undertake a course of training. So many men have said to me, "Of course if there is a war I shall do my bit but I don't see why I should do anything now". But in ARP work, as in many another job, the untrained man is more of a hindrance than a help.' In his usual outspoken manner, the Vicar went on: 'Other people have declined to volunteer because they say they are pacifist. I am always one to respect honest opinion even though I may violently disagree, but I feel compelled to say that anyone who opposed the plans that have been made to prepare us to counteract some of the horrors of an air raid, are terribly misguided. There are clearly a great many precautions which can be taken to mitigate greatly the horror and danger of such raids and it is an undoubted duty for people to volunteer for this important work.' Those who took on this completely voluntary role needed to be resilient, however – on them fell the task of harassing their neighbours about air raid warnings, gas masks and the unpopular blackout.

Babies' Gas Helmets
Many Thousands Being Issued

The Black-Out

Light Warning to Shopkeepers

Chapter Two
1939: *'So war has come to us'*

SOME THINGS YOU SHOULD KNOW IF WAR SHOULD COME

Public Information Leaflet No 1 July 1939

The fateful year 1939 opened with 'the international situation still very grim', as the Vicar put it. As the year unfolded, unbelievable things were happening – increasingly cruel persecution of Jews, Hitler gobbling up new territories, the map of Europe being redrawn, culminating in the unacceptable invasion of Poland, which finally precipitated war. At home the preparations had been going on apace – men and troops and equipment multiplying rapidly and all the horrible apparatus of war coming into being - air raid shelters, gas masks, identity cards, information leaflets, increased income tax, evacuation schemes, rationing, blackout materials, expansion of arable farming and the moving of treasures to safe places. In August, shortly before war was declared, the Emergency Powers (Defence) Bill became law giving the government unprecedented powers over everyone's lives. Then everything burst in September and war on Germany was declared. Nothing much seemed to happen at first, apart from a vast movement of evacuees, many of whom came to Essex. In the parish magazine, at the very moment when war was being declared, Rev Ernest Stone, while discussing local arrangements for dealing with 'the crisis', was also writing about the harvest and harking back to an earlier time and forward to agriculture in the future. Thus, even while the world was dissolving into chaos, he was able to remind his flock of the continuity of the rural world in which they and their ancestors had lived, and to draw an image of Clavering at harvest time, a picture of the England they would be fighting for.

Brooklands farmyard in earlier times.

When the blackout descended, many people enjoyed the improved view of the stars: 'The stars confront us with the great immensities. They turn our minds to vaster issues than our world affairs', wrote Mr Stone - as ever seamlessly linking the war, the village and the church into higher things. The Vicar also noted larger congregations than usual, as people sought the peace and reassurance of God in this troubled time. But, as the months went by, his letters in the parish magazine reflect the growing sense of anxiety everyone felt.

February 1939

My dear Friends,

The Government book on National Service is now in our hands and the census of accommodation available for evacuated children is being taken. No one can deny that the international situation is still very grim, and without being an alarmist, I am sure we must increase the efforts we are making for precautionary measures against war... As the responsible person for ARP in Clavering, I shall be pleased to help anyone who may wish to volunteer for this service to fill up their form. With regard to evacuation, certain new regulations have been dawn up since the last crisis which should overcome many of the difficulties in connection with evacuation which arose then...

The Druce in earlier times.

May 1939

I never remember the country looking more beautiful than it did this Eastertide. It was difficult to believe as we spent our holiday bathed in sunshine, as we looked at the splendour of the spring flowers in or gardens, that men were plotting to kill and maim and destroy... In quietness and confidence, in a world full of abuse and threats, the Church of God has kept her gaze steadfastly on the things that are eternal. Throughout the land it has been encouraging to read of large congregations at the Easter Services and a great help to recovering our sense of proportion. In our own parish it was good to see such a large gathering... largest number of Easter Communicants for many years...

Yours most sincerely, E.A. STONE

Condemned cottages 1939

Against a background of the developing war scene in Europe, a little local war was going on in the villages of the Saffron Walden Rural District against the government edict condemning many run-down cottages to demolition. Throughout the district this meant the destruction of 90 houses, although 279 new ones would be built. Houses were condemned, even when the occupants were happy to live in them. In January 1939, the local newspaper reported on this Clavering cottage where the owner wanted to stay (pictured much later when it was in process of demolition). This was 'Cocky' Chesham's house at Hill Green: 'One case in Clavering has quite justifiably aroused a good deal of sympathy for the owner – Mr H. Chesham. Both he and his wife are 70 years of age, and their two small thatched cottages represent their life savings. Mr Chesham has said repeatedly that a council house is not only too large for him, but of no use for an elderly couple, such as they are. Councillors and officials have openly expressed sympathy in Mr Chesham's case, but red tape decrees that the cottages are to be pulled down.' Interviewed by the newspaper, Mr and Mrs Chesham commented, 'I can't understand why they want to disturb us at our time of life. Can't we have our last few years in peace together? They turn us out of our own homes. And it is a worse crime than the Germans turning the Jews out of their own country... my wife and I have no complaint to find with our cottage: we could spend our few days here quite happily.' There were many other such cases throughout the district and appeal was being made to MPs to intervene. Stanley Wilson from Saffron Walden took up their case, saying the cottages could easily be reconditioned, commenting, 'As so many grants of public money have been given to help millionaires, peers and other rich folk, I would like similar grants to go to these deserving people to save their homes'. Another one threatened was a cottage owned by Mr Burgess. A letter in support was sent by H.G. Baker of Middle Street, who owned some of the run-down houses himself (see cutting). He condemned the 'wanton and wilful destruction of good sound homes'. Of course the war intervened before action could be taken, and other concerns took centre-stage – all available accommodation was needed for evacuees.

> I would like to thank all those who are interesting themselves on our behalf, and all help is greatly appreciated, for and on behalf of all the cottage owners in the Clavering and district area who, unfortunately, have had their property wrongly scheduled for clearance under the 1936 Housing Acts.
>
> Yours, etc.,
>
> H. G. BAKER.
>
> Middle Street,
> Clavering,
> January 24th, 1939.

May 1939

National Service. There has been a good response to the appeal for volunteers in both villages. In ARP both Anti-Gas and First Aid lectures have been held and the roll of volunteers is almost up to war establishment... The auxiliary fire brigade at Clavering still requires a few volunteers. Lectures in anti gas protection have been attended by the firemen and instruction in fire fighting has begun. We hope soon to have a trailer pump in the village. Full particulars of this service can be obtained from the Captain, Mr A. King, Brooklands. Several of our young men have answered the call to join the Territorial Army and they now belong to the company stationed at Stansted. Meetings are held on Tuesday evenings, travelling expenses are paid and there is the usual fortnight's camp in the summer. Very soon the first of our young men in the parish will be called up for their compulsory military training,.. Although the normal routine of their lives will be for a time suddenly broken, they will gain physically as well as rendering a great service to their country...

The Old House, Church End in the grounds of which an evening ARP exercise on the reporting of accidents was held for ARP wardens in July 1939 before war broke out.

Circulating among households at this time was this ominous leaflet, full of instructions about air raids, gas masks, lighting restrictions, fire precautions and evacuation. People learnt that the biggest danger was not from bombs but flying fragments; that if you throw water on an incendiary device, it would explode; and that no light at all must show outside their homes. Now, with defence services formed in every town and village, the prospect of war began to seem very real.

IF WAR SHOULD COME

The object of this leaflet is to tell you now some of the things you ought to know if you are to be ready for the emergency of war.

This does not mean that war is expected now, but it is everyone's duty to be prepared for the possibility of war.

Further leaflets will be sent to you to give you fuller guidance on particular ways in which you can be prepared.

The Government are taking all possible measures for the defence of the country, and have made plans for protecting you and helping you to protect yourselves, so far as may be, in the event of war.

You, in your turn, can help to make those plans work, if you understand them and act in accordance with them.

No-one can tell when or how war might begin, but the period of warning might be very short. There would be no time then to begin to think what you ought to do.

READ WHAT FOLLOWS, and think **NOW.**

The Fete of 1939

That last summer before the war, Clavering and Langley residents took their minds off the deeply disturbing war news by planning a great event, the Whit-Monday Fete. The Vicar forecast: 'we shall have a most successful day, always provided that the Clerk of the Weather and Herr Hitler do not upset our plans'. Planning began in January 1939, when over 30 people met at Clavering Vicarage and set up a committee to organise it. They had the kind offer of a superb venue in the grounds of Valence Manor (pictured below during WW2), courtesy of the Teale family. A new tennis court had recently been laid there and a tennis tournament would be one of the attractions. The aim was to raise money towards Clavering Church's heating system and re-hanging Langley Church bells. The event was a great success, making a profit of £121, augmented by proceeds from a village hall dance. Lady Braybrooke opened the fete, 1,000 people attended, the weather was perfect and everything went without a hitch. As well as about 30 stalls, novel attractions included 'spectacular and daring stunts' in an aeronautic display, a ladies' ankle competition, a dog show and bowling for the pig with five pigs as prizes. The Vicar felt much of the success was thanks to weekenders who supported the event. In the dark days to come, perhaps people looked back on the Valence fete as a golden day before the world changed. Indeed, a number of traditional events such as Christmas parties, cricket matches, flower shows and garden parties had to be mostly forgotten at the start of the conflict. But soon wartime needs would bring their own legion of social and fund-raising events and, with most able-bodied adults busy on war work, the young people of the village responded. In August 1943, a young Doug Luff and Biddy Glasscock ran the fete in the village hall grounds, raising £160 for the Red Cross Prisoners of War Fund and Christmas presents for locals in the Forces, who each received a personal letter from the Vicar enclosing the present. The event was repeated in August 1944, run by

Mr and Mrs H.T. Cook, Doug, Biddy and a committee. It was another huge success, attracting a crowd of 1,500 to the village hall grounds. Mr Teale again did the honours in declaring the fete open at a time when the fortunes of war had turned, commenting, 'The war news is good, the weather is fine, the organisers are waiting for you to spend your money.' They doubled the previous sum raised. Similarly in 1945, when all the money went to the Clavering Forces Homecoming Fund – for by then the troops were on their way home. But in the summer of 1939 that was all a long way off.

Farming Change 1939

Farm Workers to Stay on the Land

Food Growing Urgency

Before the war farming was in a depressed state, and in February 1939 2,000 farmers from East Anglia held a protest march in London, demanding more support for agriculture. Everything changed in September, with the subsidy of £2 an acre for ploughing up grassland to grow crops, as war concentrated minds on the vital importance of increasing food supplies and the government wanted two million additional acres for arable crops. Farmworkers were vital to the war effort - Fred Sampford, who worked at Curles Farm, recalled: 'We were advised to stay on the land, because they needed people to work it. Everything was important. Little tiny bits of field were ploughed up just for cattle feed. We used to grow a few mangels or swedes or anything for cattle feed, we didn't waste anything. The field at Marshalls Well near Watery Stones - we ploughed that up in 1939/40 and planted cabbages on it. It had never been ploughed up before.' A great change was coming and the countryside would never be the same again as old pastures came under the plough, such as those round Thurrocks Farm. Still something of the old romance of farming remained as the Vicar mused (before war was declared): 'From time to time some of our older people tell me of their reminiscences of harvesting in their young days and as I watch the modern reaping machines at work in our fields, I find myself picturing the same scene fifty years ago with the band of reapers with their scythes, led by the lord of the reapers, and leaving a swath behind they as they went across the field. The same seed time and harvest yet what a difference in the gathering and who knows what greater inventions may still be ahead of us.' He was right – war forced the pace of mechanisation. While there were still 649,000 farm horses labouring in the fields in 1939 and only 56,000 tractors, this total quadrupled by the end of the war while horses declined in number.

Harvest time old style - pitching sheaves on to the cart in the fields of The Court Farm, 1938.

August 1939

War now seemed inevitable, with the Nazis still on the march and Britain pledging to stand by its promise to Poland. On the Home Front preparations went on apace, with identity cards, the calling up of reserves, the evacuation of children and the ARP on alert. Clavering air raid wardens and others took place in the nation-wide exercise in August.

ARP. There will be a blackout over most of England from midnight on 9th August until 4 a.m. on 10th August. The ARP services of Clavering and Langley will make use of the occasion for an ARP exercise. Wardens will be at their posts and first aid patrols and utility squads will gain practice in driving through the country with no headlights. When gas masks are no longer required on account of death, they should be returned to the Senior Warden of the village who returns them to headquarters.

Clavering Parish Magazine, September 1939

The Crisis. Since this magazine went to press we have arrived at another time of crisis. When you read these words the question everyone is asking " Will there be a war " will in all probability be answered. While we all hope and pray for peace it is our duty to be prepared for war. The following information will be helpful. The Senior Warden for A.R.P. in Clavering is Mr Beamish, 4 Stortford Road, all enquiries relating to gas masks should be addressed to him. First Aid is under the direction of Mrs Slingsby. The Vicar is the Billetting Officer for Evacuation, assisted by Mrs Finzel who has enrolled a number of lady visitors to help in this work.

September 1939

On 1st September, what everyone had dreaded, came to pass: Germany invaded Poland and by the end of the month the old Poland had virtually ceased to exist. Britain and France declared war on Germany. The Vicar's October letter was a solemn one.

My dear Friends,

So war has come to us. Our prayers have been answered, but not in the way for which we had hoped. We prayed for a just peace and that has not been finally denied us. We still have our vision of a Europe free from tyranny but in the mysterious providence of God we are not permitted to realize our ideals in any measure without a grim and terrible struggle. War was inevitable if the German ruler refused to reverse his aggressive policy and this he would not or dared not do despite the opportunities that were given him, and so the hands of peace-loving nations have been forced. The British people have met this challenge to all that they hold dear with an amazingly quiet calmness, no shouting or cheering but nevertheless thousands of men and women just doing their bit efficiently and without fuss... We have been thrown into the turmoil and excitement of war. Let us look at the ordeal calmly and realistically. We shall be surrounded by mass emotions of the most violent kind – fear, hatred, foolish hopes, lying rumours, perhaps panic. One contribution which we can all make is to preserve our sanity, our calm confidence, to be centres from which cheerful courage flows to others... At the beginning of the war when everything seemed either to shut up or shut down I wondered how many of our village organisations would be able to carry on. But now that the ban on certain things has been lifted and cinemas and theatres are allowed to open again and the regulations regarding the carrying of lights are less severe, I think we should try and carry on the social life of our villages in the most normal way possible.

Yours most sincerely, E.A. STONE

The Day the War Began

The day the war began, Sunday 3 September 1939, was a day which stayed forever in the memory.

Isobel Barker: 'I had my own radio, and I was listening to it when the war was declared on the Sunday September 3 1939. I was very upset because by that time I had met my future husband, who was a soldier in the Essex Regiment and a friend of my brother. They were at Warley Barracks together, and used to cycle home on Sundays when they were not on duty.'

Des Abrahams: 'I remember the broadcasts of Neville Chamberlain that Sunday morning – everybody was extremely nervous, one cannot describe the last war because of the fear, the worry, it was an unusual time, serious time. I remember the woman across the road - her husband was a gardener for the Ackroyds at Sheepcote Green – came across crying, "My Herbert!", and my father said, "Oh don't worry about him, they won't be taking him for a while".'

Jean Abrahams: 'We were half expecting but then like everyone else it just sort of all went flat. We had a blackout of our cycles and the cars and the houses and everything. Father was an ARP warden. We went to the village hall and we were issued with a gas mask, just before the war. The searchlights were put all around here some months before the war broke out, and I shall always remember them going backwards and forwards across the sky, especially on a dark night. It was frightening at times. I was often frightened. But we went to London just a few days after the fires around St Paul's and saw all the damage.'

Douglas Savill: 'I was not very old when the Second World War broke out in September 1939, but there are memories that bring back those days and something of what it meant to so many people. There were signs that the war was coming - the Army had extensive manouvres and all around Langley and area at one point there were troops and army vehicles. I remember the soldiers showing us children some of the Rangefinders and Sound Detection equipment they had set up on Langley green. With the outbreak of war it meant the end of Grandfather George Wombwell's building firm. Some of the men had to go into the Forces; the lorry and the car were commandeered for the war effort.'

'The day war broke out I was in Sunday School, we came out about half-past-ten before morning service and there were all these people, the churchgoers waiting to go in and talking about the war coming. I was a very curious child and they said war was being declared, it was Cecil Livings who broke the news. We were coming out of Sunday school but we didn't go home because we were listening to all these people, it meant nothing to us.'

June Riley

'I was only about 4-5, but I always remember that Sunday morning when Neville Chamberlain spoke on the radio, and I sat there with my parents and when the broadcaster finished, my father looked across at my mother and said, 'Oh well that's that then, its what we've all been expecting, you know'. Every time adults met it was the same subject, the war. Being the age I was, it was more exciting than frightening, but I knew what was going on.'

Roger Petchey

13

October 1939

Prayer leaflet authorised by the Bishop of Chelmsford

Prayers

for use in War Time in the

Diocese of Chelmsford.

Services. Both our Church Councils have recently met to consider what changes were necessary in the time of the Services. At Clavering it was thought that the task of darkening the windows was too great to be practicable and it was agreed that Evensong should be at 3.30 p.m. instead of 6.30 p.m... So far the authorities have allowed the Clergy a fairly generous extra ration of petrol. While I shall use my bicycle as much as I can I hope that the supply of petrol will enable me to continue the services on Sundays as arranged... Quite a number of the boys and girls who are staying in the parish have come to Sunday School...

The men of Clavering aged over 20 were now called up, unless they were in reserved occupations. Notwithstanding the Vicar's wish to carry on with normal village life, the October magazine and most issues thereafter were filled with war-related activities and news.

Peace Bell. For several hundreds of years it was the custom of the Church to sound a call to prayer at mid-day, by the ringing of a Church bell. This call to prayer was known as the Angelus, and wherever men and women were they stopped work for a moment's prayer when the bell was heard. During the last war this custom was revived in many parishes as a call to prayer for peace. It has been suggested that we ring in Clavering a peace bell at mid-day, and so from Monday to Saturday as the clock finishes striking twelve the bell will sound, calling us to a moment's silent prayer for peace. It will be rung in the traditional style of the Angelus, namely three times with three strokes followed by nine strokes.

Knitting and Sewing. A meeting was held to consider the setting up of work parties to do knitting and sewing for the troops and the Red Cross. Would any ladies wishing to take part in this most important piece of National Service, come along on Friday afternoons at the houses of Mrs Finzel, Mrs Luckock and Miss Ackroyd.

Allotments. The need for as much land as possible to be put under cultivation must be clear to anyone... those interested should apply to the Clerk of the Parish Council.

ARP. At the time of writing, there have been very few air raids so far... Wardens will give the warning signals in more populous parts of the village... the best air raid warning for country districts is the sound of our own anti-aircraft gunfire and until that is heard

Urgent ! **Urgent !**

A·R·P

MAKE BRITAIN STRONG

little alarm need be caused... all ARP workers have given up valuable time to attending lectures and classes to fit them for their work. The first aid post at Danceys has meant that Mrs. Slingsby has given up a large room completely for this purpose and also has fitted it out, largely at her own expense.

Air Raid Precautions 1939

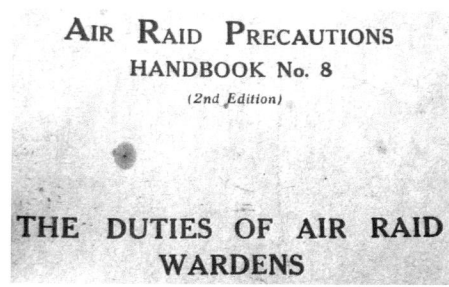

AIR RAID PRECAUTIONS

HANDBOOK No. 8

(2nd Edition)

THE DUTIES OF AIR RAID WARDENS

Because there had been a pre-war crisis in 1938, preparations for civil defence were already well in hand, with wardens recruited, when war did break out in September 1939. In this area the Air Raid Precautions were organised by a joint committee with its headquarters at Fairycroft in Saffron Walden. If there was an alert, the first notification would be heard at Fairycroft, then they would phone it through to the villages, whose wardens would blow a whistle to show alert and ring a handbell for the all-clear. By May 1939 there were almost enough wardens, and ARP lectures in anti-gas measures and first aid had already taken place, with badges and certificates presented to nine wardens, Messrs Abrahams, Atkinson, Blackborrow, Caton, Funston, Gammon, Lewis, Luckock and Lloyd. The wardens' posts were allotted and name plates nailed to their gates (see below). Some of the wardens were quite elderly, such as Alfred Prestige Lewis who before he died at the age of 72 in 1944 had been, as the Vicar put it, 'a devoted member of the A.R.P. service, he always carried out his Air Raid Warden's duties with keenness and enthusiasm, while in the earlier days of the war despite his age he was a most faithful and regular fire-watcher'.

On a summer's evening in July, the Wardens held a village ARP exercise in the reporting of accidents, and were also involved in a nation-wide exercise, involving the imposition of a blackout over most of England from midnight on 9th August until 4 a.m. on 10th August. The wardens manned their posts and first aid patrols and utility squads practised driving through the countryside without headlights. Later in the year the vicar became concerned about rumours circulating that ARP wardens received payments for storing equipment. This was completely untrue, he pointed out they gave up their time voluntarily and 'Few villages have such a loyal and faithful band of ARP workers as Clavering and Langley. For anyone to suggest that these workers are receiving money for their work is a scandalous and shameful thing.' The Senior Warden for Clavering was Edward Valentine Clutton Beamish, then coming up to about 60, and among the volunteer wardens was the Vicar himself who recalled, 50 years later, that he was 'constantly rung up during the worst of the raids to give a warning to the village. Being a very scattered community we were not an easy target and the village escaped any serious damage. With the other wardens we were expected to put on our tin hats and sound and blow a whistle in our localities. There were sirens in Stortford and Saffron Walden and we sometimes heard them if the wind was in the right direction.'

Air Raid Warden metal plaque which once adorned the gatepost of a Clavering ARP Warden (found by the author on a shed at Clavering allotments).

Evacuees 1939

By early 1939 a census of Clavering accommodation available for evacuated children was in hand and completed by the summer so all was ready when war broke out. The Vicar was the Billeting Officer for Clavering and kept the register – all who volunteered to take in unaccompanied children were given a window card acknowledging this as a contribution of National Service. Through Mr Stone's vivid description in the parish magazine, it is easy to imagine the day when they all arrived and were allocated to families:

'I don't think I shall ever forget the scene in Clavering on Friday afternoon 1st September 1939 when two buses arrived at the school bringing the children who had been evacuated with their school from Tottenham. Like many other people I had spent some time during the past year getting familiar with the various types of bombs and the horrors of war and how to deal with them, but the sight of those children getting off that bus, many of them quite small and carrying a pack of luggage nearly as big as themselves, brought home to me far more than any lectures or classes what war meant. And as we watched that little group of fifty children with their teachers make their way into the school, and thought how each of them had left behind a mother or a father, we realised how hard it must have been for the parents to part with their children, and what an insane thing war was. The children for their part were very cheerful and after some lemonade and biscuits were taken to their new homes in motor cars, thanks to the kindness of a number of ladies and gentlemen, who kindly placed their cars at the disposal of the billeting officer. I think it is very wonderful, the way in which both the people of Clavering and Langley have opened their arms to these strangers who have so recently come among us. In both villages at the last moment we only had half the number we expected and that is why several people who kindly offered billets to evacuees did not receive any.'

In Langley things were too quiet for some mums with their children and many went home again quite rapidly – as one commented to the Vicar: 'The people are so kind here that I feel I am being ungrateful to go back home, but it would kill me to stay here.' In Clavering, on 13 September 1939, 96 new children aged 5 to 13 were registered at the school. This first batch were allocated to over 50 houses around the parish, some families taking in two or three of the same family, a few accompanied by mothers but most on their own. Of these, 53 were from Bruce Grove School and were taught together in the Lower School. They lived in 28 different billets - most were aged under 10, a lot only five or six years old. It was obviously a great help that they came with their schoolmates from Tottenham, but others later on were from many different places. Out of the Bruce Grove children, half had returned home within six months, and a few even went the same week, while a quarter had gone by Christmas. But others stayed much longer, in some cases through most of the war. It was probably thanks to the Vicar that the organisation here went so smoothly, as this was not the case everywhere. The Vicar did all he could to ease the many problems that arose, and by the end of the year could report that those who were left 'appear to be very happy and comfortable. Clavering has a good record for the children remaining in their billets and not returning home, which speaks well for the love and care taken by our foster-parents.' However, Mr Stone did wonder whether so much upheaval was really necessary, since it led to the breaking up of homes not only in towns, but also in the countryside billets which had to make considerable adjustments for the strangers in their midst – although there was payment - 10s 6d for the first child and 8s 6d per head for others. 'It would seem with the course events have taken that London with its great anti-aircraft defences is one of the safest places. Time will, of course, prove whether this is true', commented the Vicar. This of course was before the terrible Blitz of 1940 that led to a second wave of evacuees.

The leader of the Bruce Grove School, Tottenham group, Mr L.M. le Plastrier, wrote expressing 'what a deep debt of gratitude we owe to the parents of Clavering, who have so willingly taken our children and teachers into their homes. It speaks for itself when I say that there has been very little shifting of billets and a very small proportion of children returning to Tottenham.' At Christmas began the tradition of parties which continued throughout the war (see p.165), and there is plenty of anecdotal evidence to suggest that many of the evacuees, particularly those who stayed long-term, enjoyed their stay here and in their future lives looked back on it with some nostalgia. The recorded memories of Eileen Clarke, Olive Revell and Elsie Kemp are the most comprehensive (see pp 18-19, 51, 114-115), but how did it look from this end? Isobel Beckwith recalled the evacuee arrangements operated by her aunt:

'She had two brothers, seven and four years old, also my sister had two girls, one was sister to the brothers and the other a cousin. They could not believe their eyes to see all the chickens, pigs and rabbits that my Aunt kept, also some of the food they had never seen or tasted. Their Mother was at Stansted with the baby and sometimes would walk over to see them, but they were very happy to stay. After some time the Mother took them all back to London and we never heard of them again.'

The family of Des Abrahams, who lived on the farm at Sheepcote Green, also took in some evacuees through the village scheme:

'They were people my Father knew, two girls came down and stayed with us for some time. We had another one, a girl with us... about the same age as I was, 12-14. Some were here a long time. I don't know how we catered for them, the house was so primitive, we had no bathroom and an old toilet under the chestnut tree, so it must have been difficult.'

Dick Law, who can recall exactly which houses where evacuees lived, felt that 'they settled in and we got to know them quite well and if they went home for a week-end we use to get invited to go up and stay with them'. But once the evacuees started coming from different places, 'there were so many who didn't even know each other because they came from all over the place'. In neighbouring Langley, Douglas Savill's grandfather, George Wombwell was involved in sorting out accommodation and reportedly was told by one lady that she could not possibly have an evacuee as she only had one bathroom, to which his grandfather retorted, 'Well Missus, I think you could manage if you tried, I always have a bath once a year whether I want it or not'.

The view of Bury Meadow that greeted evacuees as they arrived in Clavering.

Finding a billet 1939

On 13th September 1939, seven-year-old Eileen Clarke from Ponders End in Enfield was one of a large number of children evacuated from North London to Clavering. Unlike the majority of evacuees that week, who all came from the same school in Tottenham, she and her mother were private evacuees and she remembers what a muddled time they had finding a billet.

'When war broke out Mum and I were packed off to Clavering to Dorcas Livings, who supposedly had told my Father that "Should anything happen in the war, send the family to me". So we get off the train at Bishop's Stortford - the bus runs twice a week! So we start to walk to Clavering. Get as far as Manuden where this delicate small child collapses and refuses to walk any further and a chap came along and it was some kind of farm vehicle I think and he asks us where we were going. He drops us off in Middle Street. We knock on the door and Dorcas Livings comes to the door and my mother said, "Eldred said that we could come and stay with you". She says, "I'm afraid that I don't know who you are, and I don't know any Eldred Clarke. I can't put you up - I've got a houseful of children and we have got two bedrooms." So she sent us to the Post Office where there was somebody called Biddy Glasscock. "Ah", she said, "'I think you can go up to Mrs Luff who's on Hill Green". She was a school teacher. So we stayed there for a few weeks. I was in the Lower School. At the same time two of my cousins were also evacuated to Clavering - they came to stay next door at the *Fox & Hounds* for a little bit until they took up somewhere in Middle Street. And then for some reason or other, we went up further up Hill Green to the Reynolds, a little bungalow tucked back on the corner. They seemed very staid and very chapel and they wouldn't have the wireless on. So of course, this child that was brought up in London with the radio on etc - it was VERY restricting. I can remember they put the wireless on for us one day, but I think it was because Princess Elizabeth was making a speech! At that stage they stopped bombing in London so we went home again. Then we got bombed out, we had a direct hit and we had to come out of the house so the whole family came back to Clavering.'

Another long-term evacuee was Olive Revell nee Holland (b.1926) who recorded her experiences. Pictured is her ten-year-old brother Jeffery at The Nook.

'I was 13 years old when war started, and living in Tottenham. About two weeks after war was declared I joined my mother in Clavering with my young brother who would have been about 8 years old. We lived in a cottage called 'The Nook' at Valence road with five acres of ground and we had about seven evacuees staying with us at the time. Sleeping arrangements were basic, about three to a bed. There was no gas, electricity or telephone. Water was connected soon after we arrived, before that we had to go to the stand pipe down the road. We had an Elsan toilet until my uncle and father dug out a cesspit about a year later. We also had an orchard with apples, pears, plums, which my father used to take back to his greengrocery shop in Tottenham. When I was 15 years my mother died suddenly following an infection, this was before the availability of penicillin. She was only 42 years old. The evacuees all went back except Malcolm, aged 9. I looked after my brother and Malcolm and Dad came down at weekends. I coped with all the funeral arrangements and keeping the house together. We stayed in the cottage with the boys, until war ended and we went back to London. I had my heart set on joining the Wrens, but they wouldn't accept me because of the boys.' ©O.R.N. Revell www.bbc.co.uk/ww2peopleswar

Evacuee School 1939

The influx of evacuees brought many logistical problems, not least how to maintain their education. Clavering was luckier than most villages as it had two school buildings. With the arrival of all these extra boys and girls in the autumn of 1939, mostly official evacuees but also some private ones, the whole of the Lower School (photo left) in the churchyard was turned over to them, while the 64 local children, used the Upper School in Pelham Road, with the Infants for a time taught at Piercewebbs opposite.

This was to follow the Board of Education guidelines to preserve the identities of both schools. After a while, a lot of evacuees went back to London and the two groups were amalgamated – in 1940 the school inspector commented: 'Despite the admixture of London children and consequent unsettlement I can give quite a good report'. Evacuees more than doubled the school numbers early in the war but, by the end of 1942 there were only 23 (mostly government) evacuees in school. June Holland (nee Riley, b.1930, pictured left aged 12) met her future husband, Jeffery Holland (see photo opposite), when he was evacuated to The Nook in Valence Road:

'The evacuees came on a bus and were allocated to different people but there were a lot of families, not just those on the bus. They took over houses, there was not a house empty during the war. They lined us up in the playground and had the Clavering children and the evacuee children, and we as the locals had to look after the evacuees, because these children won't know about trees and grass and closing gates. We had one each and I got Jeffery, we came all through school together so I've known him since he was eight.'

Among other long-term evacuees was Eileen Summers (nee Clark, b.1932) who had an amusing memory of 1940 when she was eight years old and had moved to the Upper School:

'We had a teacher there, bless her heart, she taught us scripture so you can imagine it - a room full of children all from around Tottenham and my area. Most of them had been bombed out, a lot of them had lost parents and she said, "I'm going to give you this lesson today. You're in this house and there is a knock on the door and you open the door and outside there is an English soldier and he's got a bullet wound in his arm, but there is a German soldier there and he's got a bullet wound nearly through his heart. Now children, which one are we going to attend to first?". All these little bullies from town, we all screamed out 'KILL THE GERMAN!' So we all had to stay in after school because we should have said, "you have to go for the one that is the most badly injured". Her whole lesson had been destroyed! I can see this poor woman, she was virtually in tears because we were all shouting.'

Parish Council Digs for Victory

Clavering Parish Council was relatively inactive during the war – its members were already doing voluntary war work, and parish council business seemed to be minimal. But they were concerned about the exhortation to 'Dig for Victory', since Clavering had parish allotments. But when, in October 1939 unlet Clavering allotments were offered for this purpose, there was not a lot of enthusiasm. As there were no takers for the spare allotments, the councillors decided to plough them up and the following spring they were planted with potatoes to be sold to the Government's Food Office. Cllrs Arthur King and Vassar Rowe, who were farmers, were left to deal with this. Otherwise normal village life went on, and the minutes of the annual meetings contain no reference to the war at all. Sometimes they would not meet for 6-9 months at a time and, when they did, the most vigorous discussion related to overgrown hedges, unpaved footpaths and troublesome gypsies. The council preferred not to get involved in three war-related initiatives: in May 1940, they turned down the idea of having an additional salvage dump as they already had facilities at the Vicarage and school; five months later, they discussed a request from the Essex Village Food Production Committee to set up a depot for the disposal of surplus vegetables. But again it was felt there was no need for this in Clavering. Another seven months went by and in May 1941 the parish council, faced with a letter from the Rural District Council asking them to set up a Communal Feeding facility, again turned it down, as the parish was 'so large and scattered'. So they just went on

PARISH COUNCIL.—At a meeting on Monday, members present were Mr. J. Clarke (in the chair), Messrs. V. H. Rowe, A. D. King, H. C. Finzel, D. Morgan, J. Matthews and T. Ellis, with the Clerk (Mr. J. R. Luff). Business concerned the planting of the unlet allotments, and repair of one of the public seats, which had been wilfully broken. The Council expressed the hope that more care would be taken of the seats. A precept of £10 on the Rural District Council was decided upon.

growing potatoes and alleviating the national food shortage by selling the crop to the Ministry of Food. One year, however, the potato harvest was so poor, it was fit only for feeding stock, so they tried barley instead. This was a great success and a cheque for £68.16s resulted – in December 1943, Mr Rowe patted Mr King on the back for his good cultivation and he received 'a hearty vote of thanks'. The council raised a special rate to pay for the village Victory celebrations on 8 June 1946, to which £15 was contributed. The same year, there was a parish election which was keenly contested, with 16 nominations for the nine seats and an enthusiastic parish meeting attended by 70 parishioners. Special thanks were minuted to the retiring chairman - local cobbler, Jimmy Clarke who resigned after half a century with the council.

Above: A typical Clavering Parish Council report from March 1940. Right: Vassar Rowe and Arthur King in wartime roles as special police sergeant and fire chief.

WVS Parcels

Right, Ian & Margaret Napier; below, Apple Tree Cottage in Stortford Road as it looked in 1939.

Living at Appletree Cottage during WW2 was Ian Napier, who ran the Air Training Corps and taught navigation skills (see pp. 84-85). He was also prominent on the Invasion Committee, Pig Club and the Fire Watch committee – he often worked in London during the week and also helped with firefighting in the Blitz. Mrs Margaret Napier played piano at the village hall, knitted for the troops and worked with the WVS, collecting surplus fruit and vegetables for their scheme to help 'men of the small ships of the Royal and Merchant Navies'. People either delivered them or she cycled round the village with one of her young daughters (Jean, Betty and Brenda) to collect. They packed them into hampers and the girls would write letters to go with the parcels (and often received replies). The vegetables were then sent them off every Thursday morning in summer from Bishop's Stortford railway station, where they were conveyed free of charge to the nearest port to be 'passed on to our gallant seamen'. The scheme worked well and Clavering sent off a weekly hamper for three months. She reported, 'the cards of thanks and appreciation that the Sailors have sent are ample evidence of how worthwhile Clavering's effort has been. In a beautiful part of the countryside like this – we cannot always realise what it means to those who go down to the Sea in Ships to have fresh produce available'. When the Napiers came here in 1939 to escape the bombing, the cottage was in a poor state of repair but over the following years they gradually turned it into a comfortable home. Their domestic help was Mrs Wombwell, the chapel keeper who lived in the old thatched cottage next door. The youngest daughter, Brenda, now in her 70s, remembers waving to the troops marching past their gate, riding on Farmer King's cart in the harvest fields opposite and making do with water from a standpipe in the road, an outside toilet and no electricity or gas, just an Aga. Aged seven, Brenda fell down the stairs and broke a bone in her neck. Forced to rest a lot, one day she was sitting in the garden near the apple tree (still there) when there was a dog-fight

overhead and she was showered with spent cartridges – a frightening experience for a little girl. Having already moved to escape the Blitz, now Mrs Napier became worried by the proximity of local aerodromes, so in 1944 again moved the family away, this time to Surrey - only to discover that their new home was on 'doodlebug alley'! Their departure was a great loss to the Clavering Home Front.

November 1939

My dear Friends,

In these days of black-outs and reduced lighting have you noticed how much brighter the stars and the moon appear? With the windows of the houses showing scarcely a glimmer of light and with no headlamps to dazzle the eyes, one appreciates the light of 'the village lantern'. I find myself in these days looking up at the sky more than I did, particularly at night. Perhaps an occasional searchlight comes into view or you try to detect the whereabouts of that aeroplane you can hear so plainly; but always on a clear night there is that wonderful background of the stars... The stars confront us with the great immensities. They turn our minds to vaster issues than our world affairs... The one bright spot in the ghastly thing that has happened to us is the chance that it gives us of thinking out afresh our relations with God...

Many people have told me how much they appreciate the ringing of the Angelus with its call to prayer for peace... The change at Clavering from an evening to an afternoon service has so far not proved very popular. We are all rather conservative in our way of life and do not take kindly to change and no doubt we are accustomed to spending Sunday afternoon either in a quiet sleep by the fire or perhaps in taking a good walk... I was interested to see the other day a copy of the parish magazine for December 1914... a list of those from the parish serving with the King's forces. Now 25 years later it falls to my lot to compile a list of those now serving in the Army, Navy and Air Force... The usual Armistice Day observances are not to be held this year but poppies will be on sale and our generous help is asked for this annual appeal of the British Legion. There will be a short service of intercession for peace in Clavering Church on Saturday morning 11 November at 10.45 pm. The usual service at which we remember by name all who fell in the Great War, will be held in both Churches on Sunday 12 November... Has anyone a harmonium or American organ that they would lend the vicar? Owing to the blackout restrictions it is impossible to hold choir practice in church and it is proposed to hold it in a room at the Vicarage...

Yours most sincerely, E.A. STONE

December 1939

My dear Friends,

It is now three months since our evacuated visitors came among us and those who still remain appear to be very happy and comfortable. Clavering has a good record for the children remaining in their billets and not returning home, which speaks well for the love and care taken by our 'foster-parents'. One might well wish that the whole evacuation question had worked out as smoothly as it has done in Clavering. The details in our newspapers of the numbers of evacuees who have returned home together with the lack of educational facilities for those who chose to remain in the towns makes sorry reading. One wonders now whether evacuation with its breaking up of homes both in town and country (for a house is just as much broken up by the accepting of evacuees as by the departure of one's own children) was worthwhile.

Yours most sincerely, E.A. STONE

With the King's Forces 1939

George &
Percy
Livings, Fred
Chipperfield
and Jack
Livings

At Christmas 1939 only 17 Clavering men were listed in the parish magazine as serving with the King's Forces - but the Vicar's list must be incomplete, for instance Jack Livings remembers several other lads joining up with him in 1939: 'Percy Livings and Fred Chipperfield were step-brothers to George and I, and all four of us served throughout the War (see photos above): Percy (Essex Regt) in Italy, Fred (Royal Artillery) in Africa and George (East Surrey Regt) in Europe and Dunkirk. I joined the Territorial Army with six other Clavering boys – brother Percy, George Law, Maurice Atkinson, Jim Kemp, Stanley King and Albert Blackman. I served seven years in the Artillery, being too young to go abroad, on Bofors guns aimed at enemy aircraft at many different places on the south coast.' Jack's mother Dorcas Livings (previously married to a Chipperfield), thus had four soldier lads to worry about throughout the war – happily, all returned safely.

Ethel and Tom Barker from Church End also ended up with four sons at war. During WW2 their 3 daughters worked as cook at Langley School (Ivy), cook at a British Restaurant (Eva) and cleaner in the wounded soldiers' ward at Haymeads Hospital, Bishops Stortford (Ethelwyn). Their oldest son Sydney (pictured right, better known as Sonny, who post-war ran the *Waggon & Horses* pub at Roast Green) had been in the Army in the 1920s so was a Reservist called up the day war broke out, and when his younger brother, Henry (pictured left) was called up, Sonny 'claimed' him so they could serve together. This meant that when it came to Dunkirk they were both awaiting rescue. Their sister Ethelwyn, now 91, recalls: 'There were boats coming in to take them and they had to jump into the boat from the pier. Sonny wouldn't go as he hated water, and Henry went back for him and got him to jump into the boat.' Sonny was later sent to Burma, and after the war was still in uniform, at the occupation of the Rhine. Meanwhile, their brother Philip had worked at Brent Pelham kennels before the war and volunteered in order to work with horses. He was out in Palestine when a horse sent out the same kennels, came up and nuzzled Philip, recognising him from his days at Pelham! Finally came the day when Tom, a veteran of WW1, reflected, 'They've taken my youngest one' – Hubert, who served in Italy and did not return till the war ended. But all four did survive and came home.

Chapter Three
1940: *'These are dangerous days'*

The memorable year 1940 began with the coldest winter for a century, and it was to become a year of extremes in many other ways too - from the lows of Dunkirk and the Blitz to the highs of the Battle of Britain, words that would live on forever in the annals of British history. Two million more young men were called up. In Europe, the news was absolutely appalling with invasions of Denmark, Norway, Finland, Belgium, Holland, France, Luxembourg and the Channel Islands following in quick succession - in just a few weeks the Nazis seemed to have moved so far and so fast with their 'blitzkrieg' methods. They were also engaged in building Auschwitz and imprisoning Polish Jews in the Warsaw Ghetto, bombing Atlantic convoys to starve everyone of food supplies and attempting to destroy air power to open the way for invasion. Russians and Italians joined the Axis and, after the chaos of Dunkirk, Britain felt desperately alone and everyone expected to be invaded. The contagion was also spreading to the Mediterranean - with fighting in Africa, Greece and Crete - and to Asia, where Japan signed a pact with Germany.

On the Home Front, it was also a case of extreme measures even before the new government led by Winston Churchill acquired emergency powers enabling them to do what they liked. Rationing began to bite, postage, taxes and petrol went up, and there were shortages as U-boats took their toll. Railings disappeared and saucepans were collected allegedly to make planes. Clavering folk could see the glow of the Blitz in the sky as London was ablaze – on the night of 10 May, there were 2,200 fires in the capital affecting 155,000

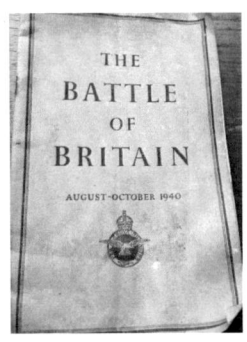

households - and another wave of evacuees was triggered. There was some good news - the ban on football was lifted, the Enigma Code was cracked and radar came into its own; factories were in full production and most people had jobs. Commonwealth troops were wading in to help, the USA was sending more aid and the RAF were fighting brilliantly against the Luftwaffe. Those not able to enlist in the Forces, were flocking to join the Home Guard prepared to put into practice Churchill's declaration to *'fight them on the beaches'*. The very survival of Christian civilisation, he said, depended on the outcome of the Battle of Britain which raged in the skies from August to October. Fortunately, it did not succeed, and became instead part of Britain's *'finest hour'* when so much had been *'done for so many by so few'*. Nor did the dreadful bombing seem to defeat people entirely. Much effort was expended on keeping up morale, both nationally and locally.

In East Anglia, invasion plans included the setting up of an office in Cambridge, linked to the War Room in Whitehall, where operations would be directed. Essex Regiment battalions were serving abroad. Not far from Clavering were two of the main fighter bases, at Duxford and Debden, the latter covering the southern area of East Anglia with Hurricane and Blenheim planes, while bombers were based in Norfolk and Suffolk. Nuthampstead was also active. People could see the dogfights and realise how Britain was fighting for its life. It is impossible for generations that followed to recapture the feelings of people in those terrible times, particularly after France fell and Britain seemed so alone. But a strong impression can be gathered from the Vicar's letters to his parishioners, which month by month, reflected the growing alarm, and often specifically addressed the issues of the day.

The parish magazine reflected the kinds of wartime activities typical of every community – ARP exercises, Home Guard training, knitting comforts for the troops, digging for victory, exhortations to save and salvage to help pay for the very expensive war effort. But many things could not be publicised – the removal of signposts, the look-out for enemy parachutists, the building of the Defence Line of pillboxes and anti-tank traps. We know the searchlight camp on Stortford Road existed by May 1940, as the magazine contained a request for books, magazines and gramophone records for the men and surplus seeds so they could make a garden there. Dunkirk is not mentioned in the parish magazine until four years later, and only briefly in the local newspaper, nor is there any specific mention of the stray bombs which fell here in 1940, as there was censorship of any publicity that might help the enemy or spread despondency. Oral sources fill some of the gaps, if impressionistically through the eyes of many who were only children at the time.

ADOLF HITLER

This wicked man, the repository and embodiment of many forms of soul-destroying hatred, this monstrous product of former wrongs and shame, has now resolved to try to break our famous island race by a process of indiscriminate slaughter and destruction.

What he has done is to kindle a fire in British hearts, here and all over the world, which will glow long after all traces of the conflagrations he has caused in London have been removed. He has lighted a fire which will burn with a steady and consuming flame until the last traces of Nazi tyranny have been burned out of Europe, and until the Old World and the New can join hands to rebuild the temples of man's freedom and man's honour upon foundations which will not soon, or easily, be overthrown.

THE PRIME MINISTER.

Early in the year it was still the period of the 'phoney war', but in February 1940 Mr. Stone warned that these were nevertheless 'dangerous days' for the country. He fervently prayed for peace, contrasting the freedom of Britain with the slavery of the enemy, and saying the Christian message was the only light in 'this murky world'. When the Mothering Sunday service, which he had instigated earlier, came around he emphasised the vital importance of mothers in maintaining family life at a time when so many homes were broken up by war. In the spring, when the Nazi blitzkreig brought them right across Europe in just a few weeks, the degree of anxiety was intense, with 'horror succeeding horror in this terrible conflict which is tearing the world to pieces', he wrote, but he counselled positive thinking in the face of 'the godless gangsters' of the Axis. In July he wrote a parish letter of such power and eloquence that it is quoted in full here (see pp 38-39). Having lived in London as a child during WW1 air raids, he realised that the worst thing was how it affected people's nerves, but courage must not fail, even if Britain was invaded. They must carry on as they were now, it was 'a people's war' and everyone was keen to 'do their bit'. He criticised pacifism, and those who talked in defeatist fashion, and praised those dealing with the London Blitz. Britain never wanted war, but they had to end the brutality. It was a crusade and they should all be prepared to be martyrs. This theme continued month by month, always interweaving strong action with Christian duty, and looking for signs of hope such as the wonderful harvest. The Vicar was constantly on call for advice on everything imaginable and said he had never been so busy in his life, with people calling at the Vicarage all day and stopping him in the street for advice. As they approached the second wartime Christmas, he acknowledged how lucky villagers were to sleep in their own beds in relative peace, but it remained a deeply anxious time and he never pretended otherwise. In 1940, as the Prime Minister stirred the nation, Clavering had its own Churchillian figure, guiding and leading his local flock and trying to inspire them with the right words. He was the clergyman that Clavering needed at this critical time, the man of the hour.

The Rev. A. E. Stone

January 1940

My dear Friends,
A happy new year! So we are wishing one another just now. A happier year most of us are hoping than the one which has just finished - a year in which peace will come and where life will be more normal than at present... we regret that the customary parties at the Vicarage must this year be abandoned but we shall look forward to their resumption at the end of the war.
Yours most sincerely, E.A. STONE

S.S. Mary and Clement. Clavering Essex

Pre-war postcard showing Clavering church across the Dam meadows. The Vicar in his February letter reminded people how churches were being closed down by the Nazis.

February 1940

My dear Friends,
'We know what we are fighting against but we do not know what we are fighting for'; this we have been told recently is a common attitude of mind particularly among the younger men at the present time. Deeply conscious of great powers of evil at work in the world and fully realising that these powers must be checked, it is natural that men should turn their minds to what will follow when their task is achieved. We fight to check an evil... Our newspapers and wireless sets are frequently telling us of the savage brutality of those who are our enemies. We contrast the liberty and freedom of our own country with the apparent slavery of body, mind and spirit of the German people, telling ourselves that after all we live in a Christian country. But what do we mean by such a statement? When we read of the closing of thousands of churches in parts of Germany or Russia or their use for secular purposes, what are our reactions? ... I think that when we do read of such crimes as the cruel treatment of Christian priests and the wilful desecration of churches and chapels we tend to shake our heads and say that such things could never happen here. I am not so sure... These are dangerous days not only physically but morally and spiritually... there is no light anywhere in this murky world except in the Gospel. There we can estimate human nature as we find it now around us and within us...
Yours most sincerely, E.A. STONE

National Savings Week 1940

THE CRUSADE

War was a costly business and an important aspect of the Home Front was the campaign to increase savings, which was urged not for reasons of personal benefit but for the country's good. The government led the way with the suggestion of National Savings Groups in each village with the motto, 'The Savers will beat the enslavers'. Thus began in the spring of 1940 the Clavering savings group, having its headquarters at The Old House where the Hon. Treasurer, Richard Luckock would sell sixpenny savings stamps on Monday afternoons. The campaign had a strong moral imperative, pushing the message home every month with such exhortations: 'our present interest in pool gambling which represents in wartime so much money thrown down the drains might be transferred to National Savings. In such a way we should be helping our country in its tremendous task of winning the war... Isn't this a thing in which grown up sons and daughters who are not of military age can yet play their part in winning the war? ... it would save the country borrowing so much, stops prices rising, provides a nest egg... come in very handy after the war when you can better enjoy spending or perhaps in your old age you may be very glad of it.' In July 1940 the cheering news that both farm workers and old–age pensioners were getting a rise was the focus: people should show their appreciation by 'lending to the government some of the increase to help in the winning of the war'. By the end of the year, the Clavering Savings Association had 63 members who between them had saved £272 and now stamps were also available from local shops – Catons, Peacock the butchers and Taylor Stores as well as the Old House. The vicar's wife, Doris Stone became Hon. Secretary and described her ambitious aims in the September 1940 magazine: 'Everyone has been thrilled in the last few weeks at the wonderful exploits of our airmen in the destruction of enemy aircraft. As a practical expression of their admiration many towns and even villages are trying to raise the money to replace our aircraft that get destroyed. What a grand thing if we in Clavering and Langley could, through our local war savings association, buy one Spitfire. Let's go to it for the Clavering and Langley Spitfire!'

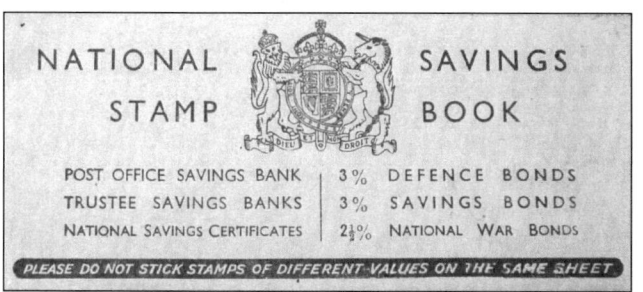

That object was not achieved, of course, but this was about morale as well as money – it was promoted as a way that ordinary non-combatants could help defeat Hitler by following the 'crusade' in their 'big battalions' of savers.

Wartime School

The war made an immediate impact on Clavering School on 4 September 1939, when headmaster Alec Richardson recorded in the school logbook: 'School did not re open this morning owing to outbreak of European war'. Sorting out the evacuees took a week and more than doubled the normal school roll. The school re-opened late, with evacuated children and teachers in the Lower School, Clavering classes in the Upper School, and infants temporarily taught in a room at Piercewebbs opposite. Lace curtains were taped on the school windows in case of glass splinters, and air raid wardens visited 'to see that the children's gas masks were properly adjusted'. On Empire Day in May 1940, 'prayers and hymns for our country and empire at this critical time' were said, and £1 6s 6d collected for the Overseas League Tobacco Fund. This resulted in a grateful letter from E.R. Spence of HMS Woolston: 'it was awfully nice of the children to give up their pennies to send us a few smokes', and in return the sailors sent the cigarette cards back for the children to keep. Similar collections were made other years. During the Blitz, lessons were disturbed three times by air raids, and the Christmas party had to be cancelled, but locals paid for sweets and biscuits instead. The children did charity work at times, and on one occasion two pupils, Joyce Murrey and Margaret Bennett, received special mention for their 'enterprise and initiative in making and selling novelties for the Red Cross'. At the special request of the Essex War Agricultural Executive, school holidays were postponed to mid-August so that older children could help get the harvest in, since manpower was in short supply. In 1942, they also helped with potato lifting with an additional autumn holiday. The school buildings were useful to the war effort - the youth centre was housed in the churchyard school (with electricity laid on for this purpose), while the Upper School was used for ATC meetings and HQ for the firewatchers – all the teachers volunteered for this. The children contributed to the war effort by their savings, gathering in savings for Warship Week and Wings for Victor Week and also collected bucketfuls of rosehips. School records are

missing for part of the war, but in 1944 the children had a lecture from the police about the dangers of touching unexploded bombs and other dangerous objects – as if to demonstrate this, the walls of the Upper School building were badly cracked when two doodlebugs dropped locally, but finally came the happy day in May 1945, when school closed for the VE Day celebrations. There was a teacher shortage during the war, exacerbated when two long-term teachers left - Miss Marjorie Somerfield after 18 years and Miss L.J. Barker after 21 years: 'One wonders how many children must have known Miss Barker as teacher and friend', wrote the vicar. 'By her infinite patience and tact she has made herself beloved by all.' Miss Barker was famous for her pageants, dressing the infants in costumes of tinsel, crepe paper and dyed stockings made by herself (see photo).

March 1940

My dear Friends

'It doesn't do to think in these days Vicar, it really doesn't.' You can probably guess what went before in the conversation. We had been speaking of some of the horrors of the recent time, of the evil in the world and my friend's mind seemed do be moving towards despair. Certainly it doesn't do to think if our mind leads us to the things that are horrible, for very soon comes panic, and panic is one of the deadliest foes of the human soul. But it does do to think in another way, to think one's way through the surface of things and to get down to the bedrock of life. We are very much under a cloud just now and we long for a glimpse of the blue sky as we grope our way along anxiously and uncertainly; we long again for an assurance of the final certainties that await our struggling race..... The call of our church to thank God for mothers and our homes comes with particular force this year. Family life in various parts of Europe has been broken up; many have been exiled; even in England the war has brought a change to many homes. In some the menfolk are serving their country on land, sea and in the air. In others we have given shelter to young children evacuated from their own homes. I hope that as many as possible of our mothers will be present at these Mothering Services and I do particularly invite all those from whose homes men have joined the colours, all those who have acted as foster parents and all children. Thus may we join in thankfulness to God for all that our homes mean to us in an age when so much is being threatened.

Yours most sincerely, E.A. STONE

PARISH CHURCH.—There was a large congregation at Clavering Parish Church on Sunday afternoon for a special Mothering Sunday Service. This was the first occasion such a service had been held in the parish, and in addition to the families of the parish, a special invitation had been sent to all evacuated children and their foster-parents and also to the families of those serving in the Forces. The service was conducted by the Vicar (the Rev. E. A. Stone), and the lessons were read by Lieut. C. C. T. Simmonds, one of the church-wardens. In addition to the special hymns the choir sang a beautiful 14th century carol about Mothering Sunday. It was pleasing to see such a good response to this revival of a very ancient custom.

Local newspaper report on Clavering's revival of the custom of holding a special service for Mothering Sunday. The photo shows one of Clavering's wartime mothers – the Vicar's wife Doris with their little daughter Judith, born in 1938.

Food in Wartime Clavering

When rationing was introduced at the beginning of 1940, every household had to register with local shops and take their ration books to be stamped according to the allowances for cheese, bacon, ham, sugar, butter, cooking fat, later tea and meat. Ration books were issued locally by the Food Office. Connie Mowbray (nee Foster, b.1930) left school towards the end of the war and her first job was for the Ministry of Food Office in Saffron Walden, which administered the ration system: 'I biked to Saffron Walden seven miles to work. One summer I did night and morning every day. I earned 19s 6d a week. It was lovely when we went out to the villages with ration books. Downstairs they sold the dried milk, cod liver oil and orange juice for mothers with babies.' The ration books had to be stamped for purchases at five village shops: Fairbanks in the High Street, Catons at the Mills, Kells at Pelham Road, Atkinsons bakers and Peacocks butchers at Arkesden Road.

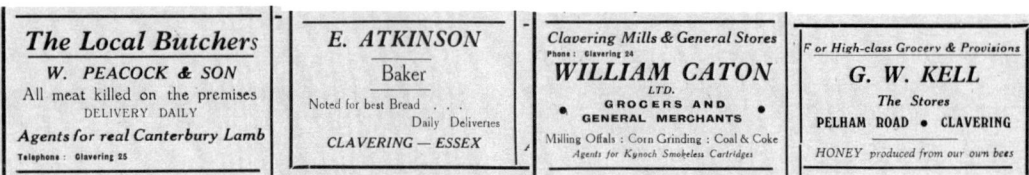

Mr Peacock also had a wartime role as the chief allocator of meat for the whole rural district. Isobel Beckwith (nee Barker, b.1918) did the butcher's rounds during the war, since Mr Peacock's male drivers had been called up: 'I started delivering the meat around Clavering, Berden, Pelham, Langley, Duddenhoe End, Arkesden and Wicken. They had two deliveries a week, and when I wasn't out on the rounds I was making sausages for the shop also for the rounds. I also had a limited number of meat pies to sell, also liver, and "lights" for cats. I drove a Ford Eight van - maroon was the "Peacock" colour, the other van was driven by Mary Martin, whose father was the undertaker, and lived on Hill Green. I enjoyed doing the butcher's round as I kept up with all the families and heard about their husbands or sons who were away in the war. By 1944 petrol was getting short so I was only working three days a week, although they were long days, 7.30 until 6 o'clock or after.'

During wartime many foods were in short supply, but country people had more options than those in town. Isobel Beckwith recalled: 'We were never short of food as my aunt kept pigs, chickens and we always had plenty of fresh vegetables as there was a large garden at the back of the house - rabbits and there were always eggs, which you could make so many different meals with. One of the favourite supper meals was poached eggs on runner beans or fresh peas.' Housewives needed much ingenuity to produce nutritious meals and one year Mrs Stone arranged a free wartime cooking demonstration by an official of the Ministry of Food, using an oil cooking stove. The 'Weekday Pages for Women with Homes' at the back of the parish magazines were full of useful ideas for eggless cakes and ingenious things to do with potatoes (see appendix 5). It is always said that people were healthier during the war because there were no luxuries and no junk food.

Mothers of children under school age could obtain an annual permit enabling them to buy a pint of milk a day for twopence – forms could be obtained at the Vicarage. There was also an allocation of fruit juice which was later extended to all children under five years old. In March 1943 this bureaucracy was simplified and mothers simply had to show the milkman their child's ration book in order to get the milk. Adults might have to put up with National Dried Milk, which was sold in cans by the Ministry of Food. Much more popular with children were the tins of sweets sent over for them by Canadian schoolchildren.

Dried milk and dried egg - essential in order to use the recipes for wartime puddings: 'one level tablespoon of dried egg with two tablespoons of water equals one egg'.

Countryfolk could keep chickens, and once a year the church collected eggs at Easter for the local hospital. A basket was left at the door of the church on Palm Sunday and in 1942 they managed to send 67 eggs, 111 in 1943, 104 in 1944 and 115 in 1945. Everyone tried to grow vegetables - Eileen Clarke, an evacuee at Clavering Court, remembers that 'the gardener was told to turn part of the herbaceous borders over to vegetables. There was no shortage of food there with the farm next door. I remember a pantry where all the preserves were kept - buckets and buckets of eggs in isinglass'. June Holland (nee Riley) recalls: 'We did grow some things, more of a barter system. Meat was rationed in money rather than weight, so we always bought stewing meat, and mum would put it in a large sauccpan with veg, and it stayed there all day, with horrible dried haricot beans, and jacket potatoes in the oven, so they were ready when we came home for lunch. We could always get potatoes and Arthur King used to drop us rabbits when he was shooting, Someone used to snare rabbits up Gipsy Lane and we used to buy off him.'

There was a government scheme in 1941 for community jam-making and Clavering set to, led by the usual good women of the village - Jean Finzel of The Court and Doris Stone from the Vicarage with a committee of seven. In June 1941 the Clavering and Langley Jam Centre was set up and a village meeting held to explain the scheme. It relied on every household sparing at least a pound of fruit but they did not need to give it away – windfall apples, plums, blackberries and even marrows would be bought at government prices, and the committee would pay ninepence per dozen for 2lb jam-jars and sixpence for 1lb jars. The resulting preserves could be sold in local shops – the intention was to expand the food supply rather than to make money. Curiously, there is little further mention of this in subsequent years, although in 1942 Langley School did something similar and produced 130lbs of jam with the help of extra sugar from the Ministry of Food. Local schoolchildren could also earn fourpence a pound collecting rosehips, used for making rosehip syrup, rich in vitamin C. Curiously, they also collected hundreds of conkers, apparently used to extract starch to make acetone for cordite in ammunition.

Clavering Pillbox

The pillbox, still very solidly *in situ* on the outskirts of Clavering along the Manuden road, is a symbolic piece of WW2 reminding us of the desperate time in the dark days of June-December 1940 when invasion seemed imminent. To boost morale and offer delaying tactics against invaders, the Government spent the huge sum of £28 million commissioning Coulsons of Cambridge to provide 22,000 pillboxes of concrete, steel, bricks and mesh. Each one cost £1,200. By June 1941 the project was complete. Wartime historian Michael Barton feels that Clavering's isolated box was probably one of the later constructions as it is not part of the 'GHQ Line' that ran on the east side of the old A11. Dick Law remembers that there were also concrete anti-tank traps shaped like large bells that could be rolled into the road. Originally the pillbox commanded unrestricted views of the road and river valley. The Clavering design, with walls only 15 inches thick, fits most closely to a bullet-proof Type 24 box (see diagram below), i.e. it was not shell-proof or blast-proof. The exterior has small square holes above and below the embrasure, which would have held a vertical rising metal shutter, the faint outline of which can be made out – perhaps to keep the draught out on chilly winter nights. The interior photograph shows the ricochet and blast brick wall in the shape of an equally-legged Y. Below the embrasures inside are four metal bolts to secure a wooden table the same width, used to rest the elbows when aiming a rifle or Bren gun. There was probably a trench running north to the searchlight camp, and the box may have been utilised as a blast and air raid shelter. After all this expense, pillboxes rapidly became redundant, as Hitler's 'Operation Sealion' was called off and the Government's approach altered from static defence to rapid response troops. But the strongly-built fortifications are very hard to remove, and many remain – although a second box, that once existed near Wicken Road, was demolished after the war. The Clavering pillbox is worthy of rescuing from the undergrowth burying it - Clavering's only remaining artefact from an extraordinary period in our island history 70 years ago.

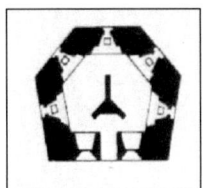

Type 24 pillbox, an imperfect hexagon, showing Y-shaped blast wall in front of the entrance and five embrasures offering viewpoints in all directions.

Searchlight Camp 1939-44

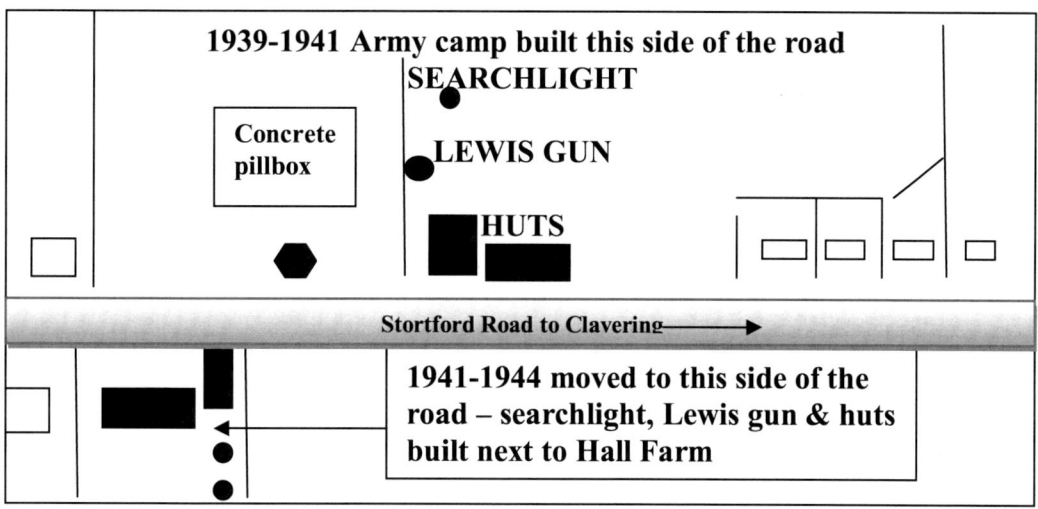

1939-1941 Army camp built this side of the road

SEARCHLIGHT

Concrete pillbox

LEWIS GUN

HUTS

Stortford Road to Clavering ———▶

1941-1944 moved to this side of the road – searchlight, Lewis gun & huts built next to Hall Farm

This diagram (not to scale) illustrates the layout of the ack-ack battery which was built in between Clavering Hall and the last house on Stortford Road. From 1939 onwards there was a whole complex of Army structures along the road, but their position changed over the course of the war. From 1939 to 1941, the Anti-Aircraft Command searchlight camp was on the same side of the road as the pillbox, with a generator adjacent to the road, then some Army huts for dining and sleeping and up in the field a Lewis gun emplacement and a searchlight. It is not clear whether it was linked to the pillbox which may have been built later (see p.32). Such camps were very common in the countryside – others existed near Duddenhoe Grange and at Hobs Aerie in Arkesden. The searchlights lit up the sky to pick out enemy planes so that anti-aircraft gunners could take aim. In 1941, the whole complex was shifted to the other side of the road adjacent to Clavering Hall Farm, possibly so that the water and other facilities at the farm could be utilised. This diagram provided by Mike Preisig, who now lives in Kent but was a schoolboy in Clavering at the time, was confirmed by Dick Law, also a young lad in the village. He remembers taking food up to the soldiers who manned the camp, and thinks there were up to 20 men there at any one time, who always seemed to be hungry in spite of army rations. In May 1940, the Vicar of Clavering put an appeal in the parish magazine for surplus seeds so the soldiers could make a garden, also gifts of books, magazines and gramophone records. Local girls used to visit the soldiers and at least two ended up marrying girls from the village (see p.100), one of them the sister of Maurice Kemp. There was a guard hut with a sentry and the men lived in the huts. John Barwood was also a boy at the time and remembers dogfights here:

'One night there was a lot of activity in the air and we went down the allotment, it was a moonlit night and we saw the beam had got a plane and suddenly this plane dived down the beam and just before he died away 'cause our fighters were after him, we heard the gunfire go, they shot him but only somebody got slightly injured. That was a sight. Then later on there was pall of black smoke and we all went hooray 'cause there was so many of our fighters after him, they surrounded him, probably several of them were gonna beat him up.'

The camp was closed down in 1944 when the Allies went into Europe and it became clear that the danger of invasion in Britain was no more.

Formation of Home Guard 1940

On 14th May 1940 the Local Defence Volunteer Force was formed, later called the Home Guard. There was a rush to join and by the end of the year it had more than one million volunteers, among them those in Newport Company to which Clavering belonged, formed in July 1940. The local unit was part of the 12th Essex Home Defence Battalion with headquarters at Stansted. The Newport Company, whose Commanding Officer was Squire Wilkes of Elmdon Bury, had detachments at Clavering, Newport, Langley, Arkesden, Elmdon, Littlebury, Chrishall, Great Chesterford and Wendon. Clavering was No 3 Platoon, initially under Platoon Commander, L.R.H. Luckock who lived at The Old House, with members from Clavering, Langley, Arkesden and Wicken Bonhunt. Able-bodied adult men were expected to do some form of voluntary service, also young men such as Fred Whyman waiting till they were old enough to be called up. Lance-Cpl Fred Sampford, who could not join up through an arm problem, recalled that HG training included 'going down the tunnels at Audley End in case there was any disruption. We all got together with the other villages.' Barry Wilson still has a bayonet that his father, Charles Wilson of Stickling Green, kept while training with the Home Guard. An account of what it was like to belong to the 'Dad's Army' has been recorded by Douglas Savill who grew up in Langley:

'Grandfather Wombwell joined the LDV (Local Defence Volunteers) who were distinguished by an armband with the letters LVD on them. The LDV later became the Home Guard, and uniforms were gradually issued, and the Home Guard began to look like soldiers. He would go on night watch. He would take with him some sandwiches and a little Camp Coffee bottle full of home-made Mead to reinforce them during the night. Sometimes the group would go on guard duty at the railway tunnels at Littlebury - and it was said that some of the stokers on the trains would throw off some coal for them to make a fire. The Home Guard was eventually issued with some rifles - old Lee Enfields. Colonel Ambrose, from Thurrocks Farm, officer in charge, had a car and a petrol allowance to visit the troops. The Home Guard was made up of men who were allowed to stay in the village because of

being in a reserved occupation, or were too old to be called up. All those in the Home Guard took it very seriously, and no doubt if the Germans had come they would have done their best to repel the enemy.'

Members of the local Home Guard practising drill on the road between Duddenhoe End and Arkesden – they include Louie Atkinson, Stan King and Stanley Neville.

June 1940

My dear Friends

Horror is succeeding horror in this terrible conflict which is tearing the world to pieces. The world has suddenly blazed up and the rapidity with which events are marching makes it impossible for our intelligence to grasp the situation... What are our reactions to the war news? Are we living generally in a state of hope or of fear - fear of death, fear of illness, fear of air raids and a thousand more ... The future of the world depends on hopeful and constructive thinking. We must believe the best, speak the best and live day by day as though the best is yet to be... There has been a good response to the appeal for volunteers for the Defence Corps and detachments under Mr Luckock and General Anderson have been formed. The air raid wardens and special constables in addition to their usual duties have been carrying out a dawn watch for possible parachutists. Our householders whose evacuated children still remain with them have received a letter of appreciation from Her Majesty the Queen. At the same time the list of names of those serving in the King's Forces grows bigger every week. I am sure that we have them constantly in our prayers.

Yours most sincerely, E.A. STONE

Silent Church Bells

The Government Order forbidding the use of church bells for any purpose other than warnings in connection with air-borne enemy troops had come into force last week-end, so that on Sunday the usual church bells were silent.

Silent Bells

The Home Front was full of irritating restrictions, none more so to the clergy and others than the banning of church bells. Not only they lost the traditional call to worship, but also the skills, which took years to acquire, disappeared as bellringers were away on war work or in the Forces. At the start of the war, bellringing was still allowed, but then in the summer of 1940 came the government edict to silence the bells, and the Vicar was deeply upset by it: 'The stopping of the ringing of the church bells has meant a real break in our parochial life'. But he did recognise that it had to be so. Now and then ringing was allowed, as in November 1940 after the victory at El Alamein, but to the Vicar's great disappointment, the band of keen young ringers he had put together before the war were all dispersed on Army or Home Guard duties and a team could not be found. So the bells remained silent for several more years.

Dunkirk 1940

Twenty-year-old Douglas Stock, Elsenham's first Militia youth, and George Livings, of Middle Street, Clavering, who is thought to have been the only man from that village, are both back safely, as is Driver H. B. Thomas, son of Mr. and Mrs. B. Thomas, of Brooklands, Wenden.

Most of the 18 Saffron Walden men have already reassured their families that they have come back unhurt. Pte. Bert Dench of

Between 27th May to 4th June 1940, 338,226 British and French troops were rescued from the chaos of Dunkirk when the British Expeditionary Force were backed onto the sea. To the great relief of his Middle Street family, young George Livings of the East Surrey Regiment (see photo p.23) was among those who came home safely, but the local newspaper report is incorrect as there were others from Clavering who were rescued, including Sonny and Henry Barker (see p.23), Sid Matthews (see p.87), John Newland (see p.144) and Driver George Barker of the Essex Regiment (pictured below). A professional soldier since before the war, he had joined the Essex Regiment in 1934 aged 19. In his 90s he recalled: 'As time went on we realised there was trouble coming, so when Mr Chamberlain announced there was a war on we were already packed. I was attached to B. Coy and I drove an 8cwt vehicle. It was a very cold winter, the coldest for years. In the spring we moved to Meurchin, and we were here when the Germans went into Holland.' The battalion moved on, but then were forced back to Dunkirk. In his 90s, still living in Clavering, George recounted his Dunkirk experiences which were typical of many.

'There were many bridges round Brussels and the Essex had to blow the last one. The time came and everybody safe, the bridge was blown, we had a meal, by that time it was dark. The Battalion started marching back the way we came, moving all night and they would somewhere take up a defensive position, nothing happened. I was driving and the Germans used to strafe the roads – that was wicked! The roads were full of refugees fleeing the opposite way to us. One day when the Germans flew over and dropped bombs, I dived out of the lorry and ended up in the side of a bomb crater covered in sand and my mate had to clean me up. The whole traffic was stopped, the road was solid and we couldn't move any farther because there was so much - the refugees were coming at us and all of a sudden there were three German tanks in the distance going from right to left. Luckily they didn't swing their guns on us! When we got to a certain position, all the vehicles had to be left and dumped.

'And then everybody walked and the Battalion kept in formation for a long time, then it was every man for himself and we eventually finished up in Dunkirk by 29th May. I was with a corporal named Percy Parker from Godmanchester and he and I kept together. I was on Dunkirk Beach. We stood there and the tide would come in, and when the tide went out, you laid down and the Germans would come over and strafe you. We lost several on that beach. We didn't have any food but we'd got our water bottles full – there was a tap where we could get some water. Percy got away before me - he got picked up the day before. There was someone rowing up and down with this little boat and he took me out to this destroyer. Sailors helped me up the rope ladder, sat me down on a bench, and one gave me a cup of tea and a corned beef sandwich. I went to sleep and don't remember any more till they woke me up in England.' **Extract from *Clavering Remembered* George Barker (2011)**.

In Memoriam Sidney Rosier

After Dunkirk came news of the death of Sapper Sidney Rosier who was aged 32 and served with the Royal Engineers. His name appears on the war memorial outside the Christian Centre in Stortford Road, but not on the wooden memorial inside Clavering Church even though his widow, Ivy (nee Newland), lived in Clavering. The reason for the discrepancy may be because he was not a Clavering resident before the war. The photograph shows him in happier times, on his wedding day in 1937. Their baby son Kenneth John was born in October 1939, but the boy never knew his father who was serving abroad up until his death - his name is on the Dunkirk Memorial as he has no known grave.

In Memory of
Sapper SIDNEY ROBERT ROSIER

1865170, 17 Field Coy., Royal Engineers
who died age 32
on 01 June 1940
Husband of I. R. Rosier, of Clavering, Essex.
Remembered with honour

DUNKIRK MEMORIAL

'During the Second World War, Dunkirk was the scene of the historic evacuation of the British Expeditionary Force from France in May 1940. The Dunkirk Memorial stands at the entrance to the British War Graves Section of Dunkirk Town Cemetery. It commemorates more than 4,500 casualties of the British Expeditionary Force who died in the campaign of 1939-40 or who died in captivity who were captured during this campaign and who have no known grave.'
Commonwealth War Graves Commission

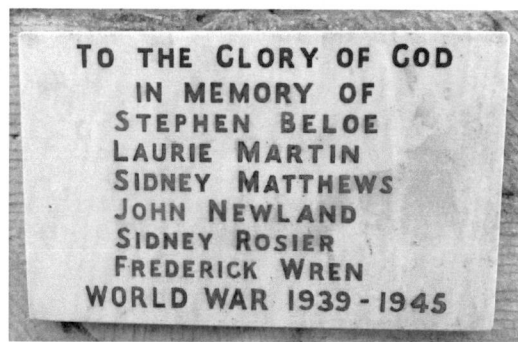

TO THE GLORY OF GOD
IN MEMORY OF
STEPHEN BELOE
LAURIE MARTIN
SIDNEY MATTHEWS
JOHN NEWLAND
SIDNEY ROSIER
FREDERICK WREN
WORLD WAR 1939-1945

July 1940

My dear Friends

The battle of France is lost. The battle of Britain will soon begin. That was the Prime Minister's message to the nation a few days ago in a straightforward, candid and heartening speech. Things certainly move quickly in these days; but a few months ago many were deploring the fact that little seemed to be happening; now every day brings news of the fresh exploits of the godless gangsters. Very soon the war may enter a new phase. The enemy has begun to deliver bombing attacks which are likely to continue. Anxiety and distress will no doubt come to all of us. How are we to face them? We can, I think, be reassured by the state of the country's defences and the efficiency of our air forces and even if German bombers are sometimes able to pass through our defences we are also able to penetrate theirs. An air attack always sounds far worse than it is... The Germans today deliberately exploit the factor of noise in order to exaggerate terror and they attach to their machines and bombs devices which increase that noise tenfold. Hitler's main object is to undermine our courage; against this we need to remember that courage can be very infectious. There is the probability also that Hitler will seek to invade Great Britain. We should look forward to that invasion without any apprehension; we must prepare for it but we should not fear it. Hitler's belief is that he can frighten the British people into surrender before the autumn. If he fails to do that he will have failed to win the war and the great tide of power will begin to turn on our side.

This is indeed a people's war and it is encouraging to see almost everyone eager to do their bit. There shouldn't be a person who is not helping in some way to carry on the war. Ours may not be a very active part. It may be only saving a few bones, a little waste paper or some scraps of old iron or perhaps buying a sixpenny savings stamp every week but we are nevertheless doing something. It is a good thing to read that some of the leaders of the pacifist movement have publicly recanted and admitted the error of their former thinking. In the last batch of men to be called up there were practically no conscientious objectors. I have read a good deal of the literature of pacifists. We are all pacifists at heart, we British folk are no lovers of war, but the man who refuses to help his country in its hour of need because he is a pacifist is both selfish and cowardly. Only last week a man said to me that he would not help on the war in any way whatever. It is difficult to see how anyone could hold such a view and still go on living in England, enjoying the security of our island, continuing his normal business and doing perhaps the better in business because of the war. It all seems very inconsistent to me and as I have said, selfish and cowardly, to allow others to give their lives in fighting so that we can be safe and then to refuse to help on the war. Why are we fighting? We are not a military nation. We went to the utmost lengths – many people think we went too far – in our efforts to keep the peace and avert war. We have gone to war because we felt we could take no other steps. We went to war so that honour, truth and justice might not perish from the earth. We went to war to put an end to oppression and cruelty and brutality and to make a world in which the nations can live in quietness and without fear. We are not out for anything for ourselves. We are not out for territory. If ever a war deserved to be called a Crusade this war - unsought by us – is such a war, for we are about to defend those values and decencies which alone make life worth living and international order possible. We can say of our cause what the Crusaders said of their adventure: *Deus Vult* – 'God wills it'. We can pray and should pray for victory and that God will bring good out of evil.

Occasionally, very, very occasionally, I am glad to say, I hear suggestions such as 'Would it be so very bad if the Germans came here?' or 'Shouldn't we stop the war and negotiate terms with Hitler?' Would to God the war would end, but to come to terms before final victory has been achieved would be to approve of barefaced lying, of slavery, of torture, of cold blooded murder, and of a regime of terror and bloodshed. Anyone making such a suggestion should certainly be reported at once to the police. They are dangerous to the community in which they live, traitors to their country and must be carefully watched... When you hear gunfire or the noise of bombs dropping do you go 'all to pieces', lose your nerve and become a worry to those you live with? No one of course feels pleased at such a time but it is a Christian duty to be calm and courageous. The nervy panicky people are usually afraid of one thing – that they are going to die. If you really believe in religion and all that it entails it is hypocrisy to have a fear of death – 'to be in great fear where no fear is'. Like the martyrs of old we are having the chance to give and dare all against the greatest organized challenge to Christianity and civilisation that the world has ever seen. The universe is so vast and so ageless that the life of one man can only be justified by the measure of his sacrifice. We are sent to this world to acquire a personality and a character to take with us that can never be taken from us. None of us knows in these days especially when our earthly mission may be brought to a close. Let us then so live each day that if it should be the last we shall be ready to cross the narrow stream of death. 'In quietness' and confidence shall be your strength' knowing that 'underneath are the everlasting arms'.
Yours most sincerely, E.A. STONE

Tea to be 2-oz. Ration

Tea is now rationed at two ounces per head a week.

Margarine and cooking fats will be rationed in association with butter in a fortnight's time.

Hotels and restaurants are not to serve both a fish and meat course in the same meal.

Icing of confectionery is to stop.

Lord Woolton, Minister of Food, announcing these plans on Monday, explained that there were adequate supplies of food in the country, but we must prepare for "a long effort of siege."

From Tuesday tea could be bought only upon the surrender of one of the spare coupons in the current ration book.

A Ministry announcement says: "You will be able to buy your tea at any shop. There will be no need to register. The price will be controlled at existing levels. The buff-coloured spare coupons are to be used either weekly or fortnightly, or the whole page can be deposited."

On top of all the other bad news that summer, came the upsetting announcement that tea was to be rationed to two ounces (equivalent today to about 15 teabags) per person per week.

August 1940

My dear Friends

A talk was given recently by the Foreign Secretary, Lord Halifax, in reply to a speech by the German Chancellor... It was good to listen to one who never lets the statesman hide the Christian... the patience, courage and cheerfulness of the people, even when taken together are not enough without the guidance and sustenance of Almighty God... So many official utterances have been very boastful almost to the extent of being depressing by placing their emphasis on our own strong arm... If we are praying for victory are we at the same time doing our best to make our country worthy of victory?...

Our children's harvest holiday has been very much curtailed. For myself, although since we came to the parish nearly three years ago neither my wife nor I have had a holiday, we feel we should remain. But if not a change of scene perhaps a short change of occupation may be possible and if I can be of any use in the harvest fields I should be pleased to give my services for a few days.

Yours most sincerely. E.A. STONE

September 1940

My dear Friends

Just now we are called to special thankfulness for the blessings of another harvest. Under ideal weather conditions, the best, so I am told, for many years, we have been able to gather in safely the fruits of the earth. At a time when the harvest in so many countries has been ruined and when because of barbaric cruelties and oppressions men have been unable to gather the fruit of their earlier labours, we should be ready to give thanks for our own. Whether it is the harvest of our garden or allotment or farm we have been abundantly blessed.... it is a very encouraging thing to count our blessings, it makes us calm and confident and just now a calm and confident person is doing as much for the country as a member of the armed forces.....

Yours most sincerely, E.A. STONE

Day of National Prayer *Sunday September 8th is the Sunday after the first anniversary of the declaration of war... since the last day of prayer in May the anxieties of the nation and empire have been greatly increased... the President of the United States has also called his people to prayer on the same day. Thus on both sides of the Atlantic the two great democracies will be joined together in their acknowledgement of God Most High.*

Harvest Services. *These were very well attended and our worship and thanksgiving in churches decorated so beautifully with such a profusion of flowers, fruit and vegetables was most helpful in these troublous times. At Clavering the large congregation at the evening parade service for members of the various village defence units made an impressive gathering. The chaplain to the forces at Stansted gave a most helpful sermon in thanksgiving and service. 'Giving up ourselves to God's service' he showed meant worship, war and work. We were glad to see the Bishop of Chelmsford at Langley although he was rather late on account of having to take an alternative route because of time bombs by the road. However his message was very heartening. The matrons of both the hospital and infirmary are most grateful for the harvest gifts and the three organisations helped by the collections are also very thankful for our gifts.*

Harvest time in Clavering

The Second World War hastened the coming of technology to agriculture. The differing atmosphere is well captured in these two pictures: (above) Walter Whyman leading the horse and cart during harvest at Ford End before the war, with Ben Rogers standing on top; (below) harvesting by steam power on a local farm.

Clavering Farms 1940

The winter of 1940 was very cold and the frozen land meant that Essex farmers had managed to plough only just over half of the expected acreage by the time spring arrived. The other big problem was shortage of labour as so many men had joined up or gone into other forms of war work which were better paid. In 1940 weekly farm wages went up from about 37 to 48 shillings, to 60 in 1941 and 65 shillings in 1943. Others who also helped were Land Girls, schoolboys in harvest camps and later prisoners-of-war. Newport Grammar School pupil, Mike Preisig who lived at Danson in Stortford Road, remembers that cattle, horses and goats were grazed on greens and wide roadside verges. Smallholder Daniel Morgan kept a few milking grows grazing on Hill Green, selling their milk from a tricycle. In Form 11C, Mike did some geography homework entitled 'Study of Farms in Clavering - 25 September 1940'. It is a remarkable piece of work by a schoolboy.

- **Brooklands Farm** – Farmed by A.D. King. 250 acres + Wayletts Farm + 14 acres Starlings Green. Labour: Oddy Rogers (horsekeeper), Derek King, Bill Newlands (beekeeper), Lionel Wombwell. Livestock: 4 carthorses, 12 bullocks, 1 house cow, 5 Essex sows & piglets. Crops: 10 acres sugar beet, 7 acres potatoes, 12 acres grass, wheat, barley, oats, field beans, red clover. Machinery: 1 International 10.20 tractor
- **Clavering Court** – Farmed by Mr H.C. Finzel and son Richard.
- **Clavering Farm** – Farmed by Jennings family. [P.W.Gammon]
- **Clavering Hall** – Farmed by P.E. Rowe. Highlands Farm & Sheepyard. Approx 40 milking cows milked by machine. 6 cart horses grazed land along River Stort.
- **Clavering Place** – Farmed by Ted Funston and family.
- **Curls Manor** & grazed Bury meadows - Farmed by Vassar Hunter Rowe. 2 farm lorries – carted milk in churns every day to Walthamstow Dairies. Drivers: Bunny Mathews & Sid Law. General farm haulage – sugar beet to Felsted factory.
- **The Grange** – Billy Williams, farmer and dealer, and son Aubrey.
- **Ford End (Yew Tree Farm)** – Farmed by Foster family.
- **Lower Ford End** – Farmed by Custerson family. [A.G. Brant]
- **Hill Green Farm** – Farmed by Reg Tinney and Hitchcock - Foreman Walt Read, the largest farmers in Clavering. Crops: picking peas and potatoes + grain crops. Employed lots of gipsy families who camped in the field opposite the *Princess of Wales*.
- **Parsonage Farm** – Farmed by Dick Bazley and brother-in-law Pinnock. Small dairy farm.
- **Roast Green Farm** – Farmed by Mr W. & A. Smith and family.
- **Sheepcote Green farm** – Farmed by Will Abrahams and sons. Vast number of pigs. Own lorry carted pig-swill – sugar beet etc. [see photo]
- **Stevens Farm** – Farmed by Woodham family.

The Harts *Directory* also lists Home Farm (F. Archer), Bird Green (F. Copeland) and Brocking Farm, Moat Farm (F. Kemp) and Mill End Farm. Of the wartime farmhouses, only about half are still lived in by farmers today, and most are now private residences.

The ATS

A number of girls from Clavering served in the Auxiliary Territorial Services, formed in 1938 to carry out non-combatant duties such as driving and clerical work. These reminiscences of Evelyn Aberneithie (pictured 2001) capture some of the flavour of life in the ATS.

'I had joined the ATS during 1938, so I and my colleagues were all expecting to get call-up notices at any moment, but it didn't come. We all sat and listened and after the declaration was over, everybody looked at one another and thought, 'well this is it - where do we go from now?' After a few minutes the air raid siren went, a terrifying noise, and everyone parted, just scuttled like rats. And of course very shortly afterwards the all-clear went, and we felt a bit guilty, we went back to see if they were all right and the horses were all right and everything. The next day I got my call-up notice and that was very disappointing because it was to go to Weybridge, and I went on a lorry with all the suitcases. I was a corporal then and I was told to go to the local policeman to find billets for the girls, and we had strict regulations that nobody was to be billeted in a house without a bath. And I traipsed round with a very large red-faced policeman with a tin hat, and it was an awful job to find a house with a bathroom who would take two girls. Another regulation was that no girls were to be boarded in public houses, well one of our girls lived in Weybridge and her people kept the pub. She wasn't allowed to go home. We were very disgusted too because the place where we had to work was an ordinance depot and it was mostly staffed by civilian workers, and you know although everything was pretty serious then, nothing much happened. We got two bob a day, so our wages at the end of the week were about 14 shillings. I remember being bombed very badly. I was camped in Gloucestershire near Pittsburgh under canvas, and when our big guns went off at on the railway we could hear all these German bombers going over in droves in the Coventry air raid, a terrible noise but when these big bombs were fired, the tent poles used to vibrate. It was really quite frightening, and of course you never knew if shrapnel was going up quite near us, whether a bit was going to come through the tent but we were lucky we never had any.'

Some of the local girls in the ATS - Marjorie Baker, Budgie Elwell and Irene Law – Irene served in Egypt as a switchboard operator taking messages. She married a soldier while out there and later also served in Palestine.

The Maines of Mill End

The war brought a number of families out to Clavering, escaping the bombing. Among them was Bar Maine (centre photo) who had a second home at Mill End Dairy Farm (pictured below in 1940s). Her husband, Henry (left photo) could be seen mowing the lawn in a Harris tweed suit and hat, but was away a lot working in London, apparently as a civil servant. In fact, after service as a WW1 Guards officer, in 1919 he had been a founder member of the Government Code & Cypher School, decrypting messages. Hence, during WW2 he was still working for the Secret Intelligence Service doing hush-hush work. Even today his descendants know virtually nothing about his wartime role – grandson Simon Baddeley recalls, 'We were taught from childhood not to talk about "the business". My grandfather moved between Bletchley Park and Broadway during the war and that's about as much as I know.' Henry and Bar, a former debutante, had bought the farm and nearby cottages in the 1930s. She used it as a country retreat, re-named it Mill End Dairy Farm and taught herself to be a dairy farmer. Their daughters Barbara and Margot grew up here in a rural idyll, interrupted in 1940, as Barbara recalls:

'The war came and my mother got scared stiff of the bombing in London and emigrated to Clavering and never came back to London again. Clavering in the war was our solace and our refuge. My father spent a lot of time in London and had an important war job there.'

Bar Maine was once told by a local official that if the church bells rang, the Germans were invading and she must pack one suitcase and go to the end of the lane to await rescue - no, she replied, she had no intention of leaving her home. She stayed and 'did her bit', collecting salvage, depositing heaps of sand for incendiaries and hosting the launch of the Pig Club at her farm in 1941. Meanwhile, daughter Barbara would crank-start her little Austin Seven to drive to Newport railway station, to commute to London with other locals, who

forged friendships on the hazardous daily journey into the war-torn capital, amid sirens and bombings. Barbara married Capt John Baddeley of the Coldstream Guards (right photo, above), but he was seriously wounded at Nijmegen, and while convalescing was also recruited into the SIS. Barbara remembers a doodlebug at Mill End: 'My son was in his cot and I suddenly heard this strange noise. I went up to see that he was ok and I heard this rattle overhead, then suddenly it stopped and rattled over the top of the cottage then dived down the road.' Her family later moved elsewhere, but Bar Maine loved Clavering and stayed on at Mill End where she died in 1969.

'Missing in Action'

This was the dreadful message received by many mothers, wives and girlfriends of young airmen who fought in the Battle of Britain which lasted from July/August to October 1940. Among them was Margot Maine who had lived at Mill End Dairy Farm, Clavering with her family since before the war. She was engaged to a distinguished pilot, Flt Lt Robert V. Jeff (DFC & Bar, Croix de Guerre), who was serving with 85 Squadron RAF, and they were soon to marry. Sometimes, Bobby flew his Hurricane over Mill End to greet his fiancée. His personal tally of enemy planes shot down had reached nine.

But on 11 August 1940, Bobby Jeff led his flight to intercept an enemy raid of 100 enemy planes and was last seen diving to attack them. Aged 37, he was one of 'The Few', described by a fellow pilot as 'very popular and loved by the men. The pilots looked up to him and he never let anyone down'. Margot was devastated by the loss of her fiancé, but eventually found happiness with another. She too worked at Bletchley Park (see p.44). Her nephew, Simon Baddeley recalls the sad scene at Mill End Dairy Farm when they received the news:

'He was due to marry my aunt Margot Maine in the summer of 1940. Presents for their wedding were laid out in her mother's house in Clavering. Then the postman arrived. My grandmother said to me many years later: "The moment I saw him coming up the lane on his bicycle I knew". Bobby Jeff - one of "the Few" - died nearly two years before I was born in the same house. He was one of 544 airmen who lost their lives during the Battle of Britain.'

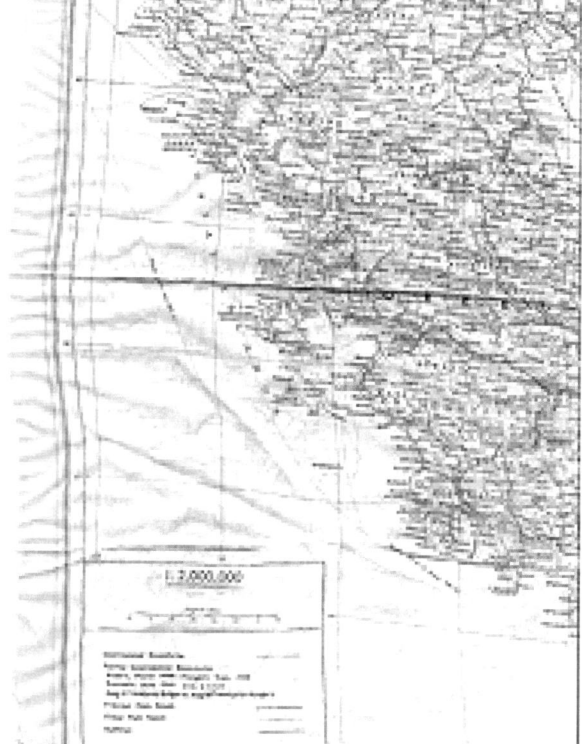

Many years later Simon found this little piece of material hidden in a drawer – it was a silk handkerchief printed with a map, half a century old but still in perfect condition. When he showed it to his mother, she produced a second one covering another area and said there would once have been two others in a set of four. Typically, they would be given to airmen like Bobby Jeff, for use if shot down over enemy territory and needing a map to find his way home. They would have been rolled tightly inside a hollow pencil with a tiny compass at one end hidden beneath an eraser.

An amazing reminder of all those courageous young men who defended England in the skies in the summer of 1940.

ARP Incident Files 1940

Thanks to the sacrifices of men like Bobby Jeff, the Nazis failed to defeat Britain in the air. Hitler then abandoned plans for invasion and decided to bomb its civilians into oblivion. ARP was stepped up as the 'Battle of London' developed from the autumn of 1940 onwards. Country villages like Clavering got off lightly, when you consider that by June 1941, two million houses had been destroyed or damaged by bombing. Des Abrahams (b.1927) remembers: 'When London was being bombed, we used to sit up nights, dozing in a chair', and when Coventry was suffering, planes could be heard going over all night long. Dick Law (b.1931) says: 'Walking home from school, we would watch the German bombers overhead, sometimes filling the sky like silver birds in the sky, we always knew they were enemy by the drone of the engines.' Mike Preisig recalls that on his way to school in 1940, he and some of his friends were actually machine-gunned - this was reported in the newspapers, he said. Len Clark (b.1931) remembers, 'On our way to school down Coley Lane in 1941-42, we saw a whole engine fall out of a Flying Fortress - there is probably still a dip where it was. It felt hot, but when we came home about 4 o'clock the authorities had been told about it and it had been collected.' The Vicar noted that a bomb at Stickling Green 'fell in a field where some cows were grazing and killed two or three. It was usually reckoned that these were from enemy aircraft returning home and unloading their load of bombs.' Being only 40 miles from the East End and very near various airfields, Clavering saw plenty of planes going over. There was a searchlight battery in Stortford Road and people were advised that, if they heard the sound of anti-aircraft gunfire, they should stay indoors. 'Our various defence services are ready for any eventuality and we can be confident of their ability to deal with an emergency', the Vicar assured. Urban sirens were no use in the countryside, so wardens would cycle round with a whistle. Senior ARP Warden, Edward Beamish (pictured right) advised everyone to keep outside their front doors a pail of water for fires, and a pail of sand for incendiaries. Heaps of sand were deposited at Brooklands Farm, Hill Green Farm, Place Farm, Mills, Grange Farm, Starlings Green and the Vicarage. The logbook of Clavering School records that the wardens sounded air raid warnings on 21 August, 3 September and 4 September

1940, although there are no local incidents recorded then. But they were called upon at least seven times during the war, according to the ARP Incident Files still preserved at Essex Record Office, most dramatically at Parsonage Farm in September (see opposite page). By then, Clavering had already experienced the dropping of two high-explosive (HE) bombs, but with no damage or casualties, on the evening of 18 September, probably just strays from a much bigger incident at Saffron Walden, where 500 incendiaries were dropped. On 22 September, an enemy HE fell on the road from Stickling Green to Clavering Mills. The road had to be closed next day as it dug a crater on the bend between the North Mill and Place Farm. On the night of 5-6 December, there was another HE in Clavering - this seems to have been a stray from a heavy bombardment elsewhere. In 1941 there was only one incident, an HE and an incendiary near Clavering Mills on 17 May – but again without damage or casualties. In 1943 there was the UXB at Blacksmiths Corner (see p.122) and in 1944 the Liberator crash at the Mills (see pp. 136-137).

Parsonage Farm destroyed 1940

This is an incendiary bomb, normally only about 18 inches long but with a flat end which blew up the fuel inside when it hit something and set off fires. Such 'IBs' were the cause of the only serious destruction in Clavering during WW2, at Parsonage Farm, most of which was burnt down by fire bombs. The ARP report makes it look as though this incident was part of a line of incendiaries with similar incidents at Saffron Walden and Arkesden:

24 Sept 1940 02.42 message: Brick Kiln Farm Thaxted Rd bombed 00.34. 4 1Bs dealt with, no damage. Wood Hall Arkesden 2 or 3 IBs at about 0.1.30 dealt with no damage. Parsonage Farm Clavering, no of IBs about 55 Fire Brigade on spot.

Parsonage Farm clearly came off worst, with 55 incendiaries falling at 1.30 am, and the Fire Brigade in attendance. Fortunately no one was hurt, but the farmer gave up his tenancy immediately, and the farm was taken over by Dick Bazley who had hitherto been a farmworker at Berden Hall. His son Colin (b.1938, pictured) was a little boy when his family moved to Parsonage Farm. He retells the story:

'A lone German bomber got detached from his main squadron and wanted to get rid of his bombs. He let off a string of incendiary bombs and most of them fell in open fields, but unfortunately some of them fell on the buildings of Parsonage Farm and most of the buildings were destroyed along with quite a bit of livestock - cattle, horses and so on Most of the farm buildings were destroyed by these bombs, but I think the cow shed must have been left, and the dairy was always there. It was a terrible tragedy really. The tenant Mr Noble did not want to carry on farming any more. Fortunately the house was not touched, but the farm stood derelict for quite a few months. My father was a farm worker earning 30 shillings a week - he borrowed £500 from his landlord at Ugley. He went after work one day during the blackout, no lights on his bike, and he biked down to Ugley, picked up £500 in cash and then biked back home again and this was in the height of the war! **Edited extract from *Clavering Remembered* by Colin Bazley (forthcoming).**

The local agricultural committee helped them replace the buildings, and they were able to buy one of the old Nissen huts then being sold off. Dick Bazley worked the farm with Jim Pinnock, and the Nissen hut was converted into a house. By 1950 the farm buildings had been replaced. This is one of Colin Bazley's 1950s photos of the Parsonage Farmhouse which survived. Colin also remembers later in the war diving under a table when a doodlebug went over, but fortunately it landed a few miles away.

October 1940

My dear Friends

We seem to be living in what has been described as a 'hell of senseless destruction', fine buildings are being destroyed, many houses are wrecked and many families bereaved. Even while I write I hear the crump of a bomb which doesn't seem very far away. It is indeed a strange kind of warfare when the enemy deliberately bombs churches, hospitals and homes, and only serves to show us more plainly the evil nature of the thing against which we are fighting. It gives us some idea of the evil which would be perpetrated in the world were the Nazi cause to remain unchecked and undefeated, and assures us of the rightfulness of our cause. It is the things that Christian people have always held most dear and sacred that are being attacked - our homes, our churches, our hospitals.

All freethinking people have been cheered by the courage and calmness of London people since the Battle of London began. In the last few days many of us have had the opportunity of hearing direct, from those who have experienced it, something of what an air raid on a large town means. We are familiar enough in our corner of Essex with the drone of German aeroplanes at night, and all too often when we hear it we imagine that a bomb will soon drop on our middle chimney. But yet compared with those in the big towns, who have been unable to sleep in their beds at night for two or three weeks, we should be very grateful. Were many of us to spend just one night in London I think we should be far more grateful and worry a great deal less. Courage and cheerfulness and deep down in our hearts a firm faith in God and the certain triumph of good are the assets we should have just now.

Yours most sincerely, E.A. STONE

Summer Time May be Extended

Postal Censorship

Rules for Letters for Abroad

War Control of Photography

Place Names Visible From The Air

Order for Obliteration

Paint Replaces Road Lights

Making Ready for " Black-outs "

Signs Invisible from Air

Defence Regulations

Gonging Forbidden

Some of the many headlines in local papers during wartime when there were unprecedented controls on almost everything – but at least church clocks were safe.

Church Clocks. We have been asked whether it would be in the interests of the villages if the church clocks did not strike at nights. We have taken expert opinion on this point and we understand that when an aeroplane engine is running it is quite impossible for the airman to hear a church clock strike and even were the engines to be shut off the aeroplane would have to be almost on the roof of the church, at the identical moment the clock struck to hear anything. From these facts it will be seen that the church clock cannot be in any way accused of helping the enemy! On the contrary, to those of us who are often on watch throughout the night the striking of the clock is most helpful...

Rescuing Londoners

The Abrahams family at Sheepcote Green Farm, as one of the few farmers to own a lorry, when war broke out were obliged to use it to help people who had been bombed and needed to leave London for the safety of the countryside. Eggie Abrahams (b.1923, pictured), describes how it came about:

'We used to cart potatoes to the London market and then when war broke out and they were bombing in London, as we were the only one with a lorry they used to ring up in the morning and say 'so-and-so was bombed out in London'. We had to go and pick them up – the Government took us over, you see. We took about four or five to Langley and of course they hadn't got much furniture. We must have brought back 10 or 15 families in this village. In London, they'd be beside the street with their little bits after the bombing. If you were close to their house, anything they had saved, we were there and brought it back. They'd tell us what house we'd got to take them to and the government just took the houses over. I suppose they got some relief, some money from somewhere. We just had to do it otherwise they would take the licence away. When we got to London, we got nearly what petrol we wanted. But it was pitiful to see them really. You always knew from the bag what little money they'd got, because the women never let it go out from under their arm. And when you moved them out. 'cause we got no cover you see, they all had to sit in the back of the lorry.' **Extract from Eggie Abrahams *Clavering Remembered* (2012).**

Villages like Clavering before the war had various empty cottages, hard to sell in the 1930s and often rather derelict, but these were requisitioned for evacuees. But in one case, Eggie recalls, this did not work out – they moved a couple to Roast Green but after they had been there about three weeks, one end of the house collapsed, leaving a bed teetering on the edge! The couple then moved to the Chequers on the Langley road, and later somewhere else. Another person brought here by the Abrahams was Harry Venthem, who had been a bus conductor in Kensington and came to live in the Lower Way. Others moved into what was not much more than a hut inside the gate of Black Lodge.

It was actually the oldest son of the family, Bill Abrahams (pictured left) who drove the lorry. Head of the family business was Will Abrahams (pictured right) who had been awarded the Military Medal for his service as a stretcher bearer with the Essex Regiment in WW1.

Evacuees in Clavering 1940

LEAVE THIS TO US
SONNY – **YOU** OUGHT
TO BE OUT OF LONDON

MINISTRY OF HEALTH EVACUATION SCHEME

The Blitz brought a second wave of evacuees to Clavering, as remembered many years later by Billeting Officer Ernest Stone:

'In September 1939 Clavering received a number of children with their teachers from Tottenham but there was little activity in England at the beginning of the war and so over the next nine months many of these children returned home. The Battle of Britain with its bombing of the East End of London brought a fresh influx of people, this time many mothers with their children. As Billeting Officers, my wife and I had power to take over unoccupied cottages which we did and furnished those which were empty with a minimum of essential furniture. Owners of bigger houses took in families and we at the Vicarage gave our basement to two mothers and their four young children. Residents in the village who had relatives in London usually had a houseful at weekends as their friends and relations came seeking a good night's rest.'

The Vicar and his wife bore the brunt of the huge logistical problems of billeting – not only finding accommodation, but also seeking surplus furniture, carpets, bedsteads, chairs and even prams. He reported:

'The population of our villages has increased tremendously in the last few days. Many have come to stay with relatives while others have been evacuated by the government because of damage to their homes. It was no small task to prepare at a few hours notice for the reception of 22 homeless persons. However thanks to the co-operation of several people we were able to give temporary shelter in the Village Hall for a few nights. The Clerk to the District Council acting under government orders was able to secure certain empty houses and thanks to the generosity of the village we were able to furnish them. To all who helped in any way towards the happy settlement of these unfortunate people our grateful thanks are due.'

Between September and December 1940 even more children were registered at the school, but unlike the 1939 batch, these new arrivals did not all come from the same suburb – they were from all over London, among them a coloured family, the Marshalls from Victoria Docks, with three little girls and other children, who were billeted in houses at Middle Street. The Evans family from West Ham lived in the Lower Way. At a place called the Nook on Valance Road were the Holland family from Tottenham with others (see p.18). Others were children on their own, placed with local families. The 1940 influx included evacuees from Chadwell Heath, Ilford, Bermondsey, Eltham, Dagenham, Walthamstow, Holloway, Camberwell, Kentish Town, Raynes Park, Stanmore, Winchmore Hill, Hampstead, East Ham and Romford. Families included some who stayed on after the war, such as the Sweetings. At least 56 Clavering homes opened their doors to evacuees, and school registers show almost 60 more evacuee pupils registered in 1940, some siblings such as Olive Bowles aged 11 and her eight-year-old twin sisters, Ruby and Rosy, all taken in by Nurse Livings at Hill Green. In July 1940 three evacuated families found they had not entirely escaped danger, as the thatched cottage where they were staying in Wicken Road caught fire. Newport Fire Brigade spent six hours extinguishing the blaze which gutted several rooms but caused no injury - the families had to be evacuated once more.

An Evacuee at Moat Farm

While a lot of evacuees came in organised groups, there were also many private arrangements, usually involving staying with a relative. One former evacuee, Elsie Kemp (nee Darlow) recalls this memorable period of her life when she was evacuated to Moat Farm, Clavering.

'When the Blitz was at its worst, my dad decided to get in touch with a relative at Moat Farm, Clavering. I think this was his first cousin, though to be honest we never even knew we had relatives living in the country. Well, it was arranged that my mum, elder sister Frances (Fran) and I went to stay there. My sister was about eleven and I was six. When you think that we lived in the East End of London and only used to seeing grey buildings and factories, it came as a bit of a shock to see so many trees and green fields all around. When we arrived at Moat Farm we were all invited in to the dining room for tea, the table was laid and I remember we all had a boiled egg. I don't think my sister or I had seen so many eggs all at one time.

The lady of the house we only ever called Mrs Kemp, to be honest we found her a bit frightening and used to stay out of her way. That wasn't hard to do with so much space to play in. It was all fun for my sister and me, but my mum did work very hard. She did most of the cleaning in the house. We used to go pea picking; I remember while my mum would fill a few sacks, we used to fill a bag between us. Can't remember how much we got for a sack, but I do remember we used to spend it on sweets, if we had the coupons... we used to sit on the big gate and wait for them to come home from the fields, Joe would let us sit on the backs of the horses and ride back to the stables. I even remember the names of the horses, Prince and Flower. The other thing that used to amuse us was playing on the haystack, when it came to moving the bales, it was great waiting to see what creatures ran out. There were nearly always hedgehogs in there... collecting the apples from the orchard that was just outside the house, we had to cross a small bridge to get over the moat that ran around the house.

The local villagers were all very nice; I do know we came home with many more toys than we went with. Harvest time when they started ploughing the fields, the men used to stand around the edge with rifles waiting for the rabbits to run out. Around that time it was never unusual to go into the kitchen with the stone floor and see hares hanging behind the door. At harvest time we walked to Rickling Church carrying something for the festival, bread, vegetable and displays that were made from the wheat and barley. For us as children it was more like a holiday, all that freedom and running around on the farm. But for mum, she worked hard in the house earning our keep.'

November 1940

One of the village shops, Baileys in Pelham Road, in the 1930s. By the time of the war it had become Kells shop. William Bailey is on the right next to his grandson, Ray Livings who later joined the Army, but died tragically at the age of 20 while home on leave in 1940.

My Dear Friends,

The last few weeks have been very busy ones for most of us. With our population increasing by several hundreds and all the houses full with people from the bombed areas, there has been a lot for everyone to do. Our village shops have stood the strain of this sudden influx well, so that no one has gone hungry; and our post offices have dealt well with their increased work.

For myself I am deeply conscious of much in the parish that I ought to have done which has just had to be left because so much of my time has been given to grappling with the many problems concerned with billeting. It has been no easy task settling so many people quite unused to country ways into village homes, but thanks to the kind co-operation of some, who have opened their houses to their friends, relatives and others who have taken care of complete strangers, the job has been tackled with a fair measure of success. Looking back over my life, I cannot remember ever being so busy as I have these last few weeks. As only those who live with me know we have had a large number of callers every day at the Vicarage at all times of the day and often at mealtimes making enquiries, not only on billeting matters, but about details connected with rationing, unemployment benefit and similar needs of the present time. And even on the rare occasions when I feel I have time either to walk or cycle it is a common thing for me to be stopped several times by enquirers. I have often thought that I should like to keep the diary of a day in the life of a Vicar! I try to help as of course anyone would, all these enquiries, but I wonder sometimes by their manner, whether they imagine that I am some highly paid official having access to untold supplies of houses and furniture, instead of an ordinary citizen doing a small job of national service without any thought of reward or payment and even spending money writing innumerable letters and making endless telephone calls...

As every night I get into my bed, the same bed and the same bedroom that I occupy in more peaceful times, I often think of less fortunate people who have to sleep in improvised beds in underground shelters and I go to sleep with the thought of thankfulness in my heart. We ought to be thankful that we live in two such scattered villages as Clavering and Langley and in what can be called as safe a place as anywhere in England just now...

Yours most sincerely, E.A. STONE

December 1940

My dear Friends

Very soon we shall be keeping our second wartime Christmas. We shall miss many of the familiar features of this season; for some the customary holiday is cancelled as the war needs must be met, while rationing will make entertaining difficult. Restricted travelling will make it hard for us to visit our friends. Many homes are broken up, husbands, fathers and brothers being away in the forces while into our own homes many of us have received mothers and children from the towns. But Christmas is still essentially the home feast... although this year our household feast may be strangely different – familiar faces may be absent and in their place unaccustomed ones. For the second year in succession, war unsought, unavoidable, destructive, is darkening the anniversary of the coming of the Prince of Peace... Just now as a result of the war there are in this country and in the countries of Europe tens of thousands of broken homes – tens of thousands of homes once happy and united that will never be restored. In those so far undamaged, mothers and fathers will be sorely missing the children sent away for safety. Wives will be lonely with their husbands on active service. Parents will be achingly anxious for their sons serving at sea, in the air and in the field... This Christmas countless rather worried men will be picturing their dear ones. It is for them to live up to the best that will be thought of them. As we gather at our home feast, broken though it will be we shall remember our absent ones...

Yours most sincerely, E.A. STONE

NEW COUNCILLORS.

The Council elected Mr. A. N. Hickley to replace Mr. C. A. Kemp as representative of Arkesden and Wicken,

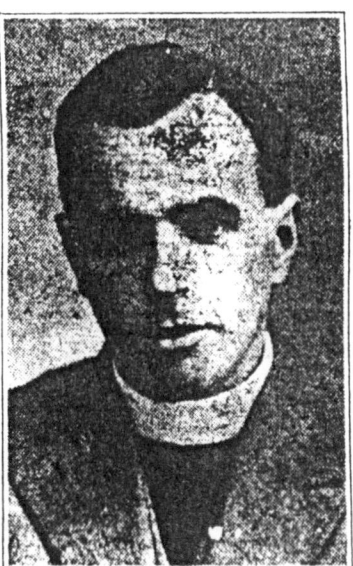

The Rev. A. E. Stone.

and the Rev. A. E. Stone to represent Langley in place of Mr. E. G. Wombwell. Both men were elected on the suggestion of the Parish Council concerned. SWWN 6/12/1940

The smart cover of the parish magazine as it had appeared since 1935 – but supplies of both cover and good paper were running out.

Rushed off his feet though he was with billeting and dozens of other duties, nevertheless at the end of 1940, the Vicar took on also the vacant position to represent Langley on Saffron Walden Rural District Council.

With the King's Forces 1940

By Christmas 1940 the number of Clavering men in the King's Forces had grown to at least 46 plus two young women serving in the ATS and VAD – although this list may be incomplete since the Vicar relied on people letting him know the names of those serving. New additions to the vicar's list were:

Joseph Atkinson, Maurice Atkinson, George Barker, Henry Barker, Philip Barker, Sidney Barker, Leslie Barnard, Ernest Beckwith, Stephen Beloe, Albert Blackman, Sidney Bowles, Wilfred Carter, William Caton, Norman Caton, Anthony Creighton, Frank Dearman, Anthony Elwell. Donald Elwell. Reginald Kemp, Stanley King, Frederick Law. George Law. Hubert Law, Dennis Ledward, Patrick Lindsay, George Livings. Jack Livings, Percy Livings, Laurie Martin, Sidney Matthews. Fred Monk, Arthur Newland, John Newland. Bernard Poulter. Fred Poulter. Leslie Poulter. Fred Revell. Claude Simmonds. Thomas Slingsby. Frank Tant, Charles Turner, Eric Turner, Gordon Turner, Leslie Turner, Maurice Wombwell, Norman Wombwell, Marjorie Baker (ATS), Laura Slingsby.

The two Caton sons from Clavering Mills were both serving in the RAF by 1940. Norman Caton (left) joined later in the war, but his brother Bill Caton (right) was in uniform through most of the war and in South Africa for part of the time. Among others on this list was Anthony Creighton (b.1922), who had lived since the 1930s in Middle Street with his mother, Elsie who was in the antiques trade. When war broke out Anthony joined the Royal Canadian Air Force, and then

the RAF as a bomber navigator, earning a DFC. He also took part in Air Force shows, playing alongside Terence Rattigan, then a wireless operator and air gunner, later to be a playwright. After the war, Creighton (photo left) trained at RADA and collaborated with famous playwright, John Osborne on two plays in the 1950s. The two were close friends, but Creighton later gave up the theatre and worked as a drama teacher in London. Also in the RAF was Peter Elliott (photo right), son of a former

Clavering vicar who lived at the vicarage from 1930-35 and joined up before the war in 1937, serving at RAF Debden.

Chapter Four
1941: 'Depths of quiet heroism'

All over the world in 1941, there seemed to be so much happening all the time, it was hard to keep up with it: Malta terribly bombed, Bulgaria joining the Axis, Yugoslavia, Greece and Crete captured. Early in the year Rommel was winning in Africa, but the Allied fortunes began to change towards the end of the year. Russia was now under attack from the Nazis, so there was a shift in British attitudes towards them. Persecution of Jews was getting worse and U-boat attacks were increasing, including the devastating losses of HMS Hood and Ark Royal, while the Nazis lost the Bismarck: thousands of sailors lay beneath the waves. With the Italians doing so badly, prisoners-of-war started arriving and were set to work on local farms. Things were also happening on the other side of the world, with Japan causing increasing alarm as the year unfolded, culminating in the devastating attack on Pearl Harbour in December and the declaration of war. Even before then, the Americans had been helping Britain, with 'Lend-lease' for armaments, food aid and protecting convoys, now they could no longer avoid participation. By the end of the year it was truly a total world war, with Japan having also invaded Malaya, the Philippines and Hong Kong. But at least advances in science, technology and engineering - penicillin, radar, aircraft production - were helping the human effort of fighting war on all fronts.

Help put the lid on Hitler
**BY SAVING YOUR
OLD METAL AND PAPER**

Meanwhile the war was taking its toll on the home front, costing Britain millions of pounds every day. Income tax was raised to 50 per cent and many people were 'browned off'. Bombing raids continued in London with a particularly vicious attack in May, in reprisal for the bombing of Berlin. By then 20,000 Londoners had been killed in the raids and 25,000 badly injured. Many other cities and ports were also bombed. There were serious food shortages, although potatoes were reduced in price to persuade people to eat more; and new controls on profiteering, as the war also offered opportunities for crooks. Fuel was rationed and clothes too from the summer, also cheese and preserves, and the shortage of materials was met with a big campaign to salvage scrap metal. Newspapers were full of notices to do this and do that - never had the population been so harangued.

**Hitler will send
no warning –**
*so always carry
your gas mask*

**"Keep
it
under
your
hat!"**
CARELESS TALK COSTS LIVES

There was a recruitment drive aimed at women to replace men in the munitions factories and auxiliary services. By the end of the year 1.7 million women aged 30-40 had been conscripted, and single women aged 20-30 were also called up for essential work in anti-aircraft, police, fire and office work. Entreaties were made for women to train as nurses, for support of mothers whose work was so essential to the home. Now men aged 18-50 were liable for service, while for others Civil Defence of Home Guard duties became compulsory rather than voluntary. So, quite literally everyone who was able to, was supposed to have a war job of some sort. Attention also turned to those too young for service, who were encouraged to join things. In 1941 the Air Training Corps was formed to train lads for the RAF and later on Army Training Corps too – both of these developments had local branches.

In Clavering the Home Front was settling into some sort of regularity – Home Guard training, blackout surveillance, fire-watching, knitting woollies for the troops, making jam, tending pigs and, to relieve the gloom, film shows, dances, whist drives and entertainments in the Village Hall. To keep the nation's children healthy, the government brought in free orange juice, cod liver oil and milk to all pupils. The great savings drive this year was known as War Weapons Week, and salvage efforts were extended to churchyard grave railings. A Clavering Invasion Committee was formed, reflecting the very real fear that Hitler's troops might arrive on our shores. As ever, the Vicar was in the thick of the action, but he continued to edit the church magazine, even though he ran out of covers and decent paper, so had to resort to thin, fragile wartime paper and a new look: this new illustration of the church went on being used on the magazine for another 40 years! The Vicar was right that the magazine was an essential part of the Home Front, and indeed without it and its energetic Editor/Vicar we would know very little about what happened in Clavering during WW2.

PARISH MAGAZINE

The Parish Church of
St. Mary and St. Clement, Clavering.

Parish Magazine. 'We appear this month in a new cover. The cover design which we have had for nearly four years is now no longer printed and the suggestion was made that we might have a cover which would be entirely our own. My father has kindly drawn the pictures of our churches and the printers blocks which have been made from them should last for many years. It is fortunate that our printer has a supply of pre-war paper for this first issue of the new cover, subsequent numbers must alas be printed on the much inferior wartime paper. I feel that this magazine has perhaps a greater value in wartime than in more normal times and therefore I hope we shall be able to continue its publication. I shall welcome your co-operation in sending to me any matters of interest to be printed so that this can be indeed a parish magazine.'

The Vicar's monthly letters to his flock as ever skilfully wove the Christian message into what was happening in both the village and the war. He sought to keep up their morale with predictions that they would win, despite it all, and he saw the war as an opportunity to re-shape society into a better mould, with the old class divisions forgotten. He sought sympathy for the feelings of the evacuees far from home, made it clear that children were welcome in church and expressed his concerns for the group we now call teenagers, that they were being neglected by society and needed outlets for their energies – this he later remedied. He asked for help with the harvest and rejoiced that farm-workers had a pay rise. He revealed his frustration at not being able to serve in the Forces himself as a chaplain – a need which he was also able to resolve later on. Mr Stone echoed Churchill's words that the Allies were Christian soldiers fighting the forces of darkness. And everything counted, including every sixpence saved and every little bit of salvage – we are familiar with recycling these days, but it was the wartime generation that got it down to a fine art.

This is what your back door should look like on collection day.

METAL   BONES   PAPER

ISSUED BY THE MINISTRY OF SUPPLY

January 1941

My Dear Friends,

At the end of a year which has brought surprises of many kinds, we can still look forward with confidence and wish our friends a happier new year. Back in July, after the collapse of France, our plight looked desperate indeed and few military authorities of neutral countries believed that we could hold out alone. But now that the months have passed, we are confident of winning through even though it may be at a great cost. The intensified attack from the air, so far from cowing us, has revealed unsuspected depths of quiet heroism and self sacrifice in our people... The future historian, looking back and writing the story of these days may well say that the issue of the war was decided not simply by the marvellous exploits of our airmen but in the soul of the British people. Something has come to us for which we thank God and take courage... This war is not going to be the end of the world. There are good days beyond when the present will only seem like some horrible nightmare. We can and must look forward. We must not wait till the war is over, when we shall be tired out. Whatever happens we must not go back to the old world with all the social injustices and national greed and selfishnesses out of which the present horror has sprung. What matters most is that there shall be a new spirit abroad. That is the vital thing. Whatever the statesmen may plan, it is only new men and women that can make a new world. So many think that you cannot change human nature. Men have always been selfish, we are told and always will be and that's just the whole trouble. We mustn't be so sure of this, it is possible to have new men and women and through them new homes, a new Britain and a new world.... Let us look forward hopefully and prayerfully to this New Year that the sufferings of these days may prove but the beginning of a new Britain where Christianity will come into its own.

Yours most sincerely, E.A. STONE

Clavering Vicarage, a centre for administering billeting and many other aspects of the Home Front during WW2.

February 1941

Happy days for Clavering children before the war - riding on Farmer King's cart to help on the harvest fields. The Vicar understood children and wrote about their difficulties in time of war. Below some local mothers at a church parade 1944.

My Dear Friends
From time to time when I hear discussions on the effects of the war on various groups of people, conversation turns to the question whether it is worse for the older people than for the younger ones. Some of us sympathise with the older ones who have already experienced one world war in their lifetime and now have to go through another; others of us feel that it is harder on the young people who have to grow amidst all the horrors of the present time. A time of war is not a happy time for anybody, but I suppose that those of us who were at school in the years 1914-18 have stronger sympathies with those who are in the same position now. Evacuated from their homes and billeted with strangers many miles away, the generation of school children today misses much that to us in our childhood was very dear, despite the great welcome which has been given them. It is a wonderful achievement that despite the many homes broken up as a result of the war and the dispersal of children over the whole of this land, the majority of them are receiving full time education. After weeks when the children of our cities have only had the streets in which to spend their days this is good news. Boys and girls as everyone knows are happier when they have something to occupy them.....
Yours most sincerely, E.A. STONE

March 1941

My Dear Friends
The call of our church to thank God for our mothers and our homes comes with even greater force this year. Family life in England has been broken up in recent months as never before. The demands of the fighting services, the evacuation of mothers and children and their reception into our own homes have brought many changes to home life. At this service we shall have these broken homes particularly in remembrance.
Yours most sincerely, E.A. STONE

Comforts for the Forces

By the spring of 1941, the ladies of the village had been sewing and knitting for six months, with three groups who would meet on Friday afternoons for two-hour sessions at the homes of Mrs. Adeline Luckock in the Old House, Mrs. Jean Finzel at The Court and Miss Ackroyd in Sheepcote Green, and there was also a girls' knitting class making squares of wool sewn together into blankets. A house-to-house collection provided the initial supplies of material and further fund-raising through socials, concerts, tea parties, donations and sales of wastepaper salvage kept the funds topped up. The output from the work parties was phenomenal – gloves, bedsocks, bandages, bedjackets, 'helpless case shirts', sea-boot stockings, oily oversocks, tropical shirts, dressing gowns, hot water bottle covers, pyjamas, pillows, mittens, wristlets, scarves and Balaclava helmets. During the first year over 1,000 items were provided, sometimes quite urgently, as when the Red Cross gave them 100-yard bales to be cut up and within three weeks they had beavered away making 21 pyjamas and 41 pillow cases. Some went to the Hospital Depot and some to the Comforts for Forces, including Royal Navy minesweepers, RAF airfields, the local searchlight camp and Clavering men serving in the Forces in response to family requests, reported Mrs. Finzel:

'We have tried to supply each person with the garments asked for and on the whole I think we have succeeded. I have had most grateful and charming letters from the all the men acknowledging the parcels we have sent them and they all ask me to thank the very kind people who have made the garments and also everyone in the village for providing the money to buy the wool. If I could show you the letters I have had from the menfolk I am sure you would all feel you should do your share.'

The work varied over time – once the Russians were on our side, they were the recipients of woollen gloves made by the Clavering ladies out of 30lbs of free wool from the RAF Depot, and this also made up socks and scarves for prisoners-of-war. Another consignment of wool was used for Merchant Navy survivors rescued after convoy sinkings. The usefulness of the gifts was underlined when the Vicar became an RAF chaplain:

'There are many members of the armed forces who have to be on duty during the hours of darkness. To these on their cold and lonely watches the added warmth of a pullover or a scarf is very welcome. At the end of the winter they are collected, cleaned and repaired and those beyond repair are salvaged to make more wool for knitting other comforts.'

One champion knitter, Miss Lucy Martin, finished six long-sleeved jerseys in just three months. Finally in October 1945, they reported the dispatch of the last bundle: 'In the six years of war, 2,050 garments have been made in Clavering for the hospitals, the three Services and the Merchant Navy. It is impossible to say how many hours of spare time went to their making'. This photo of an iced-up ship HMS Kent, on which Peter Bowles of Clavering served in the Arctic Convoys, illustrates the cold conditions requiring such extra woollies.

May 1941

May 20th, 1941.   23/5/1941
                                   Saturday

THE HOME GUARD.

TO THE EDITOR

Sir,—Britain's Home Guard, a force of over a million and a half men, has recently been celebrating its first anniversary. The high praise given by H.M. the King in his order of the day to the work of the Home Guard must be shared by everyone—they are, indeed, "making a notable and efficient contribution to victory."

Many people have been rather concerned of recent months to see that while in the other armed forces of the King every opportunity is given, where possible, for members to attend divine service, yet in the Home Guard parades are usually arranged at the very hour of the church service. In many of our villages for generations the hour from 11 to 12 on Sunday mornings has been the time of divine service. But now it is a common thing to find on Sunday mornings at the hour of service a parade of the Home Guard about to begin on the village green.

At the beginning of April we read in the Press that General Eastwood, then Director-General of the Home Guard, had issued an instruction to all local commanders that parades should be avoided on Sunday mornings during the hours of divine service. Little notice seems to have been taken of this instruction, and the practice of Sunday morning parades still goes on. Surely with the lengthening days it ought to be possible, without undue difficulty, to find other occasions than Sunday mornings for the necessary training. — Yours, etc.,

REV. E. A. STONE (Vicar). Clavering-with-Langley Vicarage. Essex.

During this time, Mr Stone was still vigorously arguing for the Home Guard to cease parading on Sunday mornings. He went so far as to send this letter to the local paper. Below, local Home Guard members in their ill-fitting uniforms.

Home Guard Parades 1941

Clavering & Wicken Home Guard practising drill near Arkesden (above); and marching through Saffron Walden led by Frank Talbot (below).

The Vicar in the parish magazine explained his feelings about the timing of parades: 'When a parade is held in the village it is of course very natural that choir boys, sisters, wives and sweethearts should want to see their men folk practising, and so instead of the parish being found at its prayers on Sunday morning, the centre of interest gets shifted to the parade ground. The defence of this land is we know vitally important but we are not fighting merely to defend a small island which is our homeland, we are fighting for everything that Christianity has taught us to value, against the forces of evil. If we are to trample on Christian tradition to disregard church and chapel services, and to make them appear of little worth, is there any point in continuing the struggle? Life in pagan England I imagine would be very much the same as life in a pagan Germany. The evils perpetrated by the German people are the result of their deliberate rejection of Christianity in the past few years. Let us pray that we may never fall into the same tragic condition.' A few months later the Director General of the Home Guard ordered parades to be held at different times.

In Memoriam Stephen Beloe 1941

BUCKINGHAM PALACE

The Queen and I offer you our heartfelt sympathy in your great sorrow.

We pray that your country's gratitude for a life so nobly given in its service may bring you some measure of consolation.

George R.I.

Two young airmen from Hill Green were killed in the war that spring, both casualties of the Desert War. Stephen Beloe lived at Derrynane on Hill Green, and was involved in village life, as the Vicar wrote: 'While our list of names of those serving in the forces grows longer every month it is my sad duty to record the first casualty through enemy action. On 28th April Pilot Officer Stephen Edward Beloe of the Royal Air Force Volunteer Reserve was killed in the Middle East. Stephen was a regular worshipper in our church, a member of the PCC and deeply interested in the affairs of the village and always ready to help in any way he could. We shall miss greatly his enthusiasm and keenness. Our thoughts and prayers are with his widowed mother and his sister in their sorrow.'

Like other bereaved families in the village, his mother would have received this sympathy letter from the King. Stephen's name is on the El Alamein Memorial, one of 3,000 Commonwealth Air Force men lost in the Africa campaigns, but with no known grave.

In Memory of
Pilot Officer STEPHEN EDWARD BELOE
80857, 45 Sqdn., Royal Air Force Volunteer Reserve
who died age 36
on 28 April 1941
Son of Edward Milligen Beloe and Edith Anne Beloe
of Cooden, Bexhill-on-Sea, Sussex.
Remembered with honour
ALAMEIN MEMORIAL

'The battlefield, across which the fighting surged back and forth between 1940 and 1942... It was a campaign of manoeuvre and movement, the objectives being the control of the Mediterranean, the link with the east through the Suez Canal, the Middle East oil supplies and the supply route to Russia through Persia.' **Commonwealth War Graves Commission**

In Memoriam Laurie Martin 1941

Soon after the loss of Stephen Beloe came the sad news that another popular young man from Hill Green, Laurie Martin, had also died on active service and also with the RAFVR. The Vicar wrote: 'We were all very sorry to hear of the death in Egypt of Sergeant-Pilot Laurie William Martin of the Royal Air Force Volunteer Reserve. Laurie comes of an old and respected Clavering family who have always been devoted to Clavering Church and have done much work in it. Our thoughts and prayers are with his family in their sorrow.' Laurie's family had been village carpenters for three generations and often did repairs in the church. They lived at what is now known as Chipperfield House and made coffins in the barn. Harold Walford (b.1913) who later took over their undertaking work, recalled in 2002 that Laurie, who had been his best pal, trained as a Bristol Blenheim pilot. This photograph shows Flt Sgt Martin just a year before, when he wore his uniform as best man at the wedding of Wilf and Gwenith Carter, his neighbours on Hill Green. On 27th May 1941, at the age of 26, he was killed in a Blenheim which blew up during a flight in North Africa. Unlike so many young men who have no known grave, his body was recovered and his last resting place can be found in El Alamein Cemetery, one of 7,240 Commonwealth burials from the Desert War.

In Memory of
Flight Sergeant WILLIAM LAURIE MARTIN
742098, 55 Sqdn., Royal Air Force Volunteer
Reserve
who died age 26
on 27 May 1941
Son of Charles E. and Agnes L. Martin, of Clavering,
Essex.
Remembered with honour
EL ALAMEIN WAR CEMETERY

Wartime village life - Spring '41

ARP Fire Watching. Volunteers are urgently required in both villages to undertake the duties of fire watching. Parties of volunteers are being organised in various parts of the villages... in the event of fires caused through the dropping of incendiary bombs during the night short blasts will be blown on whistles between 10 pm and 6 am...Three groups of watchers are now on duty every night and to all who have volunteered for this work we owe our grateful thanks.

Evacuee Mothers Club. The evacuation authorities are endeavouring to start mothers clubs in each village. The Billeting officer would be glad to hear from anyone willing to help in the running of such a club on one or two afternoons a week.

Nursing. An Appeal to Young Women. Many of the young women have had to register for National services and others will soon have to do so... the question of how best to give of one's time and service to the country must be occupying the minds of many of you. The nursing service provides a most valuable and interesting way. Not only this but the training for this work can be done in the village and Mrs Slingsby is about to arrange such a course of training now. We are sure that this appeal to help succour the sick and wounded will not fall on deaf ears in Clavering and Langley.

Salvage. A plan to overcome the difficulty of those who are unable to send their waste paper to the Vicarage stables is being formed. Mrs. Finzel with the help of her pony and cart and some boys and girls has agreed to collect from the following districts, weather and circumstances permitting. First Saturday morning in the month – Sticklings Green; second – Wicken Road; third - Hill Green; fourth – Arkesden Road. It would be a tremendous help if everyone saving wastepaper would sew a label with their name on the sack, this would ensure the right sack being returned to the right owner. Would anyone offer to collect paper in either Starlings Green or Sheepcote Green?

Jam making: a fruit preservation centre has been set up for Clavering and Langley. Mrs Finzel and Mrs Stone represent Clavering and Miss Owen and Mrs M Wisbey Langley. A village meeting is to be held in the Lower School on Tuesday June 3rd at 2.45 pm at which details of the scheme will be explained. All who are interested in this piece of National Service should do their best to be present. The time and day have been chosen to enable Langley people to get to and from Clavering by bus.

SOAP ECONOMY.—Collect all odd pieces of soap, put in a flannel bag and place in very hot water. When soap begins to feel soft, take out and flatten with a fish slice. Plunge into cold water and leave until hard, remove flannel bag and you will have a perfectly good bar of household soap. (Mrs. J. H. SMITH.)

Village Hall Dances

Village hall dances, already a fixture of the hall prewar, were particularly important diversions from the worries of wartime – they also helped to raise a few pounds for charities. In 1941, for instance, there was a Red Cross dance in March, a dance organised by the Mill End Fire Watchers in April and a Carnival Dance for the Clavering Youth Centre in November among others. In 1942 the PoW Fund was one beneficiary, in 1943 the Cadet Force Welfare Fund, 1944 Great Ormond Street Hospital and the fire service Benevolent Fund, and of course the Forces Homecoming Fund - and so it went on with dances and whist drives alternate weeks for different causes. These dances were very popular with HM Forces who got in the door at a reduced rate. Frequent visitors were Americans stationed at Nuthampstead. Eileen Clarke, who was a 10-year-old evacuee here, recalls how her mother and a friend would do the refreshments: 'Of course I had to be taken along and I was allowed to sit on the edge of the band there and told not to move and had to keep my socks on - stories used to go round that if you kept your socks on you were safe. Of course when they used to go behind to dig out the refreshments and the band would keep playing, I would take my socks off and dance.' Various bands played at the dances, among them Doug Luff's 'Delf's Band'. Doug played trumpet and other well-known local musicians included Gordon Bridges, Joyce Baker the pianist from Wicken Road, John Barltrop, a blind accordionist from Rickling and Mike Preisig on treble accordion. Mike (pictured on left of photo) also had his own band named after his home 'Danson' in Stortford Road and recalls:

'Our outfit was the Dansonian Dance Band with me on accordion, Stan Rushant on drums, Don Saggers from Newport sax and clarinet and Bettina Coombes from Langley on piano. In spite of being pretty awful, in the two years we were going we did 22 gigs mainly at Clavering Hall and Newport Studio, and we also went to Barkway, Saffron Walden and Linton. A lot of these functions were arranged by the AFS for collecting money for the War effort. Most of these gigs we got through dear old Arthur King - Fire Officer for Clavering and my cousin, Laurie Bailey from Newport AFS. Our band played at the village hall eight times in 1944/5 and we were paid £2.10s for a four-hour dance.

I also remember the American airmen from Nuthampstead, especially Frank Mulligan, a very large Irish-Yank who danced in enormous boots which made him dance in a very peculiar fashion that we named the Mulligan Hop!'

Clavering Fire Guard

Clavering's engine and firemen at Brooklands Farm, where there used to be a nissen hut used by the fire service. This picture was after the war in 1955: Arthur King, Wilf Carter, Fred Walford and George Williams.

In 1941 a National Fire Service was hastily introduced in response to the Nazi use of incendiaries and the terrible fires in the Blitz, but up to then fire-fighting arrangements were not very well-organised. In Clavering, before war began, the Auxiliary Fire Service had begun recruiting volunteers who attended anti-gas lectures and instruction in fire-fighting. Captain of the AFS was Arthur King, the farmer at Brooklands, while others on the committee were Messrs Lumley, Napier and Simmonds, and Leading Fireman Downham organising training. The fire watchers spent many a chilly night patrolling in pairs, looking out for any fires set off by incendiaries which were often mixed with HE bombs. If any nocturnal fires were spotted, there would be short whistle blasts to warn people. In 1941, the ARP wardens sent out an appeal to the village for more fire watchers and funds for equipment: 'This work is of vital importance and there must be many in Clavering and Langley who could spare a few hours once a week during the night.' Within a few weeks there were enough volunteers to set up three groups of watchers every night, numbered 1, 2 and 3 Clavering Fire Watch Districts. They were particularly alert during harvest time in August: 'we want to take very possible precaution against the incendiary bombs of the vilest enemy that civilisation has ever known'. More men were needed, however, and the point was made that 'it is not fair that one or two men should shirk their duty while others are doing their bit, sometimes watching two nights a week after working hard all day'. By the spring of 1942, Clavering had a civilian Fire Guard which supplemented the NFS. The night watch was cut back, and the fire-watchers' funds were handed over to the Invasion Committee. There were no more bulletins on the NFS until the end of the war when there was a party.

Clavering N.F.S. entertained their friends to a supper at their headquarters, and a gathering of nearly fifty people spent a very enjoyable evening. After an excellent meal Mr J. Barthrop, playing a piano-accordion, led community singing, and everybody much enjoyed the solos of Company Officer Harding and Fireman Walford... The evening finished with 'Auld Lang Syne' and 'God Save the King' which followed vociferous cheers for the guests, particularly Leading Fireman Downham, who had been responsible for the training of the Clavering men in the early stages...

Evacuee Problems 1941

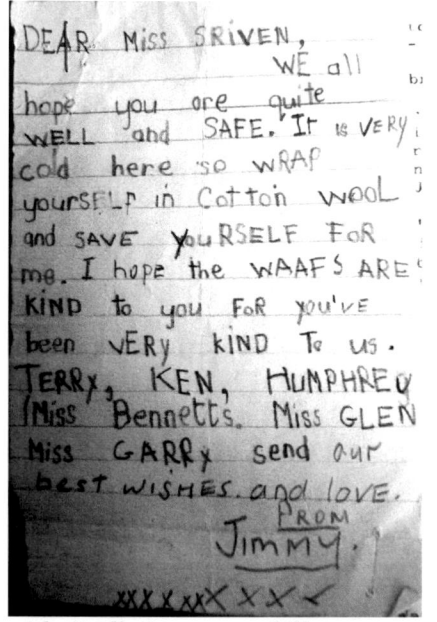

DEAR Miss SRIVEN,
WE all
hope you are quite
WELL and SAFE. It is VERY
cold here so WRAP
yourSELF in Cotton wooL
and SAVE yourSELF FoR
me. I hope the WAAFS ARE
KIND to you FoR you've
been VERY kIND To us.
TERRY, KEN, HUMPHREY
Miss Bennett's. Miss GLEN
Miss GARRY send our
best wISHES. and love.
PROM
JImMY.
XXXXXXXXX

At the start of 1941 many of the evacuees were still here and the village again put on a 'very jolly afternoon' at the evacuation party: 'After half an hour's singing which was led by Steve Arthur and his accordion, Clown Bertram, from the Children's Theatre on Clacton Pier entertained the children for an hour and a half. Everyone spent a most happy time. The afternoon was made possible by a grant from the LCC, some private gifts by friends in the village, and the officers of the village hall who being unable to give the usual children's party loaned the hall free for this children's entertainment.' This lovely letter (taken from Saffron Walden WW2 records) typifies the experiences of these youngsters so far from home.

But for those organising it, evacuation remained a massive challenge: from September 1940 to December 1941, about 1¼ million people were evacuated from bombed cities. In Clavering, the Vicar as Billeting Officer was getting rather fed up with it all. In a very different tone from normal, he criticised the ingratitude of some evacuees, and the billeting of strangers on village homes, writing in the parish magazine:

'Recently every householder in this parish as in all other reception areas, has received a Government form enquiring about the accommodation of their house... We are reminded from time to time of the town dwellers' hardship in leaving their homes to live in the country. There is all too little in official pronouncements of the countryfolks' side of evacuation and the wonderful piece of work which they are shouldering so magnificently in opening their doors to the stranger. To open one's house for a week or two to a stranger from a bombed area is what any one would do if he had room; but to do this an indefinite period, for months and years is something most noble and praiseworthy. In my work as billeting officer I have met some hundreds of evacuees. I wish I could say that the efforts of the people of our villages were really appreciated. We know that our London evacuees don't want to come into the country but we never asked them to come. We have all done our best for them but I doubt whether ten per cent are really grateful. Such cases of gross ingratitude that have come to my notice would almost make one despair of the future. Gratefulness lasts for a few days but soon what we offer in the kindness of our hearts is looked upon as a right and the country woman, giving of her time and care to look after evacuee mothers and children is thought of as doing only what she ought. This attitude of mind can, I think, be traced to the indiscriminate way in which the social services in our great cities have been administered...We in the country are not used to this state liberality. We have had to work and to work hard for the sake of our wives and families... No one knows how long the billeting problem will be with us but certainly I suppose until the end of the war. The only true and lasting settlement of the problem is of course to house the Londoner on his own. The Government I think has realised this at last and there has of recent months been a wholesale requisitioning of empty properties. This is as it should be, for the average house is quite unsuitable for two families to live in for any length of time. Of the properties requisitioned in our own villages it is good to know that the temporary loss of these properties has caused no hardship to any of the owners.'

June 1941

My Dear Friends

I have been thinking a great deal lately about the young people of our villages and adolescents generally and their place in the life of our country... The problem of the 14 to 20 age group has been with us since the last war. So many children leave school at 14 and receive no further guidance as to how to live their life. They belong to no organisation, they do not know what to do with their leisure time and a boredom and general moral deterioration sets in. But young people are most desperately anxious to be of service and to find an outlet for their enthusiasm. We see in Germany how the Nazis have exploited this characteristic of youth. The Hitler Youth Movement which demands from its followers fanatical devotion to their leader shows what happens when God is just left out of the picture and the man-made law of the state is put in its place... We should have our boys and girls of 14 to 20 very much in mind just now. It is easy to do nothing at all and to watch our young folk hanging about aimlessly on the street corner and getting into mischief because there is nothing better to do. Such a National Youth Movement as our government has started is of great importance. The government is anxious to help in any way possible the forming of youth organisations not only in town areas but also in villages. The aim is to have a youth centre in every village where suitable activities may be provided... Unfortunately just now there seems to be rather a dearth of youth leaders but that doesn't seem to be a reason for neglecting our young people. There must be some among us who could help in some branch of youth activity... The post-war years of reconstruction are not going to be easy for anyone and for our young people more difficult perhaps than for others...

Yours most sincerely, E.A. STONE

These young people parading to church all belonged to uniformed youth organisations – what worried the Vicar was the majority who did not join such clubs and were found 'hanging about aimlessly on the street corner and getting into mischief because there is nothing better to do'. Within a year of writing this, he had set up at Clavering one of the first youth centres in Essex (see p.69).

Clavering Youth Centre 1941

Juvenile delinquency became a serious problem during WW2, with convictions of under-17-year-olds rising by a third from 1939-41. The Government suggested setting up youth centres. The Vicar, who was always interested in the young, had already done something 'for our boys and girls in Clavering' in November 1939 when he converted a room at the Vicarage into a clubroom for their recreation. Two years later he pondered in his parish magazine letter on the problems of youth in wartime (see p.68). This was followed with a meeting in the vicarage garden, addressed by county and district youth organisers, who explained the Government's wish to help young people. A committee was then organised with the Clavering School head, Mr. A.J. Richardson as secretary, to look into the setting up of a proper youth centre. In July 1941 lots of young people turned up at the vicarage where the Essex County Youth Organiser 'thrilled us all immensely with his talk about the possibilities of a village Youth Club. It was unanimously agreed to form such a club and then the older people present withdrew while the young people elected their officers'. Doug Luff was chairman and others included the Misses Barnes, Caton, Glasscock, Messrs Bowles, Hill and Kybird. With a room in the school made available, all sorts of activities would be possible - sports, dancing, woodwork, needlework: 'Our young people were all agreed that such a programme was infinitely to be preferred to the aimless, monotonous idle hanging about on street corners which seemed the only alternative. The whole parish will join in wishing this new venture every success.' A carnival dance raised some money towards the necessary electric light, heating and equipment, but progress was slow due to the difficulties of war and it could not open till October 1942 (see p.99).

Clavering Pig Club

As part of the war effort, the Clavering Pig Club was set up in July 1941, its object being to collect and distribute waste foodstuffs, sort out the rations of pig meal, arrange to buy suitable store pigs for its members and obtain a licence when the club member wished to kill the pig and send it to market. The annual subscription was one shilling and the ration was 56 lbs of cereal and 7lbs protein per pig each month. Initially 14 people joined and began straight away fattening the pigs. Six months later the first batch had already been slaughtered, and the members were 'reaping the reward of their labours, either in pork and bacon for their own use or in cash by sale to the Ministry of Food'. During the first year about 50 pigs were fattened and by the second year, membership had grown to over 20 and the following year to 30. The leading lights were Mrs Bar Maine at Mill End Dairy Farm, Keith Mossman, Mr and Mrs Ledward, Mrs E.M. Caton and Ian Napier. Good reports came year after year – in 1942 they boasted:

'The Clavering Pig Club has filled a tiny corner of the national larder and when it is remembered that there are more than 2,000 Pig Clubs up and down the country, many of the them larger than ours, it will be seen that the pig club movement is playing an important part in defeating the attacks of the U-boats on our shipping.'

By 1944 there were 5,000 pig clubs throughout Britain, and the scheme contributed usefully to the national food supply. Newspaper advertising helped to boost the scheme, pointing out the quick returns on pig-keeping, as a diet of kitchen waste would fatten them so quickly that within a year a baby pig could be producing a litter herself. With meat strictly rationed, the usefulness of the domestic pig came into its own again.

MASS PRODUCTION IN 13 MONTHS. The above
photographs show the value of pigs

The 'War Ag' 1941

During the war there was strict government control over farmers, who were obliged to plough up old grassland, grow certain crops and follow numerous regulations. The Essex County War Agricultural Executive Committee – generally known as the 'War Ag.' - had strong powers, under the Ministry of Agriculture, to maintain high standards of husbandry in order to produce as much good-quality food as possible. Farmers who failed to take action could find their land taken over by the Committee (who were all farmers themselves). The minutes of the Saffron Walden District Advisory Committee from 1941 onwards, preserved in Saffron Walden Town Library, show how this affected the 480 farms in the Walden district. By April 1941, 452 ploughing orders had been served, 3,146 acres of grassland ploughed, 3,004 acres mole drained and 6,269 acres ditched in the Walden area – possession was taken of 981 acres, of which 241 were cultivated by this committee. This was the year of the National Farm Survey, when every farm had to be visited and judged on its efficiency – 'C' grade meant they were failing to maximise their crops. In Clavering the inspections came under Rickling farmer, Mr J.R. Tinney (pictured), who sorted out any number of problems, commenting that farmworkers did not appreciate 'the gravity of the national food position'. There were worries about incendiaries damaging crops. Mr Foster was granted permission to sow barley on part of his fallow land at Ford End. Miss James' land in the village was transferred to Mr R.E. Baker provided he ploughed it immediately, but when he objected since the grass was

needed for cows, he was told 'no concession whatever can be made' and the committee took possession. Just in time, Mr Baker let it to another farmer, Mr King and this was allowed so long as any ploughed-up footpaths were restored after the war. Mr Tinney also told Mr Webb to plough up four derelict acres on the Herts border. In June Mr Tinney reported that Mr Rust at Clavering wanted compensation for young apple trees destroyed when the committee had his land ploughed over. In September there was criticism of a derelict market garden at Clavering Hall and the manager was ordered to tidy it up and threatened with possession and reversion to arable. A farm at Ford End was told they needed a good foreman, and orders were also served on a smallholding at Butts Green, and Grange Farm

standards were criticised (see photo). It is clear from the very personal comments in the minutes that the wartime rise in production, although it brought extra income to farmers, also started a trend of increasing interference in their traditional independence.

Grange Farm, where production was criticised in 1941 - the tenant blamed this on the 'shirking and laziness' of the Italian prisoners-of-war he had to employ.

September 1941

My Dear Friends

Clergymen and other ministers of religion are the only people who do not have to register for military service and consequently are never called up. At the same time the government are rightly mindful of the spiritual needs of those in the forces and a number of chaplains are required. During July I was recommended by the Bishop to the Air Ministry for a chaplaincy in the Royal Air Force. I was passed fit by the Air Force doctors and after an interview with the Chaplain in Chief received a pressing invitation to join the RAF as a chaplain and to accept the necessary commission... As a young man I welcomed the opportunity of working amongst the gallant young men and women of the RAF. At the same time I realised that it is now four years since I became your vicar and practically all my time has been given to the life of the two villages so that I have never taken a holiday nor been away for one Sunday... Since the outbreak of the war I have undertaken various unpaid jobs of national service which I felt I could do in addition to my work as Vicar of two villages. When I came to arrange for someone to carry on my work as Vicar during my absence and to try to find in addition people willing to undertake all the jobs of national service that I do at present I was up against a great difficulty. I have after much thought and prayer decided to remain in the parish and have informed the Air Ministry that I cannot accept their invitation. If it were just a question of pleasing myself I should be off tomorrow as a chaplain. But we are warned that there are difficult days ahead and so I have chosen what is perhaps the harder part and will remain the parish.

Yours most sincerely, E.A. STONE

Day of Thanksgiving: Sunday September 21st is to be observed as a day of united thanksgiving for the great deliverance from a terrible danger which was wrought a year ago when the Royal Air Force fought and won the Battle of Britain. The Bishop of Chelmsford says: 'Had we been defeated the war was lost! The German bombers would have been over our great cities all day long bombing us into ruin and extinction day and night until complete submission was inevitable. this would have ended the War, the British Empire, and all hope for the future! Under God, the People who saved us were a few hundred British boys in their fighting planes. Those lads saved Britain and the world!'

Clavering Invasion Committee

The danger of invasion was acutely felt in the early years of the war and villages, just like towns, had to put together plans to deal with every scenario. Thus, in August 1941 the Clavering Parish Invasion Committee was set up. Chaired by Ian Napier who ran the ATC, the committee also included the parish council chairman (Jimmy Clark). the village constable, the local food controller (Mr Luff) and assistant organiser (Vicar), Mr Luckock for the Home Guard, Mr Beamish for the Air Raid Wardens, Mr King for the village Fire Brigade, Mrs Slingsby for the Red Cross and residents Mr and Mrs F. Anthony, Mrs Simmonds and Mrs Finzel. The schoolmaster Alec Richardson was treasurer and Mrs E.M. Caton secretary. The Committee had no powers to dictate but drew up detailed lists of how invasion would be dealt with locally, for instance assessing that the Village Hall could become a rest centre capable of feeding 80 homeless persons and 50 sleeping. Mr Luff as Village Food Controller had a key role: 'His powers at such a time will be extensive and his work is to see that everyone is fed. There would be, in an emergency, no deliveries of bread or milk, these would have to be fetched from specified centres'. A year later the Invasion Committee sent a circular round the village telling everyone about arrangements (see p.93). No local records seem to have survived, but as in other places they would have dealt with the role of the police and special constables (traffic and roads etc); ARP wardens (incidents, rescue parties, etc); casualty services (first aid posts, stretchers); fire brigade; civil arrangements (water supply, food office, burials); homeless (rest centres and billets); and also messengers for taking messages between the various groups. Minutes of meetings do survive for neighbouring Langley, detailing their discussions on all such matters, and a fragile document regarding medical arrangements, found inside a clock at Danceys, may well relate to this committee (see p.129). To fund all this, the Clavering Invasion Committee organised dances and gathered subscriptions to buy stretchers and carriers, and the Fire Fighters and Fire Watch Committees raised money too. One of their invasion exercises must have caused some damage to Brooklands Farm where Mr King lived, as a sum of 25 shillings was needed for repairs (as shown in this final 1944 balance sheet). The committee then stopped meeting but went on giving advice, such as how to dig a slit trench in the garden, and in March 1944 the Home Guard dug a sample to demonstrate the method. However, by November 1944 there was no longer any threat of invasion and the committee was disbanded. The equipment was given to the Red Cross and remained in use after the war and the remaining funds given to Mrs Slingsby to start a depot of equipment for sickness and convalescence run by the District Nursing Association.

Invasion Committee Balance Sheet.

Receipts.	£	s.	d.	Payments.	£	s.	d.
Profit on dance	10	4	6	Hire of rooms			
Fire fighting fund	1	12	6	for lectures,			
Fire Watch Com-				etc.	1	17	0
mittee ..		9	6	2 Stretchers ..	3	15	0
Subscriptions ...		9	5	0	Stretcher car-			
				riers ..	10	0	0
				Repairs at Brook-			
				lands (after			
				Invasion Ex-			
				ercises) ..	1	5	0
				Cheque book ..		5	0
				Balance ..	4	9	6
	£21	11	6		£21	11	6

The Blackout

This little boy, Denis English, was one of the East End evacuees sent *c.*1940-41 to the London County Council nursery school housed during the war at Wood Hall, Arkesden, on the border of Clavering. Behind him can be seen the multi-windowed building which was a nightmare when it came to maintaining the blackout – a very strict aspect of wartime Britain. Wood Hall had 52 windows which needed covering, and in 1941 they were given their 29th warning over infringement of the regulations. This resulted in £4 fines with the LCC criticised for not doing it properly when the blackout was first introduced two years before.

The blackout had begun one night in August 1939 as a dummy run with ARP members attempting to drive through the countryside with no headlights. After war broke out, the Village Hall committee blacked out the hall windows, although this was not an easy task to enforce with so many different people using the building. No attempt was made to black out the numerous church windows – the Vicar just gave up winter evensong in the evenings, and going about to sing carols was difficult in the blackout. All householders had to do the same, since it was felt that any source of light could alert an enemy bomber. It entailed covering every window with black material or paper after dark. June Riley recalls: 'My stepfather made a plywood square that fitted into the window with a handle on it, and we would draw the curtains over it. We didn't go out at night - we had an oil lamp and used to play cards or dominoes, or play schools. or read a story.' In the summer of 1940, the Vicar sent a reminder because 'many of us have got just a little careless about our windows'. It was hard to escape detection, since policemen, specials, wardens and even Home Guard helped to enforce the strict regulations, and even the tiniest chink of light brought a knock on the door. Those who enforced the rules inevitably became unpopular, particularly when offenders found themselves in court: nationwide, over the course of the war, almost a million blackout offenders were prosecuted. In 1941 Special Sgt Vassar Rowe brought a case to the Walden Divisional Bench relating to a house at Hill Green (see newscutting), while in another case one of the Clavering shopkeepers was fined 30 shillings after the village policeman, PC Barker spotted two electric lights illuminating the road. A week later a member of the Home

> Special Sergt. Rowe said that he saw lights coming from five windows at the rear of the buildings. Four were partly blacked-out, but the fifth was unscreened. When seen defendant said, "Yes, they are terrible." He had been warned about three weeks previously.
>
> In a letter defendant admitted the offence.

Guard reported a similar infringement and this time the fine was £10 – a lot of money in those days.

Gas Masks

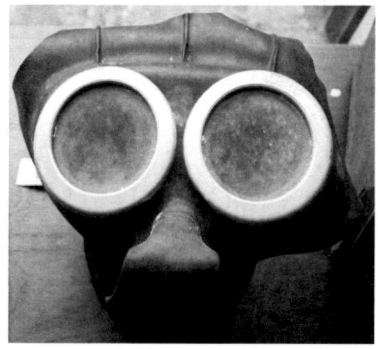

Gas masks were smelly, uncomfortable things but the very real fear of gas attacks had led the Government to issue 38 million of them even before the war started. In March 1941 the village wardens were advising the public to carry their gasmasks with them always and carefully examine them for defects to be pointed out to the wardens. The wardens must also be familiar with all the literature on the subject - the Government issued various Air Raid Precautions handbooks including one on 'Personal Protection Against Gas', and you could buy little tins of Anti-Gas Ointment in several varieties to rub on the skin if there was a gas attack – all very chilling (see illustration below). Isobel Beckwith, remembered, 'We always had to carry our gas masks with us, they were in a small cardboard box on a string which we put over our heads.' Douglas Savill recalled, 'We had all been issued with gas masks - and the first time the warning was given we all put on our gas mask - but that did not last very long'. There was also an anti-gas protective helmet for babies, to add to the family collection – there were already special masks for children, commonly called Mickey Mouse masks (see photo above). June Holland (nee Riley) recalls: 'A mobile van came to the school playground and we were all fitted - you had to go into this old caravan thing to each get fitted because there were several sizes. They put tear gas in and asked us to put our finger in the gas mask to see what it smelt like.' Responsibility for overseeing the system fell on the ARP Wardens, and Mr Edward Beamish, the Senior Warden, arranged gas-mask afternoons at the Lower School for 'anyone who wishes to test the efficiency of their mask and to see that it fits properly and to have it changed if necessary', also to repair any defects, for which a charge was made. In the summer he issued some new additions to the masks. If someone died, their gas mask had to be returned to Mr Beamish who sent it back to headquarters.

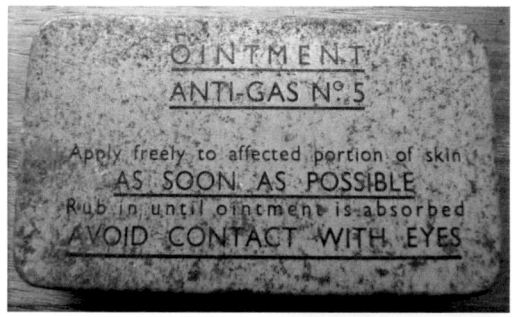

Wartime Regulations

The government seemingly controlled everything and over the course of the war the number of indictable offences grew from 300,000 to 478,000. This case from August 1941 illustrates the restrictions practised on aliens. Although this Russian was working in Clavering legitimately as a farm manager and had lived in Britain for 22 years, he still needed permission to go anywhere. By the time this came to court, Russia had switched sides to the Allies, so this may explain the smallness of the fine. But it does not give details of the mysterious Scottish rendezvous with 'the President' or why he was in a protected area.

More often, the local courts were full of blackout infringements (see p.74), and sometimes rationing offences. Petrol was rationed and allowed only for necessary journeys. In October 1943 the landlord of the *White Horse* at Starlings Green was one of those before Walden Borough Court for buying fuel using petrol coupons given to him by someone else – this was strictly against the rules and he was fined a total of £9 with additional costs. Farmers were allowed petrol for essential needs, which might include running

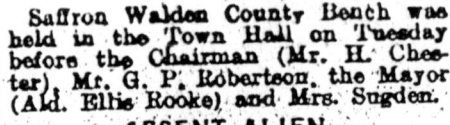

Saffron Walden County Bench was held in the Town Hall on Tuesday before the Chairman (Mr. H. Chester), Mr. G. P. Robertson, the Mayor (Ald. Ellis Rooke) and Mrs. Sugden.

ABSENT ALIEN.

Peter Zelenoff, a Russian national, now a farm manager at Hall Farm, Clavering, was charged with being absent from his registered address without permission from June 28th to the 30th. He admitted the offence.

P.C. Southgate gave evidence that at 7.20 p.m. on July 25th he saw defendant at Clavering and told him that he had information that he had been absent without permission from June 28th to June 30th. Defendant then stated that he was in Scotland with his President. The President had sent a telegram from London telling him to visit him immediately and he went not knowing that he would be away for the night.

Supt. Faulkner stated that defendant was found in Scotland by the police, and probably other proceedings would be taken by them for being in a protected area.

Zelenoff told the Court that he had been summoned to London by his President, but he did not know he was going to Scotland with him.

He was stated to have been in this country for 22 years, and he had given no previous trouble.

A fine of £1 was imposed.

lorries for agricultural and other approved purposes (see p.49). However, Mike Preisig, who lived in Clavering during the war and attended Newport Boys' Grammar School with Ted Rowe, recalls a story about Ted's father, the Curles Manor farmer and special police sergeant, Vassar Rowe, pictured here leading a church parade. He gave a lift to the boys when they needed to play an away game.

'Vassar ran two Bedford lorries, doing general farm haulage. He was a great pal of our sports master Spud Taylor. We were drawn to play a cricket match against St Edmund College, but we had to lay down in the back on straw and be covered over with a tarpaulin so we couldn't be seen. All highly illegal – using a farm lorry on rationed petrol to carry a cricket team and being driven by a Special Police sergeant!'

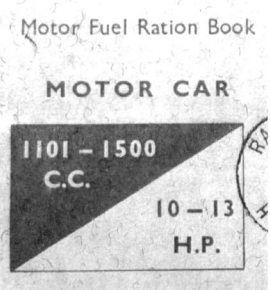

Motor Fuel Ration Book

MOTOR CAR

1101 – 1500 C.C.

10 – 13

H.P.

December 1941

My Dear Friends

I am sure we all rejoice with the farm workers in their good fortune in being granted a minimum wage of £3 a week. To have their wages nearly doubled since the beginning of the war is a fine tribute to the magnificent contribution which farmers and farm workers are making to the national effort... there has been almost universal approval of the proposal that, like carpenters and bricklayers, farm workers should receive a due reward for their labours... this rise will not come out of the farmers' pockets, otherwise one section of the village would be better off at the expense of another; but rather will the cost of the rise be spread over the whole country. Just now there are not many things to spend one's money on. Most essential goods are rationed and we are asked not to indulge in wasteful or luxury spending. May I commend the Government's appeal for war savings to all who will benefit by this wage increase?... The timely recognition of the value of an ancient industry which this wage increase brings will I think in course of time bring changes in our village life. When some fifty years ago a farm worker's average was ten shillings a week and a horsekeeper's perhaps twelve and sixpence, there were few amenities and comforts he could enjoy. But now some of the up to date amenities of the town should come to the country – better houses with electric light and fitted with a sink and hot water such problems as these should be tackled as soon as conditions allow. In the days of the small wages it was natural to look at the larger houses, perhaps to that of the Squire to provide recreational facilities and for help in time of illness. Now that we are becoming more and more equally blessed with the world's goods, we are able to support more equally village institutions. The old distinctions between rich and poor will disappear from our villages, and life will be lived on a practically level plain by all. This will mean an increase in our responsibility towards the community in which we live... now with our larger wages we may be asked to give a little more...

Yours most sincerely, E.A. STONE

Pitching sheaves by hand during steam threshing. Below, 1944 photo of a binder machine and tractor on a local farm.

Essential War Work

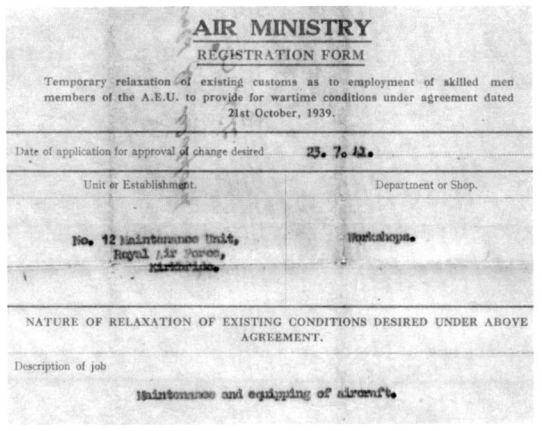

AIR MINISTRY
REGISTRATION FORM

Temporary relaxation of existing customs as to employment of skilled men members of the A.E.U. to provide for wartime conditions under agreement dated 21st October, 1939.

Date of application for approval of change desired   23. 7. 42.

Unit or Establishment.   Department or Shop.

No. 12 Maintenance Unit,   Workshops.
Royal Air Force,
Kirkbride.

NATURE OF RELAXATION OF EXISTING CONDITIONS DESIRED UNDER ABOVE AGREEMENT.

Description of job

Maintenance and equipping of aircraft.

MINISTRY OF LABOUR AND NATIONAL SERVICE.
Essential Work (General Provisions) Order(s), 1942.

Date....28.7.45....................**CARLISLE**....Local Office
Employer ....No. 12 Maintenance Unit,.....
Address ...........R.A.F., Kirkbride......
Worker ....HAROLD JOHN WALFORD.....
Address ....Red House, Kirkbampton.......
Worker's Dept....No. M.U.............Check No...D.26.
Occupation ....Fitter A.

I, the undersigned, a National Service Officer, hereby give **permission** with
1. † TO THE ABOVE-NAMED EMPLOYER effect on and after
† *a.* to terminate the employment in the undertaking of the above-named worker
his   30. 7. 45
† *b.* to cause the above-named worker to give his services to the undertaking of
their

at

2. TO THE ABOVE-NAMED WORKER
to leave the employment of the above-named employer
† Delete as appropriate.   *[signature]*
                        National Service Officer.
E.D. 342A   (SEE NOTES OVERLEAF).

Being in a reserved occupation lacked the glamour of a uniform, but was not an easy ride, and could at times be more fraught than serving in the Forces. Those who had skills were regarded as essential to the war effort, and many were away from home for years working in industry. Among them was Harold Walford (b.1913), who was married in April 1940 to Gladys Reed, but scarcely saw his wife for the rest of the war as he was doing essential war work in Cumbria. Both came from Methodist families - Gladys was the daughter of Ephraim Reed, who was killed in WW1 and whose name is on the village war memorial. Not long after his wedding, Harold applied to the Ministry of Labour & National Service for government training under the Essential Work (General Provisions) Order 1942 (see left). By September 1941, he had moved to RAF Kirkbride to work in No 12 Maintenance Unit as an aircraft fitter, maintaining and equipping the aircraft so vital for winning the war. RAF Kirkbride was a large establishment in Cumbria built in 1939 specifically to repair and store the whole range of aircraft, in an area safe from enemy attack. Four years later in August 1945, now aged 32 and the war over, Harold applied to the Ministry to be released from service because his wife was ill, and there were domestic reasons 'due to prolonged absence from home'. This was granted even though there had been some opposition due to a shortage of craftsmen. So Harold came back to spend the rest of his long life in Clavering, where he was a stalwart of the Cricket Club and helped to build the pavilion on Hill Green and served as Churchwarden. In his trade as builder, he constructed a number of local houses, including the one in Arkesden Road where he lived until his death in 2004, aged 91 - although sadly afflicted by blindness for many years, he remained a cheerful man known for great warmth and friendliness. He spoke little of the war, but these documents remind us that it was men like Harold who kept the RAF planes in the air, and capable of dealing with the Luftwaffe.

With the King's Forces 1941

By late 1941 the list of Clavering men and women serving their country in uniform and printed in the parish magazine had grown to 64. It included four Barkers, four Barnards, four Laws and many other familiar village names. Additions since 1940 included:

Frank Baker, Reginald Baker, Dennis Barnard, Reginald Barnard, Walter Barnard, Stanley Chipperfield, Peter Cleasby-Thompson, Frederick Gilbey, Percy King, Kenneth Law, Leonard Monk, Jack Peacock, Sidney Player, Ralph Rogers, Harold Walford, Derrick Wilson, Eric Wilson, Frances Riley (NAAFI), Irene Law (ATS), Dorothy Whyman ATS.

Leading Aircraftman Dennis William Barnard (above left) served in the RAF from 1940-46, and was a plant operator with the airfield construction squadrons, stationed in Europe and Singapore. Others in the family in uniform were Reginald Barnard (above right), Leslie Barnard and Walter Bernard. Young able-bodied women had also been called up in 1941, and among those from Clavering serving abroad was Cpl Irene Law, pictured here in ATS uniform, riding a motorbike in Egypt.

Chapter Five
1942: 'A time of stern testing'

As the Vicar put it, the New Year opened with 'the world in all its five continents at war'. He remained optimistic - at least in print - but things were still very grim early in the year. The Battle of the Atlantic was going better, but both British and German cities were being devastated by bombing, and the Desert War was fierce and unrelenting – although now Monty was in charge and American equipment available. The Nazis had adopted their totally shocking 'Final Solution', aiming to exterminate all eleven million Jews in Europe – a million had died already: Auschwitz began operating and thousands were dying in the Warsaw Ghetto. All was still chaos in the Far East, with Japan invading Borneo, New Guinea, Sumatra, Singapore. The good news was that Britain was no longer alone as it had seemed 12 months earlier, since there were now 26 countries opposing the Axis, including Russia which had changed sides and the USA, precipitated into commitment after the carnage of Pearl Harbour. The victory at El Alamein on 15 November was a tremendous boost to morale – *the end of the beginning*', as Churchill said.

On the Home Front, crime was on the increase, with particular worries about aimless youth. Road accidents were worse than ever in the blackout and, for the minority who had cars, they were of limited use in the face of petrol rationing, no signposts and unrepaired roads. Daily life was even more irritating - one tablet of soap a month, sweets rationed and milk allowances cut, while razor blades were in short supply and baths were to have no more than five inches of water – naturally this last item could not easily be policed, so it was only a recommendation not a requirement. The various wartime campaigns intensified, especially paper and metal salvage. But rosehip syrup and cod liver oil came into the lives of children and, to keep up morale, there was much discussion about creating a better society after the war: a major post-war house building programme, the Beveridge plan for a Welfare State, family allowances and free medicine for all: a brave new world beckoned once Hitler was defeated.

At home the Vicar was rushed off his feet, but was still becoming restless – he was quite a young man, aged only 30 at the outbreak of war, and he saw his contemporaries in uniform serving their country. The clergy were one of the occupations exempted from national service, but on the other hand there was a great shortage of Forces chaplains and this he very much wanted to do. Arrangements for filling in during his absence were complicated but eventually with the Bishop's help and his young wife's co-operation, he managed it and off he went to be an RAF chaplain, with the letters AKC and RAFVR after his name. Then for a while his contributions to the parish magazine were written from a Bomber Command station 'somewhere in England'. It helped him understand how 'our local boys and girls' felt, he said, gave him the novel experience of writing to his wife and made him realise how much the airmen needed the warm woollies being made by the village knitters. But alas his service soon came to an end, since the clergyman who replaced him went himself to be a chaplain, so Rev. Stone had to return to Clavering much to his disappointment. He decided to be frank about the reasons why he could find no one to stand in.

Community life in the village was completely geared up to wartime needs. Comforts for the Forces, Saving Weeks and salvage campaigns, Nursing Association, Invasion Committee Pig Club, Children's Red Cross Club, dancing practices in aid of Mrs. Churchill's Aid-to-Russia Fund, collecting eggs for the local hospital, Ministry of Information film shows, uniformed parades, concert parties and village hops – busy times indeed.

Rev. Stone was delighted by the success of the ATC, the appearance of the boys in the harvest camp at his Sunday morning service, and at long last in October the opening of the Youth Centre on which he had worked so hard. But the inability to find a team of ringers to mark the El Alamein Victory was disappointing. The Fire Guard wound up its night watches, there was a fund-raising appeal to send a Christmas postal order to each of the village people in the Forces, and that year was another fantastic harvest – God seemed to smile on the English weather through its most important harvests in the war years. By now the magazine was printing 200 copies a month, some being sent all over the world. The big social change of the year was that the Americans were 'over here' – welcome them into your homes, said the vicar. After the publication of the Beveridge and other reports, he was cautious about the emphasis on post-war needs in material terms, when what was really needed, as he repeatedly wrote, was a new attitude and a new spirit.

In spite of the paper shortage, there was no curtailing of official paperwork during wartime – identity cards, ration books for food, clothing and fuel and other documents filled up coat pockets and handbags.

January 1942

My dear Friends,
The New Year opens with the world in all its five continents at war... Twelve months ago it seemed that our Empire was fighting for its life alone. One or two nations were supporting us with materials but they were more or less dubious as to the possibility of our survival. In the spring and early summer further defeats confronted us in Libya, Greece and Crete and then at last the tide began to turn. The broken German army is in retreat in Russia and Libya. The Battle of the Atlantic has gone steadily in our favour for months past. We are the best fed nation in Europe and our courage is unshaken and our hopes are high. Though fierce battles may still rage in the Far East, the balance of profit and loss is definitely on our side...
Yours most sincerely, E.A. STONE

'Old Tombstone' Clavering Churchyard.

Clavering churchyard as it looked before the war.

February 1942

My Dear Friends
It is rather strange to be writing to you from my room here on an RAF Station of Bomber Command somewhere in England. With the engines of Wellington bombers roaring all around me it seems a far cry to the quiet of my study at the Vicarage. But though perhaps far from Clavering and Langley I do feel a much closer bond with our many boys and girls in the services; I know how they are thinking and feeling and how service life is affecting them... It is an unnatural life we are leading but it is for our country, the safety of our homes and families that we are fighting and it is right that we should often give a thought and a prayer for those at home... It is indeed a far cry from an Officers Mess to a country vicarage and equally far from a NAAFI canteen to a cottage kitchen... You at home have often told me how you look for a letter from your husband or the children, but it is not always as easy as it may seem to get the time and quiet to write one. Conversation with airmen and WAAFs often naturally leads to a talk about their homes and I frequently mention the duty of writing home. To so many it is rather strange at first to write home; for myself I have never had occasion to write to my wife since our marriage until recently but there is a thrill and joy in doing so. You must forgive me if I have appeared a little sentimental but so often we get a truer value of things and appreciate them more when we see them at a distance...
Yours most sincerely, E.A. STONE AKC, RAFVR

RAFVR Chaplain

The Rev. A. E. Stone.

In 1942 the Vicar, Rev. Ernest Stone was able to spend about eight months serving as a Forces chaplain, leaving wife Doris to take over his many local wartime duties and replacement clergy to run the services. There was a big shortage of chaplains, and he first expressed a wish to be a chaplain in 1941 but, to his great disappointment, found it impossible to make arrangements. However, in 1942 the way was cleared for him to become an RAFVR Chaplain, initially at St Athan in Glamorganshire: 'As a young man I welcome the opportunity of working amongst the gallant young men and women of the RAF', he wrote – particularly since, during four years incumbency, he had never even taken a holiday or missed a Sunday service. However, the work lasted only a few months, as described in his letters that year.

The Bishop made it possible for the difficulties to which I have referred to be overcome, I felt that I could perhaps make my greatest contribution to the war effort by going as a chaplain to the boys and girls of our Royal Air Force. By the time you read these words I shall have taken up this new work. I hope no one will misunderstand my action. At the moment, owing to the vast expansion of the armed forces there is a serious shortage of Church of England chaplains and something like 300 priests between 26 and 40 are needed to bring the war time establishment up to full strength. As in every other department of life the war is making demands which have never before had to be met. Nothing is normal and the church cannot remain unaffected. The time has come therefore for church people to make sacrifices in spiritual things as they have already made in secular things... The needs of the forces must be met and if it means the lending of our Vicar for the duration of the war that will just be another inconvenience which we will endure gladly for the sake of our young people in the army, navy and air force... Mrs Stone is remaining at the Vicarage and hopes to carry on most of the wartime jobs that I have been doing ... I am sure you will give to her that same help and understanding that you have always given me. I shall have you all continually in my thoughts and prayers and will look forward to a speedy return to the parish ...

While away he continued to write letters to the local 'boys and girls' in the Forces, and often sent missives to the parish magazine. The Vicar of Arkesden, Rev. Stares and a retired Chesterford priest, Rev. Gofton, took over services - the chaplain's extra salary had to pay for this. Unfortunately these arrangements fell apart within a few months because the former also went off to be a chaplain: 'I am sorry that the plans I made for the care of the parish during my absence in the R.A.F. have collapsed so soon', wrote Reverend Stone in June, and by the autumn he was back in the Vicarage: 'These difficulties have not become any easier and I have therefore been granted permission by the Air Ministry to return to the parish for some months. While it is very pleasant to be back in the quiet and peace of this corner of Essex with one's own family again, yet it is, as you can imagine, a great disappointment to me to give up even for a time a work which has such vast opportunities for good among our boys and girls.' The rest of 1942 and the whole of 1943 were to pass before Rev. Stone, in 1944, found another opportunity to work as a chaplain (see p.133).

Air & Army Cadets

During wartime there were far more outlets than in Clavering today for young people's activities. The spectre of the Hitler Youth movement, with its corruption of young minds, worried everyone and motivated adults to organise more wholesome youth activities. Nationally, the Air Training Corps (ATC) had been set up in 1941 and proved enormously popular, growing to 200,000 within six months. The 1824 Squadron was formed at Saffron Walden with Flights at Thaxted, Great Chesterford and at Clavering in January 1942. Army Cadets followed in June 1943 under Aubrey Williams of The Grange at the Lower School, while the Clavering Flight met at the Upper School under F.O. Ian Napier, who lived at Appletree Cottage in Stortford Road, and Mr Richardson, the school head. The Flight attracted lads aged 15½ to 17½ who were required to undertake instruction and who had to be 'keen on flying and are prepared to work hard'. The Vicar was delighted with the response.

'The formation of a junior branch of the RAF is to me one of the good things that have come out of the war, for what boy is not interested in aeroplanes and flying and anxious to know more of them? It is something that we as a nation are very proud of, that in the Royal Air Force everyone who is a pilot or member of an air crew has volunteered for this work. We can also be very proud that so many of our boys up and down the country are anxious to carry on this high tradition by giving up their leisure time to learning something of the subjects which pilots and observers must know before they can embark on a course of flying... there are grounds for congratulation that in a rural area such as Clavering we have a small branch of this nation-wide movement serving neighbouring villages.'

A fund-raising dance at the Village Hall in September brought in a goodly sum with which to buy equipment and text books, since joining the ATC meant a full programme of work in preparation for joining the RAF: 'The motto of the ATC is "Venture Adventure" and the present Cadets fully live up to all that these words imply', said F.O. Napier. In the autumn the boys had the first of many visits to an RAF base where 'meals in the airmen's mess and a flip for everyone in a plane' thrilled them all. The first anniversary of the Clavering Flight was celebrated with a dinner for all the members, supporters and officers:

'Glowing tributes were paid by the Inspecting Officer to the work of the flight and the capacity for overcoming the many difficulties associated with a rather isolated flight some distance from its squadron headquarters, was warmly praised. Mr Napier has done a great job of work with our lads and he can be well be proud of the boys of the Clavering Flight.'

By spring 1943, the ATC had extended to three evenings a week, with 14 boys from Clavering, Wicken and Berden receiving instruction in Morse code and squad drill conducted by Anthony Williams, mathematics and English by Mr Richardson, and navigation and current affairs by F.O. Napier, plus a monthly Sunday visit with other Flights to Debden Aerodrome. Cpl Jim Jackson (pictured outside his Druce home) became the first cadet of the Flight to enter the RAF where he trained as an armourer. Next to go was Cpl Bert Hill, entering the RAF for aircrew duties. 'Everyone has made good progress and is as keen as the day he joined', reported Mr Napier. The meetings were suspended during harvest time, but the Cadets did take part with Thaxted Flight in a week's camp at a RNAS station – this was probably at HMS Kestrel near Winchester where cadets flew in a Swordfish and a Miles Magister. They 'returned with memories of thrilling experiences and high admiration for their older brothers in the Fleet Air Arm. Each Cadet has added valuable hours to his personal flying experiences and now knows the feel of .303 kick.' They also had a day out in London visiting Madame Tussauds and Nelson's *Victory*. By then the village also had a platoon of Army Cadets, aged 14-17, attached to the 12th Cadet Battalion of the Essex Regiment, covering Clavering, Langley, Arkesden and Wicken Bonhunt. The Cadets joined others in the Farm Sunday church parade, after which 'the organisations paraded in the churchyard and Lieutenant Ledward of the Home Guard spoke some inspiring words regarding the importance of the day and of the part young people must play in planning the future'. Among those joining the ATC was John Barwood (b.1925) who still today remembers:

'I joined the ATC when I was 16 – the ATC was like being in the Air Force, though only amateur. I enjoyed that. One week we had a sergeant and another week a low-ranking officer and we used to say 'don't know who was the worst', and it was the sergeant, he was treating us as though we was in the Forces. They'd bawl out quite loud. We met in the Lower School playground and building, we used to march round the playground about 20 times 'cause it was only small, we enjoyed that.'

Others who belonged to the Flight included Bill Newland, Derrick King, Fred Fish and Ben Ruse. Bill Newland recalls: 'We used to have different lessons at Saffron Walden and every fortnight we used to pushbike to Debden RAF Barracks, and do various things there. Once we went to Winchester and I did 8 hours flying.' Ben Ruse enrolled when he was 16 and later began training as a flight engineer, but his bakery work took precedence and he joined the Home Guard instead. The Clavering Cadets used bikes for their visits to RAF Debden to watch Spitfires, Mustangs and Thunderbolts and to Nuthampstead to see the Flying Fortresses. Ben remembered the dog fights when Debden was being bombed, and seeing a Halifax on fire over Newport - it crashed at Wicken. The lads enjoyed American hospitality, including ice cream, oranges and bananas. The Clavering ATC unfortunately lost their enthusiastic leader, Mr Napier in May 1944 when he moved to Surrey (see p.21). But the Flight kept going under Mr Richardson, taking part in the splendid Empire Day Parade (see pp. 134-135) and had another summer camp at North Weald Aerodrome.

The Bowles family at sea

Left to right: Chief Petty Officer Sidney Bowles (joined 1940), his son Marine Peter Bowles (joined 1941) and his other son, Leading Signalman John Bowles (joined 1942).

By 1942 the father and both sons of the Bowles family were serving at sea – it must have been a deeply worrying time for Mrs Bowles who lived at Hill Green, but fortunately they eventually all came home to Clavering. Her husband, Sidney joined the Navy aged 35 in September 1940 and remained throughout the war, serving on minelayers and ending as a Chief Petty Officer. Their younger son, John joined the Royal Navy as a boy sailor in 1942, the start of a 14-year service, reaching the rank of Leading Signalman. He served on HMS Cumberland in the S.E. Asia Command and during wartime was based in Columbo, visiting the Nicabar Islands, Java, Sumatra, Australia, Aden and all points east. John Bowles was on the Cumberland when the atomic bomb was dropped. Meanwhile his older brother, Peter had joined the Royal Marines in 1941, serving aboard HMS Kent on the freezing Arctic Convoys, earning Arctic Convoy and Russian medals (pictured).

When Peter came off the Kent, he trained to be a sniper in the Special Boat Service, but the war ended then. On one occasion both brothers and their father were in Scapa Flow but on different vessels. At least they all came home - John's cousins had all joined the RAF and sadly two of them were killed. After the war, John remained in the Navy and, while stationed at Plymouth, met a Wren called Margaret Sinden, who worked as a cook on HMS President. They were married at Clavering Church in 1948 (see photo right), had three children and their entire married life has been spent in Clavering at Skeins Way.

In Memoriam Sidney Matthews 1942

This is Sidney Matthews pictured home on leave on the road to Stickling Green, where his family lived. Before the war he had worked for the Finzels at Clavering Court as a chauffeur, 'such a likeable chap', remembers John Barwood. Sidney Raymond Matthews was a driver with the RASC, aged only 25 when he died on 15 February 1942. He had gone through Dunkirk and managed to survive, but then was sent to Italy. The story that went round the village was that Sid was captured by the Italians and put on a hospital ship, which was mistakenly torpedoed by an Allied submarine and went down with much loss of life. News of such events was obviously suppressed in wartime, and is still difficult to verify today. But such tragedies did happen, and Allied servicemen were lost in this way including those, like Sid Matthews, who have no known grave, but are commemorated as names on the Alamein Memorial.

In Memory of
Driver SIDNEY RAYMOND MATTHEWS
T/155461, 384 Gen. Transport Coy., Royal Army Service Corps
who died age 25
on 15 February 1942
Remembered with honour
ALAMEIN MEMORIAL

Warship Week 1942

The war effort was still costing a huge amount, so the savings campaigns intensified and in 1942 there were two campaigns. National Savings had actually been falling, down from £11m. to £8m. a week, and so a new five-shillings savings stamp was introduced. Every year there was a special savings campaign with a memorable name. In March 1941 it had been 'War Weapons Week', in which the Saffron Walden town and rural aim of raising £40,000 was reached on the first day of the week. Unfortunately, Clavering's contribution amounted to a miserly £137 of that total. In February 1942 it was 'Warship Week'. aiming much higher – to raise £120,000, the price of a Corvette to be named Marjoran. The Chancellor of the Exchequer promised: 'If we invest freely for our own benefit in years to come our taxation will be correspondingly less severe'. Mrs Stone, the Vicar's wife, was secretary and stamps could be bought for 6d or 2s 6d in various outlets. During Warship Week, there were afternoon screenings of films at the village hall about defence services. The ambitious target was not only reached but doubled, and the town and district were able to buy two corvettes. Each village set its own target and Clavering had aimed to raise £4,625, but again was one of the few villages that fell short of target, although still saved a creditable £3,416 – a huge improvement on the year before and showed people were getting the savings message. However, an analysis in the local newspaper revealed that Clavering people were still some of the least thrifty in the district. In the summer and autumn, the focus was on 'Tanks For Attack'. Often the campaigns were targeted at the young – at Clavering School, June Holland (nee Riley) remembers winning a competition.

'Once there was a competition for a slogan for National Savings I won a propelling pencil for writing "*Lend your money, all you can, to help the Airforce, everyman*". National Saving stamps were sold for 6d, a card full of 40 could be taken to the PO to go into a Post Office Savings Account.'

WARSHIP WEEK

FEBRUARY 21st to 28th, 1942

"FIGHT THE GOOD FIGHT WITH ALL YOUR MITE"

VIOLET CHAMPION (14 years),
Chapel Hill,
Stansted.

This space has been generously given by:
MESSRS. MYHILL & SONS, Agricultural Merchants, SAFFRON WALDEN.

March 1942

My dear Friends,
We are passing through dark days and a time of stern testing. Wherever people have been gathered together in recent weeks the common topic of conversation has been the latest war news. Criticisms have been many, and no doubt mistakes have been made, but so often criticism does not take account of the many and vital things which have been well done and have turned out successfully. What are your actions? Do you sometimes feel that the chief ends of existence are material prosperity and comfort and get impatient because they are not close at hand? Or, when the news of enemy successes comes, do you feel the need for greater effort in the crusade against the citadels of evil? ... Almost every day on the same page of our newspapers we can find instances of these two points of view. In one column we may read the story of some deed of heroism at sea or on land or in the air, while in another is an account of the work of those who are more interested in getting than in giving – those engaged it the 'black markets'... In such times, to be apathetic and lethargic even to see some personal advantage is unpardonable treason. In our conflict with the world-rulers of darkness all who rejoice in the name of Christian must prepare for a stern crusade...
Yours most sincerely, E.A. STONE

April 1942

My dear Friends
It was in the peace and calm of a well-kept cemetery in an English country town. Officers and men of the Royal Air Force have gathered to pay honour and respect to one of their number who has been killed on active service. A few days before, a plane crashed and a flying officer, a Rhodes scholar of Oxford university and an international rugby-football player had been killed. The service is over, the firing party have fired their volleys, the notes of the Last Post and Reveille are dying away and I glance at the officers and men still standing at attention. Among them is a woman, a young WAAF officer, a pathetic figure, for she has come to be present at her fiancé's funeral...
Yours most sincerely,
E.A. Stone.

A funeral ceremony conducted by a naval chaplain, echoing the Vicar's description of an airman's burial above. This poignant photo was among those saved by Royal Marine Peter Bowles of Clavering, who was with the Arctic convoys during WW2 and perhaps attended this burial of one of their number in a frozen landscape.

Wartime Salvage

"UP HOUSEWIVES AND AT 'EM!"

YOU can have a "smack at 'em." There are war weapons in *your* household waste. Every scrap counts, so save every scrap — of paper, metal, bones. ★ Keep them separate and put them by the dustbin every collection day. They are wanted urgently to make munitions. Let's all get right into action *now!*

By 1942, Clavering had dispatched over seven tons of wastepaper, earning the princely sum of £22 for the Red Cross Comforts for the Forces Fund. But now it was illegal to burn paper so even more must be gathered, and the Vicar said that refusal to salvage was 'surely a crime against our country'. The drive to help the war effort by collecting salvage – what we now call recycling – had begun soon after the start of the war, with the public admonished at every opportunity with posters and adverts. It began with wastepaper, piled up in sacks at the Vicarage stables, and taken to Saffron Walden by Mr Caton. Metal was also needed, to make munitions. On a summer's evening in 1940 large crowds had attended an outdoor meeting in Bury Meadow to explain the arrangements: there were five dumps for scrap iron – at Starlings Green, Brooklands Farm, Hill Green, Sticklings Green and the Mills - and four salvage controllers – Messrs G. Piggott, E. Chapman and S. Smith and Mrs Maine. Older children volunteered to flatten tins, call at houses and later on helped Mrs Finzel on her pony-cart circuits collecting wastepaper. June Holland (nee Riley) remembers the Slingsbys helping too.

'The only way to go round the village to collect was by wheelbarrow. Col and Mrs Slingsby at Danceys had a nice long barn and we used to pick up the wheelbarrow and then wheel it all round to the people and get paper tied up with string and back to Slingsby's barn so it didn't get wet, then we had to stack it in the barn. And the tins to Arthur King at Brooklands Farm, they supplied a wooden mallet and we had to squash these tins flat.'

In addition, a lorry-load of old iron went out from Clavering and Langley, and a survey was made of iron and steel gates, posts and chains - all were required to be sacrificed and most churchyard railings disappeared (but not all! – see photo taken 1942 – the remains of these railings are still there today). At the end of two years, the total was 10 tons and £30 raised in the two villages. By now salvage was deemed too vital to be left to local volunteers, and the job was transferred to the Rural District Council, with a van visiting by rota, and sums collected going to the rates rather than local causes. Collection facilities were still available for old rubber goods and bones', pointed out Salvage Stewards, Jean Finzel and Doris Stone. In 1943 there began also a book drive to provide reading matter for the Forces and restock libraries damaged by air raids – 810 books were collected but most ended up as salvage, after being examined by a Scrutiny Committee consisting of the vicar, a local author and a museum curator. It was said that 'every ton of salvage means one ton of shipping space saved', and although later research queried this claim, it gave a sense of involvement in helping the war effort.

Wartime Waste

GOVERNMENT CONUNDRUMS.

TO THE EDITOR.

Sir,—I have been trying to solve some conundrums propounded by the Government, and failed. By advertisement, and other means costing taxpayers thousands of pounds, the people are urged to save this, save that, save everything; economise every day in every way. How does the Government set an example in complying with its own exhortations, to which heavy penalties are attached for non-compliance?

Some months ago householders in Clavering and other villages received a notice, in a ½oz. envelope, that the postal town in future was to be Saffron Walden instead of Newport, with a request that the recipients should inform their correspondents. Last week the Post Office sent out telephone accounts, and they were addressed to "Clavering, Newport, Essex." The P.O. ignored its own instruction. Query: Did the P.O. waste paper, envelope and postman's time in notifying a decision it takes no notice of itself?

Communal kitchens — beg pardon, British Restaurants—have been established to save food and fuel. People who have meals at these centres have their full rations at home, requiring fuel to cook. Query: Does this save or increase in the consumption of food and fuel?

To save petrol our only direct connection with London, the Friday bus, has been stopped by order, yet petrol may be used to take people to sports up to a distance longer than our bus journey. Query: Which of the two was of greater service to the general public?

So one could go on, but your space is valuable, your newsprint being rationed in order that the Government may have enough for forms. Can you wonder that I sign myself, —Yours, etc.,

"PUZZLED."

Clavering, —— ? Essex.

Some wartime regulations made no sense, was the gist of this sarcastic complaint by an anonymous Clavering letter-writer to the local paper in July 1942. Signing himself simply as 'Puzzled' of Clavering, he pointed out how government wasted resources that householders were exhorted to save – advertisements like this one, featuring the 'Squander Bug', appeared in the local and national papers all the time.

MORE WAGES THIS WEEK – YOU CAN BUY LOTS OF AWFUL TRASH !

DON'T LISTEN TO THE SQUANDER BUG!

BEWARE the treacherous Squander Bug! He's the prince of fifth-columnists—doesn't believe in a nest-egg for the future — doesn't believe in making money fight for Britain. He's all for chucking good money away on useless things that don't help to win the war. Don't let him fool you. Buy Savings Certificates with all you can spare. Join a Savings Group to defeat the Squander Bug!

Savings Certificates cost 15/—and are worth 20/6 in 10 years—increase free of Income tax. They can be bought by instalments with 6d., 2/6 or 5/- Savings Stamps through your Savings Group or Centre or any Post Office or Trustee Savings Bank. Buy now!

'Beware the treacherous Squander Bug! It's the prince of fifth-columnists – doesn't believe it's a nest-egg for the future – doesn't believe in making money fight for Britain. He's all for chucking good money away on useless things that don't help to win the war. Don't let him fool you…'

May 1942

Tidying Clavering churchyard before the war – Edward Beamish, later to be Senior ARP Warden, and Church Sexton, George Livings, with help from young John Barwood.

My dear Friends,
I was glad to be able to be present at our Annual Parochial Meetings. In both parishes the fabric of the churches was reported to be in good order while the income showed an increase over previous years. Several speakers at Clavering spoke of the excellent way in which the church and churchyard were kept and I heartily endorse their remarks; those responsible for this work can well be proud of their labours.

I was very touched at these meetings by your kindly references to my wife who as one speaker mentioned is in my absence 'bearing the heat and burden of the day'. Your appreciation of her efforts in trying to carry on some of my work was very encouraging.
Yours most sincerely, E.A. STONE

June 1942

My dear Friends,
At the present time we all know more or less what we are fighting against, but not many seem to know what we are fighting for. It is vitally and urgently necessary that we know both and then put everything we have into this life and death struggle... Hitler has taught his people a religion of hate and if he is to be defeated finally and completely, it can only be by a nation which has not only better and more tanks and aeroplanes, by a nation which has not only greater courage and endurance, but by a nation which has a better and stronger faith. Our physical courage has never been higher. Did any nation ever exhibit a grander spectacle than that seen in the autumn of 1940, when a few score British boys, outnumbered often by ten to one defeated the German Luftwaffe and drove them from the daylight sky? Did any nation ever show greater courage than the men and women of London, who night after night listened to the whine and the crash of the German bombs? ... If we feel tempted sometimes to bale out, to give up our practice of religion, our churchgoing, let us first get clear what is at stake and what would be the consequences of such a loss, to ourselves and our country. At all costs we must stick to the controls.
Yours most sincerely, E.A. STONE

July 1942

My dear Friends,
We are continually being reminded in these days of the importance of these summer months in deciding the issues of the war. Not that we are promised an early finish to the present struggle but that the enemy will put forward his greatest efforts on the various battlefronts in the hope of achieving a decision. Our friends as always are eager to pass on their views as to the future. For some, as they look forward, there is a confident optimism, for others the outlook seems long and grim... In any life or death struggle such as we are engaged in just now there are always moments of brightness and darker times when the sun seems to go and we are left groping. Some glorious victory raises our hopes, some sudden set back seems to shatter them equally quickly... Many people feel under the weather these days... And then there is the constant strain of the war, friends and loved ones on active service and a continual dread of the future. It makes all the difference to our troubles the attitude we take up to them. Let us take up the attitude of gallant acceptance regarding them not as oppositions but as opportunities for further knowledge of God, for further growth in the courage and patience of Christ for further helping on His kingdom.
Yours very sincerely, E.A. STONE

Clavering Invasion Committee. The Invasion Committee are greatly encouraged by the support they have received in many ways from all and sundry in the Parish. Particularly has the response to their appeal for Funds given them renewed zest. The proceeds from the very successful Dance held at the Hall recently together with many personal subscriptions and donations have enabled the Committee to acquire some much needed stretchers and carriers. Balances of Funds from the Fire Fighters Committee and the Fire Watch Committee have also been handed over to the Invasion Committee for the benefit of the Parish.

As is now well known, the Committee possess no executive or dictatorial powers. They are purely a co-operative and advisory body and depend on the goodwill and helpful criticism of the Community at large. Much useful work has already been accomplished by the various Services represented on the Committee. Much still requires to be done. The meetings so far held have been entirely free from 'panic' decisions, each member has offered his utmost service to ensure a smooth working of the many intricate and detailed matters that call for attention, and the Exercises that have already been held have shown the readiness of everyone to learn from mistakes and rectify wherever possible errors of judgment.

Further Exercises will be arranged in the near future for the benefit of the Parish as a whole and so long as the Committee retain the goodwill of the Community its labours generally will not be found wanting.

N.

In 1942, the Invasion Committee, which had been set up the previous year (see p.73), published this update in the parish magazine, which is unfortunately the only surviving local record of the 'many intricate and detailed matters that call for attention'. But the minutes of similar committees elsewhere reveal that they had a huge amount to do, to cover every eventuality in the event of invasion. In 1942 the outcome of the war, as the vicar wrote above, still hung in the balance.

The War Resisters

Down on the Farm

The Lansbury Gate Farm

THE WAR RESISTERS' INTERNATIONAL
11 ABBEY ROAD, ENFIELD, MIDDLESEX, ENGLAND

Spring 1942

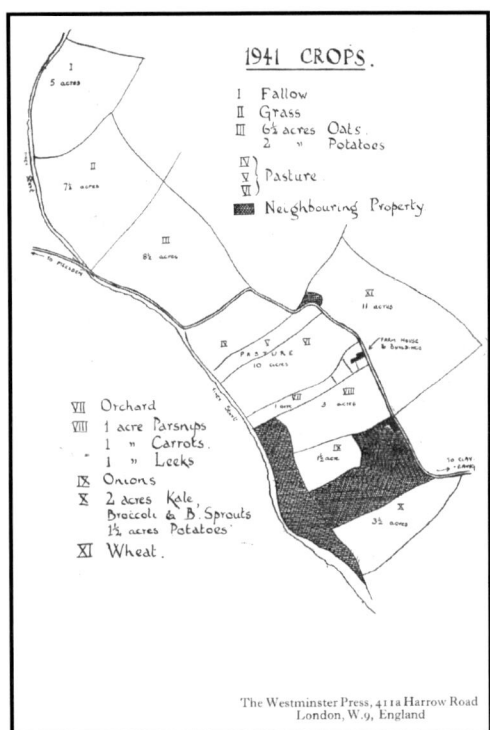

1941 CROPS.

I   Fallow
II Grass
III 6¾ acres Oats
    2   "   Potatoes

IV
V   } Pasture
VI

■ Neighbouring Property.

VII Orchard
VIII 1 acre Parsnips
     1   " Carrots.
     1   " Leeks
IX   Onions
X   2 acres Kale
     Broccoli & B. Sprouts
     1½ acres Potatoes
XI   Wheat.

The Westminster Press, 411a Harrow Road
London, W.9, England

In 1942, a group called the War Resisters International published this little booklet called 'Down on the Farm'. It recorded the results of the first full year of work at a special farm at Further Ford End, Clavering, set up to accommodate 'war resisters', better known as conscientious objectors, who were allowed, if they could prove they were genuine, to work on the land instead of in uniform. It was named Lansbury Gate Farm in memory of George Lansbury, the noted peace campaigner who died in 1940. The publication described the work on the farm, its staff, philosophy and activities with photographs of farming operations. The farmhouse (now called Barnsford) had fields running down to the River Stort, about 50 acres, part of it hired and had previously been mostly used for pigs and poultry with the arable rather neglected. Most of the old pasture was ploughed up for the war effort and the war resisters had to work hard pulling out bindweed, thistles and nettles in order to grow crops including vegetables. Surnames were not revealed in the booklet but one was a Mr Paul who married Miss Petter who lived at Seven Willows in Roast Green. The workers brought with them practical skills such as bricklaying and carpentry, and came from varied backgrounds – City worker, electrician, schoolteacher, scientist - and they employed a local farmworker called Cyril who had worked on the farm before, plus Dick the horse. Together they carted dung, pulled weeds, harvested crops, drilled wheat or pitched sheaves, fed the thrashing drum, collected eggs, milked cows and toiled on many other tasks.

In the first full year, 1940-41, they harvested five tons of wheat, six tons of carrots, three-and-a-half tons of onions, ten tons of potatoes plus parsnips, broccoli, brussels sprouts and leeks, as well as grass silage, hay and kale for cattle food. They also tended two cows and four young heifers, in addition to poultry which produced 20,000 eggs a year. They dealt with building repairs, hedging, ditching and laid a new roadway to deal with the knee-deep mud. The War Resisters were anxious to stress that 'it is no mere spirit of non-

cooperation and unhelpfulness that we withhold our support from the national effort', but they were seeking to promote brotherhood in the face of a corrupt civilisation in collapse: 'The task so urgently facing mankind today is the integration of society... this is our aim, to make our experience in communal living an offering to the new society.'

These high ideals were not entirely shared by the Essex War Agricultural Executive, whose Saffron Walden Advisory Committee had draconian powers over failing farms. In 1941 it was reported that 'much of their labour is useless' and they would be sent off to the army unless it improved. Mr Tinney, the local inspector, reported that the community farm was slipping down to Class C standard, as 'labour is constantly changing and the manager, though willing and zealous, has little experience'. They decided to watch its progress closely. For his part the farm manager asked if the committee would take an interest and give them advice. Then came a letter from the Ministry of Labour who were concerned at the numbers working there – the committee agreed that 50 acres did not need seven workers, and four would be ample so the other three would be released. When he visited again in January 1942, Mr Tinney found the 'land is well done and lays well' but in the spring he reported that it was 'not being properly farmed and the fields are in a bad state, the workers very slack'. Orders went out that the land must be thoroughly cleaned within ten days. The last surviving report was in November 1942 when the committee compiled a list of Conscientious Objectors coming to the Community Farm as market gardeners. After

this the committee became busy with other matters, and the farm was not mentioned again.

Above, ploughing at Lansbury Gate Farm. Below, harvest time 1941 at Lansbury Gate Farm, the War Resisters' farming project at Further Ford End.

95

August 1942

My dear Friends,
August as usual will be a very busy month for us all. In days of war the ingathering of the harvest is a work of the greatest national importance and on its success will depend a great deal of the rest of our war effort... the corn crops generally promise well and the wheat looks exceptionally good... not so in other parts of Europe. There is evidence of conditions approaching famine in several countries because of the shortage of labour, manures, seeds and fuel for tractors. The plight of our allies and the inhabitants of the occupied countries is indeed pitiable... I am sure that everyone who possibly can will respond to the Government appeal for help in the harvest field...
Yours most sincerely, E.A. STONE

irse Pond, Clavering.

Postcard sent to London during wartime showing the Horse Pond as it looked then.

September 1942

My dear Friends,
With deeper sincerity than ever before we ought this year to go down on our knees to thank God for a magnificent harvest. No one who has moved about the country will doubt that the English fields are bearing a record crop, and there seems every prospect, too, that it will be speedily and safely gathered in. In fact a farmer remarked to me the other day that he had never farmed through three successive years where the harvest weather had been so favourable. For us in rural England, harvest time is essentially the festival of our work...
Yours most sincerely, E.A. STONE

Italian Prisoners-of-War

The Government wanted even more grassland to be ploughed up, but there was a shortage of labour, hence the necessity of using Italian prisoners-of-war on the farms. They were now to be paid 40-48 shillings a week, and farmers had to provide board and lodgings although this might be only wooden huts. But this requirement discouraged farmers from taking on individuals in order to avoid providing transport from their quarters, and they preferred gang labour. Even when these difficulties were sorted out, there were still complaints that they were not doing the work properly so needed close supervision – although some locals quite liked the young Italians for their friendliness and would invite them to tea on Sundays (see p.115). Those who worked in Clavering lived at Meesden Manor, says Dick Law, who as a child remembers the Italians making craft items from mica out of crashed planes and giving them as presents to people.

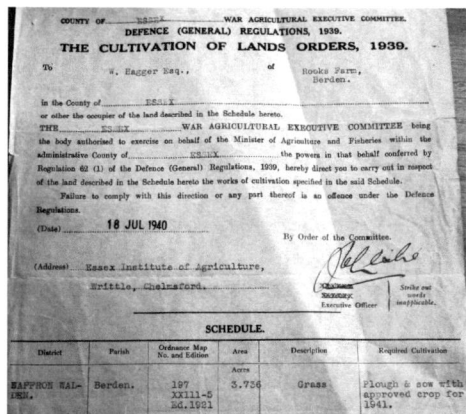

The sort of document farmers received, pointing out Defence Regulations regarding the cultivation of their land, and requirement on every occupier of farmland to make a return about proposed cropping and to apply for fertilizer permits.

The use of PoW labour was just one of the many farming operations overseen by the Saffron Walden Committee of the Essex War Agricultural Executive. Most of the Clavering farms were not in the lowest 'C' category, but several farmers were upset at being told to grow crops not suited to their land, for instance Arthur King at Brooklands had to plant five acres of beet even though he pointed out that the land suited potatoes better. When the bean crop failed at Clavering Hall, they were told to sow peas instead. The committee did agree that Mr Copeland, who farmed at Brocking and Bird Green, need not increase his wheat acreage as the land was not fertile enough and they also let him devote slightly less to sugar beet. Complaints about wasting precious petrol taking lorries long distances to be weighed, worries about gipsies and the depredations of rooks and rats - all on the agenda of the 'War Ag.' So essential was farm work that employers could seek Forces exemption for their men. One example was Bill Newland (b.1926) of Starlings Green, who left school at 14 and went to work for Arthur King at Brooklands Farm who successfully retained him (see p.117).

'I got a job with Mr King and stayed 31 years, starting off with horses, then he had one International tractor we started to drive. Then everything was done by hand, it wasn't mechanised so it was a lot of work, but I had marvelous tuition because he was very good and very clever. I did spring corn work with two horses to a plough. Then I passed the test for tractor drivers and that meant rolling. Then we used to have the binder to do it, all the sheaves were pitched by hand, then thatch the roofs of the corn stacks. It was a wonderful life in farming, everything came round different times but you enjoyed it. During the war you had to grow a certain percentage of sugar beet, potatoes and peas and they were all hoed by hand. You had a horse cultivated in between but had to stand there all day singling sugar beet. Mr King made all the hoes, we'd got the handles and the framework but they needed welding on and they were angled at a point so you could single them. We worked really hard during the war with not a lot of money attached to it.'

Schoolboys' Harvest Camps

Not a WW2 scene, but depicting similar labour, stacking at Mill End.

By 1942, schoolboys' harvest camps were an established part of the wartime scene in Clavering. The desperate need to maximise home food production, coupled with the shortage of labour as so many were in the Forces, led to some novel ideas, such as schoolchildren's labour, suggested by the Board of Education, although there was considerable opposition at first in case it interfered with their education.

The local arrangements were sponsored by the Essex War Agricultural Executive Committee, and farms wanting labour had to apply in advance. Typically the boys were paid sixpence an hour for under-16s and eightpence an hour for older children (less than Italian PoWs). The first such camp locally was in 1941, when the local Agriculture Committee noted it would need 'considerable supervision'. In addition to the boys, 80% of the pupils at Newport Grammar School would help on farms during their summer holiday. In 1942 the school holidays were fixed to match the cereal harvest from 31 July to 24 August, then again for the potato harvest from 25 September to 12 October.

In August 1942, Clavering had one of a total of 654 camps organized nationwide. The boys came from the Watts Naval School, part of Dr Barnardo's Homes. On Sundays they attended the Clavering church service and their superintendent, Capt Lewin R.N. preached the sermon. The Vicar was delighted: 'What a difference in our congregation with these additional 70 boys – would that there were 70 Clavering residents who could be present every Sunday!' In August 1943, there were 1,068 such camps and this time the 34 boys came from Twickenham Technical College and camped in the Village Hall grounds under the direction of one of their masters, Mr Fisher – even though one member of the Village Hall committee had objected because they paid only £10 to use the hall and it would reduce income from other lettings. The same college sent boys again in August 1944 (when there were 997 camps altogether) and 1945 (when it slipped to 774), and received a good welcome in the village, according to Mr Fisher, being shown much kindness by village people. For their part, the boys who came from towns by all accounts enjoyed the experience of working on the land and contributing to the war effort.

October 1942

CLAVERING YOUTH CENTRE

Opened by the Mayor of Walden

There was a large attendance of young people between the ages of 13 and 20 at the Lower School, Clavering, on Friday evening at the opening of the Village Youth Centre. The Vicar (Rev. E. A. Stone) presided, and was supported by Ald. Rooke (Mayor of Saffron Walden and chairman of Saffron Walden and Dunmow Youth Committee), Mr. W. J. Finch (secretary-organiser), and Mr. B. E. Chapman (officer commanding the A.T.C. Squadron). The Chairman having referred to the delays in establishing the Youth Centre, said they were fortunate in having such excellent premises put at their disposal free of rent by the Church authorities, and the County Council had agreed to light and heat them. He read a letter from the President of the Board of Education (Mr. R. A. Butler) regretting his inability to be present, and expressing his keen interest in the new project. They were very grateful, said the Vicar, that the Mayor of Saffron Walden was present, and his keen interest in the welfare of young people was an inspiration to everyone.

My Dear Friends

A great deal of space has been given recently in our daily press to the place of youth in the life of the nation. Everyone I think is agreed that over many years we have as a country neglected our youth... Voluntary organisations like the Boy Scouts and Girl Guides have gallantly endeavoured to repair the omission. In their work of caring for youth, in developing and providing outlets for its energies and abilities they have done incalculable service but they have only really influenced a fraction of our boys and girls. The appalling increase in juvenile delinquency has led some people to be horrified at our rising generation but I cannot share that horror. When we consider that at fourteen, the age when some children are just beginning their life at a public or secondary school our boys and girls have been hurled into the labour market of the world with few if any to care how they spent their adolescent years, it is not surprising. Of one thing I am very sure and that is, that our young people are desperately anxious to be provided with opportunities for service to the state. The registration of young people of sixteen years of age and the opportunity it provides for an interview and personal contact is a tremendous step forward. I recently spent an interesting couple of hours on a Saturday afternoon as a member of the panel of interviewers of the young people who were registering that day. While there was ample evidence of the desire for opportunities of service there was a pathetic lack in our villages of youth leaders and youth organisations to which young people could belong... I hope that our Village Youth Centre at Clavering will coordinate all youth organisations of whatever kind and be a real means of developing the individual youth in body, mind and spirit. At the moment membership of the A.T.C. and the junior section of the Home Guard is not obligatory; nevertheless I think that every lad of sixteen should join one of these branches of pre-service training... Some people would have us believe that this is just an attempt to form a similar organisation in this country to the Hitler Youth movement in Germany. I have no fear of that, provided that we of an older generation are prepared to answer the calls for leadership. The first step in any nationwide youth movement is the finding of the right youth leaders... For myself the cause of our boys and girls and lads and lassies is very dear to my heart.

Yours very sincerely, E.A. STONE

Romance at Searchlight Camp

Romance stirred at the Clavering Searchlight Camp and in October 1942 Francis Jee married local girl Violet Wisbey. Frankie had joined the Army before the war, serving with both the Royal Engineers and as a Gunner in the Royal Artillery. It was while stationed at Clavering that he met and married Violet, and these photos were probably taken there. Frankie and Violet are 2nd and 3rd from left at the front in the top picture, and Frankie is back row, 2nd from left in the lower picture.

Another camp romance between Bill Burton and another local girl, Vera Kemp, resulted in their marriage in October 1944.

Yanks Over Here

In October 1942 the Vicar wrote about the large number of American troops due to arrive and asked his parishioners to make them feel welcome by inviting them into homes in order to promote friendship between the two countries 'for the future rebuilding of the world on more Christian lines'. With the help of three village ladies, Mesdames Caton, Finzel and Sheldon, he started a hospitality scheme to entertain American soldiers. The nearest American base was Nuthampstead near Langley where woods were rapidly bulldozed and large concrete runways laid down. At first it housed American fighters, but later became Station 131 of the US Eighth Army Air Force 398th Bomb Group, with B17s ('Flying Fortresses'). Local girls found the Americans great fun and there were lots of romances, four of which ended up in Clavering Church: Cpl Charles Hart of the USAAF married Eileen Pearce in May 1944, followed in October by Capt Aubrey Creyts Crosby of the U.S. Army marrying Ethel Elwell. In 1945, US Army Cpl John Samery married Edna Rogers in January; and in June USAAF Master Sgt Ralph Peacher wed Joan Savage. One who did not go back to live in USA was M/Sgt George Cuda (pictured), an aircraft fitter at Nuthampstead, who married Joy Sibley of Berden and they settled there after the war. John Barwood remembers that George liked to drink at the *Fox & Hounds* here and would buy him and his friends lemonade and crisps, while telling them hair-raising stories of the war. Apart from pubs, the other meeting place was the Village Hall for the Saturday night 'Clavering Hop', where bands played popular tunes of the day. The Americans liked children, and those who were young then remember them well. Lads from Clavering would hitch a ride to go and watch the new airstrip at Nuthampstead under construction. Later, they would cycle up to Langley to watch the planes going to and from daylight raids over Germany, and learnt to recognise the flashing lights that indicated an emergency landing. Others remember visiting the bases at Christmas - June Holland (nee Riley) recalls: 'The Vicar used to go to the American camps and give a service and he used to take the choir with him - Americans used to send a truck for us, when the service finished we were served doughnuts and hot chocolate.'

Eileen Clarke (b.1932): 'After a dance, an American offered us a ride home in his jeep... and he decided he was too drunk to drive it - mum said, "I'm not driving it", and Nellie said, " I can't drive it". So he said, "Well, let the girl drive it". So, I got behind the wheel and there was a pond on the other side, put my foot straight down on the accelerator – straight into the horse pond! Of course he's beside himself because he will now be on a charge. The three of us got out, ran down Sticklings Green road and all the way back home and locking the door - and between our panting, Mum saying, "Don't tell your dad about this!" '	**Des Abrahams** (b.1927):' We went up to Debden on a Sunday occasionally - the Americans used to take us up to have a look round. We were very much backward and rural, and they were brash with smart uniforms and a great attraction to the girls. They used to have their own trucks and pick them up. The dances at Clavering were packed out with troops all the time - Clavering village hall had a lovely oak floor but they tore it to pieces with the nails in their boots. At Nuthampstead they had their own entertainment halls where they used to take the kids.'	**Dick Law** (b.1931): 'About 1942-43 the Americans built Nuthampstead aerodrome. A lot of ballast came from Wicken pit - about 70 lorries took it via Pelham Road, Brent Pelham to the 'drome, they returned via Langley and Stickling Green. On Sundays we would visit the 'drome and watch the planes return, sometimes damaged making pancake landings on the grass. The Americans would take us to the cinema to see the latest films, and give us an orange or banana, a rare treat. Afterwards they would take us back to Langley to walk home.'

November 1942

My dear Friends,
Do you ever feel rather impatient when you read of some of the public utterances that refer to what must be done after the war? I am afraid that very often I do. When clamour, hatred and passion are destroying lives, homes and lands, our first great hope is that the war should soon be finished and thoughts of reconstruction in the post war world seem rather unreal. Of course we ought to look ahead, for all thinking men and women are agreed that vast changes must come, and to come to a time of change without knowing which reforms would be most beneficial would be a pitiful state... In wartime we see clearly that to be a profiteer – making money out of other men's blood – is a very real sin... compare the wartime profiteer with the men in our fighting forces, who in the face of grim perils and constant hardships, are offering all they have and are to this country... there is a challenge to us to work for a better spirit in the world. If when the war is over we go back to a life of 'smash and grab' each thinking only of himself, we are heading for early disaster... There will be so many who are weak after the war, so many helpless, so many lonely, so many poor, so many at their wits' end that we shall be faced with a problem which will be too much for us unless the new spirit comes in...
Yours very sincerely, E.A. STONE

On the same afternoon we laid to rest in Clavering Churchyard, Gladys Constance Anderson known to most of us as Gladys Riley. Gladys was in our Sunday School and sang in our Choir in her younger days and at the early age of 21, within seven months of her wedding she was killed in an accident at Cambridge To her husband, her mother and brother and sisters our sympathy goes out in their bereavement.

In December 1942 there were two obituaries of church members in the parish magazine, one of them for 21-year-old Gladys Anderson who had only just got married and was working in the civil service in Cambridge when her bicycle was involved in an accident with a bus.

December 1942

My dear Friends
I get all sorts of letters from people who are scattered here, there and everywhere in this war and most of those letters end in the same way. 'Well I hope it won't be long before we are all home again'... to our boys and girls away from home the most precious thing is the folk at home. More than once a young fellow on the eve of some hazardous flight or perhaps embarkation has come to me and said 'I wonder padre if you could say a prayer for my home tonight, in case they are worried'. There are thousands of homes today that are missing and thinking of someone who is away... Christmas Day - we shall all be thinking of those near and dear to us and from whom we are separated...

As his parishioners celebrated Christmas in Clavering, Rev. Stone was serving as a chaplain abroad, and took six Sunday services, the last an evening service in a Nissen hut with officers and men of the American forces, where they gave thanks for recent victories, most notably Al Alamein.

IF I CAN'T GET HOME IN TIME. HERE'S WISHING YOU A HAPPY XMAS

With the King's Forces 1942

By late 1942 the list of Clavering men and women in the King's Forces had grown to 74, although the Vicar no longer listed all those doing civilian war work as almost everyone was now doing war-related work of some kind. Among new additions in 1941 were 16 Clavering men and two women:

Fred Atkinson, William Atkinson, William Bailes, Hubert Barker, John Bowles, Peter Bowles, Percy Burgess, Cyril Elwell, Jack Howard, Eric Peel, Jeffery Poulter, Kenneth Poulter, Leonard Poulter, Stanley Poulter, Alfred Smither, Cecil Stone, Jean Cooper, Olive Nicholson (WRNS).

William Atkinson (brother of Molly Law nee Atkinson), served in the Far East but like many in that distant theatre of war, he suffered some bad experiences in Burma. His sister recalls him telling her that one night they heard that the enemy were planning an attack, so they surrounded their camp with electrified wire. Next morning they found the Japanese soldiers all dead on the wire. When Bill came home, he took a long time to recover from his horrific war experiences. Other members of the Atkinson family were also in the Forces, including William's father, Fred.

The Bakers were another family with several members in uniform. Reg Baker served in the RAF transport section, in Burma and the Far East. His sister Marjorie was in the ATS (see p.43) and cousin Jean Cooper became a sergeant. Reg's brother, Leading Aircraftman Frank (known as Bob) Baker was also in the RAF throughout the war and afterwards, working as maintenance crew in South Africa and the Middle East – he did not return home until 1947, and in 1949 married a former Land Army girl who had worked on a farm in Berden during the war. Left to right: Reg, Bob, Marjorie, Jean.

Chapter Six
1943: 'To rid the world of devilry'

The fourth year of the conflict was when the fortunes of war finally began to favour the Allies and the threat of invasion faded – indeed there was active planning going on to reverse Dunkirk and take troops back into Europe. At sea, German U-boats were still causing losses, but air cover and radar were helping a fight-back and many were sunk. Another invention, penicillin, was saving many lives in the conflict. By the end of the year Rommel was defeated in Africa, the Russians were pushing the Germans back and Italy had changed sides with the downfall of Mussolini. Merciless bombing took a shocking toll on German cities, with thousands of dead, as well as the bombing of 2,000 factories on the Ruhr – the Dambuster raid was a brilliant initiative but the destruction was huge. Jews continued to suffer terribly with the final obliteration of the Warsaw Ghetto, although they bravely rose up against their oppressors. A War Crimes Commission was compiling a growing list of war criminals to be prosecuted after the war.

There were tragic losses in London too – a class of 38 little girls and six teachers bombed to death at a school, and 178 crushed in a tube shelter accident. At home, thoughts were now turning to the needs of the post-war world with the announcement of a National Health Service, expansion in free education and council housing, PAYE tax reform and the suggestion of an International Monetary Fund. But the irksome impositions of wartime only got worse in the meantime – the rationing of shoes, a 100 per cent tax on luxury goods, continued emphasis on savings to finance the march to victory, the order for all women aged 18-45 to do part-time war work (but at least they were now much better paid than before the war), and the call-up of 'Bevin Boys' to work in the coal mines. It was getting easier to find your way about, as signposts were once more allowed in rural areas. Dig for Victory was a byword with a million tons of vegetables grown in 1943, but there was a reaction against the draconian powers of the Essex War Agricultural Executive, whose interference was much resented by farmers. With the declining threat, fewer volunteers were needed for the ARP or Home Guard. At long last church bells were allowed to ring out again on Sundays – thanks to a campaign by church leaders.

The Church was in the news for another reason, when they criticised the rise in promiscuity that had let to a worrying increase in venereal diseases during the war, a theme that was taken up by the Vicar of Clavering in one of his parish letters. As ever, he wrote eloquently of what needed doing to rid the world of Fascism ('this devilry'). But he constantly emphasised the need for reform inside hearts and minds, otherwise 'a multiplicity of Beveridge Reports' would be a waste of time – if people just went back to the type of selfishness common before the war. With the expansion of war-related employment, he also urged people to save more (this time for 'Wings for Victory') and give more to good causes – there were numerous appeals in wartime. The Vicar, normally very fit, was struck down with jaundice in the summer and local folk must have missed his customary letter, particularly as it was replaced by a rather pessimistic one by the Bishop. He was soon back in action, however, celebrating yet another record harvest in autumn and, as the fifth wartime Christmas approached, writing letters to 140 Clavering and Langley residents serving in uniform, and collecting money to send them all a pound as a present. It was a thoughtful gesture, but very typical of Clavering's vicar who himself was still unable to make arrangements to return to the Forces chaplaincy work he loved so much.

January 1943

My dear Friends,

It was good to hear the church bells ringing again, calling us all to worship. There were hopes that we should soon be able to ring them every Sunday but that is not to be. We are warned that there still exists a real danger of invasion by the enemy and so the bells must remain silent. The singing of the choir at the annual carol service at Clavering was greatly appreciated by the large congregation. We were glad that despite difficulties of transport a number of friends in the neighbourhood were able to give us their help in the choir. The carol service was later repeated for the benefit of allied troops somewhere in England... We have received a number of letters from our boys and girls in the Forces in reply to the Christmas presents we sent them. Everyone is most grateful for the kindly thought shown to them and asks us to pass on their most grateful thanks... our boys and girls are in good heart and are looking forward to their next visit home.

Yours very sincerely, E.A. STONE

Clavering Church bells in the tower – in 1943 the ban on bellringing for services was eased but not entirely lifted until May, when the threat of invasion (of which the ringing of church bells would have been warning) had finally faded.

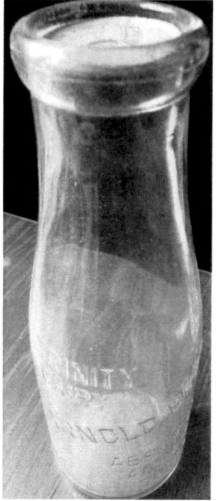

Milk Permits and Fruit Juices. Mothers of children under five were reminded that 'the permits for the supply of a pint of milk a day at 2d... expire early in February. Forms of application for the continuance of the permit may be obtained from the Vicarage. Mothers are also reminded that the allocation of fruit juices has now been extended to children under five instead of under three. Applications should be made on the same form as for the milk. When the permit arrives back at your house you should take it with two 2½d stamps to the Saffron Walden Food Office when you will receive a fortnight's ration.'

In March, however, the rules were changed and it was no longer necessary to apply for these permits – but simply to show the milkman the child's ration book.

Wartime Youth Work

By January 1943 the Clavering Youth Centre, was meeting two or three evenings a week in the Lower School, offering activities for young people aged 13-20 for an annual sub of two shillings. One of the first village youth centres in Essex, it was formed in response to the government's Service of Youth scheme, aimed at remedying the rise in juvenile delinquency. Rab Butler, local MP and President of the Board of Education, praised Clavering for 'giving a valuable lead to other rural districts'. It had not been easy – the project faced 'almost unbelievable' delays before getting off the ground. Supervision was shared between the Vicar, the headmaster and the chief ARP Warden. Getting specialist instructors was a problem because of transport, but various classes were organised - table tennis under Mrs Sheldon, play reading with Mrs Stone and a weekly talk by local men about their jobs. Tennis started up on summer evenings on the Vicarage tennis courts, and the club joined in a big rally for all youth organisations in Saffron Walden. As winter returned, the Youth Centre acquired 'a wireless set to form a listening group to discuss some of the special broadcasts for young people'. One of the members, Dick Law, remembers playing billiards and darts: 'Alex Richardson [the school headmaster] was in charge, we played him about – he couldn't discipline there as he did at school! It was somewhere to go, there was not much else to do.'

Dick was also a member of the Boy Scouts - there had been Scout and Guide units in Clavering before, but the war stimulated their revival. A Brownie Pack was difficult with the blackout, but in 1941 two village ladies, Miss Barker and Mrs Simmonds started Monday afternoon meetings for the younger girls to do crafts and other activities. Two years later a Wolf Cub Pack (photo right) appeared thanks to the Congregational Minister, Rev. W. Morley Worsam who started Monday evening meetings at the Lower School. By June 1943 there were 15 boys enrolled, all very keen and working towards badges. At the same time a Clavering Scout Troop was formed, meeting at first in the Church End clubroom until turfed out for wartime needs, after which they met in two rooms at Curles Manor farm. But a Girl Guide Company proved more difficult to get going, although one existed in Langley. At church parades their absence was noticeable, so the Vicar turned to his wife for help once more.

'From time to time I have received appeals from our girls that some such organisation should be started and quite recently a deputation of girls waited upon me and expressed the position in no uncertain terms... the only person who has had practical experience of this work in Clavering is my wife who has been the Captain of a Girl Guide Company... she would be willing to accept the leadership of such a movement in our village if there was some guarantee of assistants. I therefore appeal to any girls of say 17 or 18 upwards who feel an interest in this work and would be prepared to act as assistants to let me know. I would then ask Mrs. Stone to arrange for a short course in the work of Girl Guiding and leadership... here is an opportunity on the home front to do a grand job as important in war as in peace.'

Volunteers appeared and enthusiastic Brownies and Guides started meeting, with Mrs Stone as Captain and three Lieutenants in training - Biddy Glasscock, Faith Goodwin and Joan Ward: 'Deaconess Chapman, District Commissioner for Guides, thrilled us with the picture of guiding that she put before us to help every girl to attain the highest development of which she is capable'. In wartime, it was difficult to get hold of uniforms but within a few months 16 Guides were enrolled, a successful dance had raised money to meet the expenses including a new flag dedicated with the other colours at the monthly parade. June Holland (nee Riley) recalls: 'The Guides met in the Lower School, we went camping with Mrs. Stone, in big bell tents.' Barbara Baddeley (nee Maine), whose family had homes in both Clavering and London, also remembers guide camps here.

'I became a Girl Guide in London and took them to Clavering to camp in the field in front of Mill End farm. There were 25 guides and rather a strict captain - one evening I found that my sister had secretly taken a hot water bottle from my mother's house and those sort of luxury goods were not allowed in camp, you had to be very hardy.'

In the autumn Deaconess Chapman took over as Captain of the Clavering company. By the time of the great Empire Day parade in 1944 (see pp.134-5), the Guides were flourishing and are shown here marching with their flag past Bury Meadow (below left) and entering the church (below right). The Scouts are shown entering behind them with Scoutmaster Dan Sullivan – out of sight is troop leader, Peter Goodacre. Among the Scouts (pictured right) is Dick Law, without a hat, while the others are about to remove their three-cornered hats before entering the church.

Military Policeman

Fred Whyman comes from an old Clavering family, inter-connected with many other village families. Born in 1924, he worked in farming, gardening and building and has spent most of his life in Clavering, apart from the war years. He was called up halfway through the war and served in the Royal Artillery and then the Military Police, an experience he greatly enjoyed. Post-war he started Whyman's Nursery which he still runs today with son Gerald. As part of the Clavering Oral History Project, Fred described his memories of wartime service:

'I was 18 and I was called up in January 1943 in the army, then I had 4½ years. I was all over the country, different places. One place was in Upminster and there was a convent down the street where we used to billet and we used to go to Clacton for firing courses. I had one narrow escape there, I was on ack-ack guns, and we went to Clacton on a course, firing at a wreck in the sea. We were clearing out and going up to Northumberland and the night we moved out Jerry bombed the place. You think to yourself - how lucky we were!. I went into the Military Police, because they were short of recruits. I went to Normandy and I was on Juno Beach. It was such an experience. Before we went we had to waterproof the vehicles, blocking them with plasticine for when they went in the water. We followed through and a lot were killed. We were strafed by Gerry planes on the beaches. I was on duty on Pegasus Bridge and I heard the machine guns across the field, that was as close as we got to the fighting at Caen. 'We were attached to the Canadians and we then went up to Amsterdam and then went through Belgium. Then it was all over and they brought us back to Ostend. The next thing I was in the New Forest. We were going out to the Far East to help them out there, but then it was VJ Day and that all finished in the time of our transit, and we had disembarkation leave. Then we had an embarkation leave, and I was sent to Egypt for 15 months. I came out the army in May 1947 when I was 24. I often look back and think, well, if it wasn't for the army I don't think I would have ever moved out of Clavering, but it was a great experience, I wouldn't have missed it for the world really. I enjoyed it.'

[Extract from *Clavering Remembered* © Fred Whyman 2011]

Fred with the MPs in Egypt in 1945

'Wyngate's Chindits' 1943-44

L-Cpl Alfred Smither: left, after joining up, 1942, right in jungle gear, 1943.

The bombing of Pearl Harbour not only brought the Americans into the war, but also sent British troops out to fight the Japanese, in a distant conflict that few people at home thought much about. Among those sent to the Far East was Alfred W. Smither who lived at Stortford Road, Clavering. He joined up in February 1942, having previously been deferred for occupation as a baker, during which time he served in the Auxiliary Fire Service. L-Cpl Smither trained at Tidworth as a tank driver in the Royal Armoured Corps, then in May 1942 was sent to India for training. Here he joined the 26th Hussars near Poona and was corporal in charge of the HQ cookhouse staffed by young Indians called 'boppengees'. He then joined the 14th Battalion of Lt Col Orde Wingate's Chindits in Burma - famous as 'Wyngate's Chindits' who had already carried out a heroic expedition in the Burmese jungle, from which many were captured. Their brief was to disrupt the Japanese supply system and generally cause havoc behind enemy lines. Alf began his training in September 1943, but this was interrupted by an expedition walking 400 miles to capture an airfield at Indore - very tough going in jungle conditions and many became ill with tropical diseases. The only way to transport goods in such a place was by mule, so Alf found himself driving mules instead of tanks! In notes he made about his experiences, he emphasised: 'We did NOT take the airfield due to no communication to GHQ which went back to India the same week'. The Battalion returned to bas Aberdeen in Burma and while awaiting flyout were asked by Brig. Mike Calvert to march three days to relieve the 77th Brigade at base White City. Many were lost during this exercise, but it did succeed. They then marched to base Broadway, survived a monsoon and were flown to Comilla in India to recover. Here in hospital, Alf met the 'Forces sweetheart', Vera Lynn. He then went to Rawalpindi to join the South Staffordshire Regiment, 'to whose rescue they went', as he put it. Finally, he was due to go back to Burma but fortunately the war ended and he stayed in India. Safe but much affected by the deprivations of jungle warfare, Alf finally came back to Clavering in 1946, having not seen his family for three years. Alf, his wife and children (Malcolm, Maureen and Barbara) moved to Berden where they became well-known shopkeepers, trading as H.J. Smither & Son, eventually retiring to Clavering. Opinion remains divided as to the effectiveness of special forces like these – some military historians feel the Chindits operation was very wasteful of men and resources: 1,396 were killed, 2,434 wounded and half hospitalised. But others point out that the operations were good for morale and did help pave the way for the Allied invasion of Burma in March 1944. What an extraordinary story of courage and endurance these men could tell, however Alf was always reticent in dwelling on the past, except when with other Burma Star veterans, and his daughter Barbara was able to glean only the bare essentials of serving with the famous Chindits.

March 1943

My dear Friends

'What shall I do?' you may say, 'Well, let's win the war first'. I quite agree. This evil in the world is a most frightful thing. To drive it out is going to take a mighty effort and we have each got to make that effort, whatever it may cost. By God's help this devilry shall go. But victory can never be enough. We are fighting to make injustice a forbidden thing, to stop persecution and cruelty in every shape and form – nation with nation, man with man. But we can only do it if at one and the same time we can claim all the vast energies of the world for the doing of things worthy of our humanity, things that make for love and service and not for bitterness and hate. If we can do that, then there is our new world. If we can't then chaos must come... While there is a crisis on – like this war – and we are in a common danger, we are kinder to each other, much more human, much more helpful in every way. But when the crisis is over, we may try to settle down again as we were before – each of us living for himself. No. We've got to change people. Nothing less will do. We've got to change all our ideas of life – the things we live for and the things we live by. We've got to change a good many of our aims and motives. We've got to think differently, very differently about what is success in life, for instance –what success really is and what failure really is... I have been reading recently the discussions in Parliament on the Beveridge Report. I have even read some of the report myself although I cannot claim to understand it all. But clever brains are busy planning a new world. We must be grateful to them. We shall need a lot of new plans. But you can't change this world by planning. You can map it all out, you can produce a multiplicity of Beveridge Reports, you can put it all down in black and white, but it won't work unless you can change the people who are going to work it... We must gird ourselves to our two-fold task – to rid the world of devilry and to fill the world with Good. Are we ready for that?

Yours most sincerely, E.A. STONE

As well as the Vicar's exhortations for a change in attitude, the public found notices like these every time they opened a newspaper.

Weekend Cottages

In 1943, it was reported that Clavering had 18 'weekend cottages' occupied no more than once a month by people who lived elsewhere. With the need to get out of London to escape bombing, such cottages became a refuge, as at Mill End Dairy Farm (see p.44), and The Nook on Valence road: Mr Holland, a greengrocer in London, had bought The Nook with five acres in the 1930s. When war came he moved all his family there. Various other evacuees, via his shop customers, found their way here, and would help with minding his children (see p.18).

Sometimes evacuee billeting could prove more troublesome, however. As recorded in this local newspaper story, in 1941 Mrs Queenie Wombwell (pictured 1950s in Women's British Legion uniform) had to go to court to get back her cottage at Hill Green from an evacuee, because it was needed when husband Norman was home on leave from the army.

Possession of a Clavering Cottage

His Honour Judge Lawson Campbell presided at the County Court at Saffron Walden Town Hall on Monday. Mrs. Queen Wombwell, wife of Mr. Norman Wombwell, of Hill Green, Clavering, applied for a possession order in respect of a cottage at Clavering occupied by a London evacuee, Mrs. Curtis.

Mrs. Wombwell claimed possession, saying that her husband, who was a member of the Forces, was home more than she had anticipated he would be, and she wanted a home for him.

The local Billeting Officer gave evidence revealing how the premises had been secured by Mrs. Curtis.

In evidence the defendant stated that she had been given to understand that the premises she occupied were for the duration of the war.

The Judge made an order for possession in 28 days.

As well as evacuees, there was a great shortage of housing for the farm-workers who were essential to increasing food production. This became the particular concern for the Essex War Agricultural Executive, whose Saffron Walden committee took up a number of cases locally. The problem was compounded by the number of tumbledown cottages which, before the war, had been so bad they were supposed to be demolished. Nationwide, it was estimated that hundreds of thousands of people lived in such homes. There was one family at Sheepcote Green, whose home was so dilapidated that part of it collapsed, and they all had to move to separate lodgings as there was no other cottage available. The committee looked into a 'weekend cottage' at Mill End which had been let to evacuees who had not been there for a year so it was left empty at a time of desperate need. In this instance, the committee decided to ask the Ministry of Health, who had the powers, to requisition it. However, once they got wind of this, some owners might use a 'deliberate ploy' to move in a different tenant, as a requisition order could not be served on another person having already served it on the previous tenant.

May 1943

The sky's the limit in our—

WINGS FOR VICTORY WEEK

Now in the fourth weary year of the war, there was no let up in the demand for savings to help finance the war effort. It was the turn of the RAF to be the focus of Wings For Victory Week in May 1943, the aim being to lend money to ensure that there were enough planes – and again with the promise of individuals reaping the benefit after the war from their thrift at this time. With 145 members, only a quarter of the people in Clavering belonged to the savings group – this compared to three-quarters in Debden, for instance. This time the target for the Saffron Walden borough and rural districts was a massive £200,000 to which Clavering planned to contribute £7,237 so that in conjunction with Arkesden, Langley and Wicken, they could provide two fighter planes. In the event, Clavering was only just over a hundred pounds short of target. The Vicar wrote that most workers were earning more because of the war so should put the extra into savings to help the war effort.

My dear Friends,

We all owe so much to our gallant Air Force. As you sit by your fireside on a winter evening and hear the roar of aircraft overhead as the RAF go out to attack some distant target, what are your reactions? Do you just remark 'there's a big raid on tonight' and go on reading your newspaper? Or do you in imagination put yourself in the place of those flying the planes? If you do the latter and realise that these gallant boys, who have all volunteered for air-crew duties, are giving everything they have for us (for many may never return) then we must ask ourselves what we can do to help. Here in Wings for Victory week we have our chance. Most people in civil employment are considerably better off now than they have ever been in their life. What are you doing with this extra money which has become yours through the war? Haven't you an obligation to lend some of it to the Government and so provide more and more aircraft as a tribute to our gallant airmen? The target for Clavering is £7237 and Langley £2314. I hope both villages will easily exceed these figures but to do that means everyone having a share. We are asked to invest our money through the Village Savings Group but if anyone should lend their money through their bank at either Saffron Walden or Bishops Stortford would they ensure that the amount is credited to the village so that it will help towards our target. If we all do our share then the money target will be achieved and to use an R.A.F. expression 'it will be a piece of cake'.

Yours most sincerely, E.A. STONE.

June 1943

As well as savings, another regular call on income was the increased number of charitable appeals, many related to wartime needs. In his June 1943 letter, the Vicar described some of these worthy causes and the essential work they did.

My dear Friends

Hardly a week goes by in which I am not asked to organise a collection for some most worthy object. To many of these appeals I have alas, to turn a deaf ear or we should be having flag days and house-to-house collections almost every week. The appeal, however, of the Church Army for providing mobile canteens for visiting lonely units of H.M. Forces is one which will appeal to us all. Will you read the leaflet enclosed in his magazine and having done so ask other members of your household to do the same and then pass round the envelope for any gifts for the work? The envelopes can then be brought to Church or given to the lady who brings your magazine and she will pass them on to me. On June 5th our help is asked for the flag day of the Red Cross and St John joint war organisation, an object which needs no words of mine to commend it. Alexandra Rose Day is on June 22nd and by buying one of these roses you will be helping the work of our own Nursing Association. As the treasurer of this Association I can say with authority that we are in urgent need of funds, and we hope for your generous support on this occasion. Finally on July 3rd a flag day is being arranged thorough the British Sailors' Society for work among Seamen. We owe so much to our Seamen who have kept us so well fed during this war...

Yours most sincerely, E.A.STONE.

HOUSE-TO-HOUSE COLLECTION

In Aid of CHURCH ARMY WAR WORK for H.M. FORCES

RECREATION AND REST CENTRES
MOBILE CANTEENS AND REFRESHMENT CARS
CLUBS AND HOSTELS FOR MEN AND WOMEN ON LEAVE
EVANGELISTS WORKING IN MANY CAMPS
HOMES FOR AGED AND BLIND MEN AND WOMEN EVACUEES

This work is being carried on in the Camps, and frequent visits paid to Anti-Aircraft Batteries, Searchlight Crews, Listening Posts, Barrage Balloon Units, etc. (many in lonely places far from human habitation), providing refreshment and the hundred-and-one needs of the Service men. In addition the ordinary work of the Society goes on unimpaired.

Contributions will be called for in a
few days
Thanks for help and goodwill.

Evacuee Memories 1941-43

Having come and gone as an evacuee twice before, in 1941 aged nine, Eileen Clarke and her mother from Ponders End in Enfield evacuated themselves again and this time remained in Clavering until 1943. They lived at Clavering Court (pictured here in 1943). Now Eileen Summers, in her 80th year, she has recorded vividly her memories of what to her was a magical time.

'We stayed with Mrs Finzel of The Court at Sticklings Green - her two maids went into the WAAFS, and she had two rooms at the back of the house which we could have, which was rather nice. And that's where life in the country began for me because I ran absolutely wild – had a wonderful time. I think we were there for at least 3½ years at The Court. I was so lucky to be with my mum and living in The Court was lovely because you had the freedom. And we made very big friends with the people at Court Cottage [pictured bottom left as it looked then], Nellie and Alfie Clark. She was a housekeeper there and Alfie was the gardener and they had one son, Len who was a year older than me and he teased the life out of me. At the back of the house you went up between the two rooms. I think there was a little bathroom and a toilet. We must have eaten in one of the rooms. It was a lovely view out the back because there were all the herbaceous borders. There was a tennis court at the side – I think they must have lived quite well before the war. There was a vegetable garden at the side, we did eat well and my dad used to bring things from London – I'm sure it was all black market stuff but as a child you don't know. My mum wanted to do war work, wanted to do something to help. The Finzels had lived in India, they were landed gentry really. She said to him she wanted to do some work, she didn't just want to be here - and he gave her a pair of scissors and told her to cut the heads of his dahlias! And she wept, she really did because this isn't what it was all about.'

114

'There was a German prisoner-of-war camp not too far away from here and because she was Dutch they assumed she spoke German, and she was asked to go to do translation but she refused, she hated them so much. All her family were occupied and she lost lots of cousins and people like this, and it was a pretty sad time when Holland was occupied. The Germans were working on a local farm, but they were very well guarded and kept well apart. We saw them but my Mum would hurry me by. She didn't want me to be anywhere near them. But we did have other prisoners-of-war there, they were Italians and they were lovely. They were only youngsters and they were really nice. The Italian boys came on Sundays and Nellie used to have some of these youngsters in for tea. They didn't speak any English... I was able to go to school on a bike down Coley Lane opposite the Court. We had a very, very cold winter and I can remember having terrible chilblains, because we couldn't get proper shoes - they were made with some kind of American cloth or something like that that. My mother made all my clothes and she knitted my stockings. Now all the evacuees in the school came from Tottenham and they all had black woollen stockings, and I was desperate for black woollen stockings but my mum insisted on knitting these wretched things. They were brown wool – I HATED them and I used to say to her, "I shall never grow", and of course I haven't, have I! Then one day, a parachute was given to some of the ladies and my mum had some pieces of this so of course we all had blouses made out of a parachute... The Court was in its own farm. We spent a lot of time stooking, where they used to put the sheaves of corn [see photo]. Also did pea picking, we used to get fivepence a sack.'

Eileen Clarke playing in the harvest field near Clavering Court in 1942.

'As a child I never got the impression that anybody didn't want us they all seemed to be friendly. Mr Piggott the postman who lived up the green was a delightful man and he used to let you ride on his cross bar... my mum liked to help at the village hall... it was a social gathering and you met people, there were sewing things going on here. She may well have done these things while I was at school. Then the Americans came and that for us was quite interesting, there were loads of them. The Americans came to Clavering on Saturday nights because Doug Luff had this little band in the village hall. My mum and Lennie's mum, Nellie Clark used to do the refreshments for the Americans.... So we stayed until the end of '43. It must have been when they stopped the bombing - it was just doodlebugs and rockets after that, which felt easier to cope with although we did get bombed out by a doodlebug when I was in London and went to another house. We didn't come back to Clavering any more to live after that. For me it wasn't a hard time, it was a wonderful time because I had a freedom that I would NEVER have had in London. I absolutely loved it and the freedom. People didn't seem to be afraid of letting you run loose and come home when its dark – great stuff really...'

July 1943

My dear Friends

'I like to have my wireless on most of the day. It keeps me from thinking' – more than one person has said this to me of recent years. Do you ever feel the strain of being alone, as we say, with your thoughts? In these days, when so many are away from home, those who are left must often find themselves alone with their thoughts. While we know that we must fight our way through this way it is equally true that we must think our way through it as well... As we look back to the years immediately before 1939 we can see now that we didn't think much. Ease, pleasure, our own selfish pursuits were the chief guiding influence of many people's lives... How - after the war - can we get lasting peace?

The week before Whitsun was indeed a sad one for us in Langley as we laid to rest in the churchyard Patrick Cassidy of the Essex Regiment, killed by enemy action in the South of England buried with military honours... Paddy was a popular fellow not only at Langley and Berden, where he worked until the outbreak of the war, but also among the officers and men of his regiment. Like so many others he has given his life that we may live. As we cherish the memory of a brave soldier our sympathy is with all who mourn his passing.
Yours most sincerely, E.A. STONE

All out for the 1943 Harvest

INCREASE THE YIELDS OF ALL YOUR FIELDS

This is the most critical year in our history. Hitler still aims to sink our ships—to starve us out. You are fighting the "Battle of the Fields" to defeat him. Every possible ship that might bring us food must now carry tanks and planes and guns. Every extra acre of tillage crops you can grow in 1943 will help to release ships and bring the day of victory nearer.

The bumper 1943 harvest led to a government edict to churches to celebrate by holding special Farm Sunday services. The Vicar of Clavering obliged, with a big parade of all the local uniformed organisations, reported here in the local newspaper. The newspaper did not report that a party of American troops on their way to the service, which coincided with their National Day of Independence, never arrived since their truck collided with a lorry.

CLAVERING

FARM SUNDAY.—The request of the Government to observe Farm Sunday was carried out in Clavering by a special service in the Parish Church on Sunday morning. Attending the service were members of all the youth organisations of the parish, including Army cadets, Air Training Corps, Boy Scouts, Wolf Cubs, the Langley Company of Girl Guides and members of the Village Youth Centre. The service was conducted by the Vicar (Rev. E. A. Stone), who briefly explained the significance of the day, and an address was given by the Rev. W. M. Worsam. After the service the parade of youth organisations was addressed by Lieut. Ledward, of the Home Guard.

Bumper Harvest 1943

During wartime many old meadows were ploughed up for the first time.

There was a bumper harvest in 1943, brought about by the good weather, the hard work of farmworkers and the continuing government drive for efficiency by ploughing up old meadows and maximising crop production. The local branch of the 'War Ag' continued to apply Government edicts, and set up a new Clavering farm discussion group with 16 members – but in Essex generally farmers were growing critical of how the 'War Ag.' operated. The local committee used its powers widely, for instance in 1943 Mr Tinney, their inspector, said that the management of the Clifton Agricultural Company at Clavering Hall Farm was not satisfactory, with an increase in vermin caused by stacks of unthreshed corn deteriorating fast, and 'an acre of wheat very foul with pepperwort'. Orders were also served on a farmer who had not cleared a river, another who had failed to cut a hedge and clean out a ditch, and on the conscientious objectors' farm at Further Ford End, said to be over-staffed. A request from Mr Ambrose at Thurrocks Farm to employ child labour was refused.

But the committee also helped farmers - they could apply to the committee for tractors and drills and, after incendiary damage at Parsonage Farm, they helped the new tenant, Dick Bazley obtain the timber to repair buildings. The committee also concerned itself with those who deferred call-up because of essential work on farms – employers could apply for exemption and one who benefited was Bill Newland who had worked for Arthur King at Brooklands Farm since 1940 (see p.97). Tragically, his older brother John was killed in September 1944 (see p.144), just about when Bill reached the age of 18 and was liable to call-up: 'my brother was killed then and Mr King got me off otherwise I would have gone in the RAF because I was doing a good job there providing food.' Thus he was able to stay on the farm.

August 1943

At this time, the Vicar was seriously ill with jaundice, and unable to write his customary letter to parishioners, so a letter from the Bishop was substituted, in which he criticised the French for their weakness and more or less said that youth work was a waste of time! All rather pessimistic in tone compared to the Vicar's letters, and people must have been glad when normal service was resumed in September. No sooner had he recovered, however, than the Vicar had to fend for himself in the big bleak vicarage as his wife was needed to run the new Land Army hostel in Langley (see p.119).

September 1943

My dear Friends,

Thank you all for your most kind enquiries during my recent illness. Being ill was rather a new experience for me, for since my childhood days I cannot remember even spending more than a day in bed at any one time. Although jaundice is not a serious complaint it can be a very painful and unpleasant one, as some of you probably know well. I shall certainly have a greater understanding of the feelings of sick persons in the future when I visit them, than I have had in the past! ... all took a lot of arranging and I was grateful for my bedside telephone. Difficulties of transport were overcome by my wife acting as chauffeur...The end of the present military conflict may still be far ahead and any relaxation of our national effort would be fatal to our cause; but at the same time our leaders are speaking of the present stage as a possible beginning of the end... Every effort must now be put forward to achieve a victory which is sure and complete... I would like to think that more and more people were asking themselves honestly why the world should be in its present state... The atmosphere of the world between the two great wars was poisoned by a number of acts of aggression committed by various nations, but little was done to check them. The war is not the fault of any one person or of one nation and so the sorrows and sufferings of war fall upon the whole human race because we have failed to order our life in accordance with God's laws. Too often we have thought about our dividends and profits and markets to the exclusion of everything else. There can be no final victory which can bring peace to the world until we become fit to bring about the triumph of God's righteousness over the evils

of the world. When that victory is won justice and freedom and equity will be the basis of peace for all people... Once again there are on all sides, accounts of record harvests gathered in under ideal weather conditions. God has indeed crowned the year with his goodness...

Yours most sincerely,

E.A. STONE

Harvest time at Lansbury Gate Farm, Further Ford End, early 1940s.

118

Women's Land Army

Land Army girls do not seem to have been a noticeable feature of wartime Clavering, although some of them worked on local farms, but the nearest WLA hostel was at Brent Pelham until 1943 when the Essex War Agricultural Executive decided to take over the old vicarage in Langley as a hostel for the Women's Land Army. There was some urgency in getting the building ready to meet a government deadline, but by September 1943 there were 20 Land Army girls in residence. Due to the remoteness of the village, it was difficult at first to find a warden and (as in many things) a problem which the Vicar solved by seeking the help of his wife Doris (pictured in 1943), a former primary school headmistress. She 'agreed to act for a time as Warden of this hostel and she will live there most of the week; Judith [their five-year-old daughter] will go with her and Faith our maid and they will be assisted by a cook. For myself for part of the week, it will be a return to bachelor days, but I shall do that gladly knowing that the national effort is being helped on in a small way by my household. I am sure than in both Langley and Clavering a welcome will be given to these girls, most of whom are new recruits from London and quite unused to life as we know it in a village.' In Mrs Stone, the girls found a caring overseer of their welfare. After a few weeks, a warden was found and she moved back to the Vicarage. Des Abrahams (b.1927) recalls 'I had Land Army girlfriends. Some of them had no idea about land work, one had worked in an office in London – I used to go up there sometimes, Clerkenwell ... some of them were good, strong, we never had any on the farm. There were a lot in Langley - by that time the Americans were at Nuthampstead and they were entertained by them.' But some of the girls did know about farmwork, among them Nancy King (b. 1924), later better known as Mrs Nancy Caton of Catons Stores at Clavering Mills. Her father was a farmer in Manuden, and her mother had been maid, then cook at Clavering Court for the Finzels. Nancy decided to join the Land Army: 'I worked on the land all during the war. I went to work 7 o'clock in the morning till 5. I enjoyed it, used to bring up the lambs if the mother couldn't take them and they would follow me around. I fed the chickens and the pigs and did hoeing

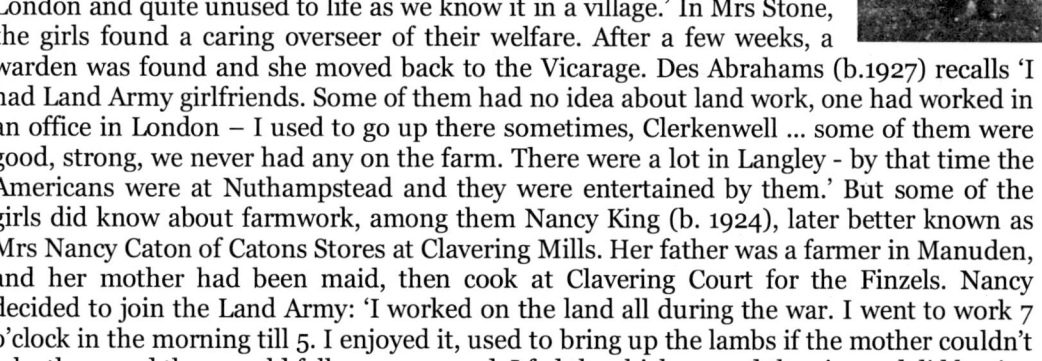

and manure spreading and things like that, planting the potatoes and gleaning them - always lots left over and they used to feed the pigs with those. There used to be a big boar and none of the men would go near it because it had big tusks, but it loved to have its ears scratched.' Nancy's family all did their bit in various wars - her father had served in WW1 and her grandfather took part in the Boer War at Mafeking. In ww2 her brother was in the RAF and flew numerous hazardous missions. In 1945 she married Norman Caton who also served in the RAF during the war, as did his brother William (see p. 54).

October 1943

My dear Friends
We are familiar from the daily press of the great campaign now going on to combat the scourge of venereal disease which has increased by 120% since 939... Ignorance is so often the cause of evil in the world that no longer must we allow Victorian taboos to allow young people to grow up in ignorance of the consequences of ill-considered actions. Our boys and girls in the Forces receive instruction in this matter and the large factories lectures are arranged by the welfare officers and given by competent people. In a rural area the problem is somewhat different. The responsibility for publicity is laid by the Ministry of Health upon the local government authorities and the Public Health Committee of our Rural District Council has spent some time in recent months discussing the best means of publicity. It was agreed at a recent meeting to ask leaders of youth organisations and the clergy to speak of the matter to their young people and to distribute some of the excellent leaflets that deal with this subject...
Yours most sincerely E.A. STONE

November 1943

My Dear Friends
In times like these there are strange ideas as to what enjoying oneself means. The increased wages, the break up of homes, the utter boredom of life for so many people all tend to a search for enjoyment in a way which would be shunned in more normal times. Standards of conduct, the sort of things we would do or wouldn't do, get put on one side all too quickly. So that even to talk of a standard of conduct raises in some people's mind the idea of something that interferes, that stops you having a good time... When people say that we are fighting for Christian moral standards, they usually mean that we are fighting for kindness and fair play between nations and classes and individuals...
Yours most sincerely, E.A. STONE.

December 1943

My dear Friends,
I don't think I have ever written so many letters as I have during the last few weeks. Our family in the Forces is indeed a large one, in the two villages nearly 140, but I have managed to find time to write a few lines to each one of them in addition to my normal correspondence which is never very small. I have enjoyed doing this tremendously even though it has meant writing far into the night on several occasions. The letters to the boys and girls overseas have already been posted and those for the home forces will be sent about the middle of December. I have tried to make my letters as personal and individual as I could and as I know all our boys and girls in the forces or their families, this was not very difficult. My main task I think was to assure them in the name of the village, of our thoughts and prayers especially at Christmas and to hope that before another Christmas it may be for them 'home again'... Our boys and girls in the Middle East, on the sea or in the air can cheerfully endure the fatigues of their work because of their folk at home and the knowledge that they belong to a home...
Yours most sincerely, E.A.STONE

Note: fund raising round the village raised £98 so that a postal order for 20 shillings could be sent to every Clavering person in the Forces, enclosed with the Vicar's letter.

Wartime Entertainment

By autumn 1943, the war had been going on for four years and everyone was fed up with it. But people did know how to have fun, notwithstanding the blackout, the regulations, the rationing and so forth. There were two cinemas in Bishops Stortford, the Regent and the Phoenix, with programmes changing every three days, and you could get to Stortford on Wilson's buses driven by Tommy Ellis or Ronnie Atkinson (pictured). In June 1943 James Cagney in 'Yankee Doodle Dandy' was all the rage, and this was the era of Laurence Olivier, Joan Fontaine, Greer Garson, Walter Pidgeon, Robert Donat – amid the glamour of the silver screen, briefly in a darkened auditorium, people could forget the war in escapist romance, drama, comedy and music. At home there was also the wireless, and Tommy Handley on ITMA was particularly popular. Home-grown entertainment came via the village hall, with its regular whist drives and dances, and occasional socials, concerts and Ministry of Information film shows. The constant need for fund-raising for various wartime causes ensured there was plenty going on, and the war itself generated talent. A concert party group from nearby RAF Debden, the Debdenairs, put on a show one Christmas. Another Christmas, the Pelham Amateur Dramatic Society did a concert, and another year 'Mrs Chappell and her trio of evacuee boys from Great Hormead' provided much hilarity, while Mrs Simms gave a selection of songs from her E.N.S.A. performances. Children had their own annual parties

> MINSTREL ENTERTAINMENT.—There was a large and appreciative audience in Clavering Village Hall on Wednesday evening for the entertainment given by the "Black-outs Nigger Minstrel Troupe" accompanied by the "Black-outs" band. From start to finish the performance went with a swing and was thoroughly enjoyed by the large number present. Mr. Buck was "Mr. Interlocutor."

shared with evacuees, paid for by London County Council (see p.165), and were included in the village hall all-age socials which started in 1944, while the teenagers and youths entertained the village at the end of the war with their Cheerios Concert Party (see p.164).

One concert, held in aid of the parish church heating fund, featured a visiting troupe whose name would not be thought politically correct today (see newscutting). Day to day socialising, of course, was centred on the pubs like the *Fox & Hounds*, seen here in the background of a wartime photo taken on the Bridges, with three local girls enjoying the company of a soldier and a sailor on leave.

UXBs Blacksmiths Corner 1943

On 3 November 1943 two bombs fell from an Allied plane at Blacksmiths Corner and settled as unexploded bombs (UXBs) in Brooklands Farm meadow. The ARP incident gives the details:

Message 15.15: 'About 14.45 today two UXBs were dropped in a field at Brooklyn Farm, Clavering near Blacksmiths Corner. Further investigation proceeding approximately 10 people evacuated.
Message 16.02: ' 10 people evacuated. Further investigation proceeding.'
Message 16.45: 'Roads blocked B1098 Clavering to Pelham. Unclassified road B Stortford to Langley. Position of bombs (first) 4 yds east of road junction (second) 20 yards east of road junction. First bomb unburied approx 4ft by 18 ins diameter, markings 2 yellow and 1 about 1½ ins wide & 1 about ½ ins wide. British wording painted on it and bands visible... Box Containing 2nd bomb buried, 3 people evacuated & accommodated by neighbours. Road diversion being arranged by police. UXB report will follow when further particulars obtained.
Message 16.11: evacuated people accommodated in neighbour's house close by.

A few people remember the incident. The late Isobel Beckwith (nee Barker) recalled it as she was coming home on a bus: 'As we came up the Wicken Road, the bus was stopped and we were told bombs had been dropped at Stortford Road, which of course made me feel awful. But after a while we were allowed to carry on home, as the bombs were safe and had dropped in the meadow at the Blacksmiths Corner. I was so pleased to get home again as I felt safer there.' Mike Preisig, who with others was threshing in Brooklands yard at the time, thinks they came from a Marauder plane from Nuthampstead airfield that happened to be over Clavering when they let their bombs go. June Holland (nee Riley), who was a teenager at the time living in the Druce, also recalls the incident: 'There were two big elm trees on the corner and two 1000 lb bombs hit a tree and it broke the fall - they embedded in the meadow and we were all looking at them. The Air Raid wardens bought in the bomb disposal people.' In the parish magazine, the Vicar commented: 'We can now reveal the fact of the merciful deliverance we experienced when two bombs recently fell by accident from an allied aircraft close to the centre of Clavering and fortunately did not explode. Our ARP wardens acquitted themselves nobly and had the position well in hand until finally the bomb disposal squad rendered the bombs harmless. In Church on the following Sunday we gave thanks to God for safe deliverance from what might have been a great tragedy.'

Photo taken from Brooklands Farm, showing the large elm trees which used to dominate Blacksmiths Corner – one of them deflected a bomb in 1943.

With the King's Forces 1943

By Christmas 1943 the numbers serving in the King's Forces had grown again, now reaching 94 on the parish magazine list – some names came and went as people moved away. There may be omissions, as the vicar appealed: 'I do rely on the cooperation of others to help in keeping this list up to date. To all those whose names appear this month we hope to send a letter and present of twenty shillings to reach them at Christmas.' Among them was Jim Jackson of The Druce (pictured), the first Air Cadet from Clavering to enter the Forces – he had joined the RAF to train as an armourer and eventually reached the rank of sergeant. Other new names on the vicar's list this year included two women, Joy Revell and Joan Simmonds, and two dozen men:

Reginald and Walter Barnard, Albert Buckley, Ernest Butler, Victor Clarke, Cyril Davis, Duncan Elwell, Alexander Greenfield, Bert Hill, Jim Jackson, Francis Jee, Percy Kemp, Richard Kybird, Herbert Lane, Hazel Martin, Ernest Matthews, Charles Seabrook, Joseph Sweeting, Alec Turner, Fred Whyman, Leslie and William Woods – and two more Law brothers, Robert and Sidney.

So now Fred and Clara Law had four sons away at war, travelling all over the world - fortunately all returned home safely. Freddie (b.1919) served under Montgomery in the Desert War; Kenny (b.1921), who had volunteered for the RAF aged 18, served in Burma; Sid (b.1923) joined the Army in 1941, visiting Gibraltar, Germany and Africa before being taken prisoner in Italy; and Bob (b.1925) served in the Queens Army Scottish Borderers and while in Germany had the traumatic experience of entering Belsen. Fred's brother William Law, who had been seriously wounded in WW1 at Ypres, and his wife Emily, also had several children in uniform, including daughter Irene (b.1920) in the ATS (see p.43); Robert (known as George, b.1924) who joined the Essex Regiment at the age of 17 along with Jack Livings and other village lads – he had some extraordinary experiences with the sea defences in 1940; and Bill (b.1926) who joined the East Yorks Light Infantry aged 18 in 1943, was promoted to corporal and served in Palestine.

Left to right: Kenny, Sid, Bill and George Law.

Chapter Seven
1944: 'Mercifully delivered'

In the same year that Britain was planning a better world for its children - with extended free education, free health care and the promise of millions of new homes - Hitler was calling up all young people aged ten upwards for military service. It was now certain that the Allies would win the war, it was just a matter of time, but the Nazis still had some wicked aces to play, most notably the V1 and V2 rockets which rained down and caused much damage and loss of life. So did the RAF bombing German cities into oblivion, with 20 million made homeless. The war was also being won by starving the enemy of food and fuel, but the Nazis continued their shocking atrocities in areas they still controlled – persecuting Jews, razing the Warsaw Ghetto, and now the world was finding out about the Nazi death camps. It was like 1940 in reverse, with the Allies pushing the enemy back in all directions – the Pacific, the Atlantic, the Mediterranean - Russia, Burma, Czechoslovakia, Yugoslavia, Lithuania, Poland, Greece and finally in Germany itself. The D-Day strategy for 6 June was the best-kept secret of all time, but with large Allied losses. Rome, Paris, Brussels and Athens were liberated one by one, to scenes of great rejoicing, and the Germans gave up their occupation of the Channel Islands. There were still reverses – the failure of Arnhem, the Japanese *kamikaze* pilots - but there was no doubting the unstoppable trend to victory.

At home, however, people were getting very 'browned-off' as shortages were increasing – but lemons were available again and the 'austerity suit' was no more as clothing restrictions were lifted. It was a relief to have the blackout largely lifted in September, and road signs restored, after five years of great inconvenience. There were breakthroughs in science - the discovery of DNA and the synthesising of quinine. In Essex, the signs of imminent D-Day were everywhere – troops practising, vehicles amassing, the air full of planes. But there was now no further need for the 'Dad's Army' and they were stood down. The announcement of a post-war United Nations gave cause for hope that world war would never be possible again.

Post-war planning was also being talked about in Clavering. The Vicar was a member of Saffron Walden Rural District Council and on the delegation which spent three days touring all 33 villages in the council's area to look at sites allocated for council housing. He commented on the sad statistic of wartime divorce rates, the longing for peace and the great need for faith when the invasion of Europe was likely to lead to so many casualties. He said little about the war news but in the summer on the eve of D-Day, Rev. Stone announced that, for the second time, he was leaving the parish temporarily to become a Forces chaplain, this time with the Royal Navy. The Vicar of Berden filled in for services, and the stalwart Mrs Stone held the fort at the vicarage. The Rural Dean asked everyone to pray for the difficult life he had chosen as a chaplain: 'It requires tact, sympathy and endless patience. In many cases the Chaplain has literally to build up his 'parish' from nothing amid all the terrible distractions of war.' From his ship, the Vicar still wrote for the magazine. He may have gone to Norway, as he mentions fjords and snowy mountains. He wrote of life at sea and how odd it was to take a harvest service in a barren land far from home. As always, he sat up far into the night writing a personal letter to all 120 Clavering and Langley residents serving in the Forces while Mrs Stone sent everyone in the parishes a 1945 calendar. It was his first Christmas away from home but for many they had spent every wartime Christmas away from their loved ones. At least the end was in sight.

Wartime routine went on in Clavering, reflected in the pages of the parish magazine – there was bellringing again and village hall shows and dances, meetings of the various organisations – Scouts and Guides, ATC, Youth Centre, savings groups, knitting for the Forces, the schoolboys' harvest camp, the village fete, the evacuees' Christmas party – though there were a lot fewer evacuees than before. The Invasion Committee and the Home Guard were wound up. The doodlebugs, so devastating in some places, did not cause much damage here but brought another influx of evacuees. Another young man from Clavering lost his life in the war.

Two events stand out in the memories of those who later recalled 1944 Clavering – the parade of organisations on Empire Youth Sunday, so memorably captured in a photograph published in *The Times*; and the crash of an American Liberator bomber at the Mills, without loss of life but with a scattering of plane parts that are still sometimes found today.

Dropping in on Clavering in 1944 - the American Liberator and its crew from 93rd Bomb Group, 409th Bomb Squadron who baled out safely over Clavering Mills: Pilot Lt Irwin H. Fruchter and Lt Sam Burgamian from New York, Lt Davenport, J. Karow from Florida, Lt Alfred R. Thompson from Massachusetts, S.Sgt Joseph A. Novak from Connecticut, S.Sgt. Henry G. Belzer from Ohio, Sgt Harland Wilkinson from Wisconsin, S.Sgt Paul S. Elatoric from Ohio, S.Sgt Donald H. White from Kansas and Sgt Joseph T. Doyle from Panama (see pp.136-7).

February 1944

My dear Friends

Amid a great deal of talking and planning for the post war days it is good to find that the provision of new houses has a high priority...With two other members of the Rural District Council I was asked to go to each of the 33 villages of the Council's area and view the sites that had been purchased for houses and in villages where no land had been bought to recommend the purchase of some. It was a very interesting task and took us three whole days. On some sites work had already started, the foundations were laid but then war came and everything had to stop. As one looked at a piece of ground producing during the war a food crop, one's imagination ran on to when one hoped that same piece of ground would have on it a home and the desperate shortage of houses in our own area would in some degree be lessened... We know of course that every house is not a home but the encouragement of a stable, simple, cultured home-life for everyone must be a chief aim of post-war planners. I read some alarming facts about the break-up of homes quite recently. The list of divorce cases set down for hearing in the current law term reached the record total of 3,399. A year ago the figure stood at 2,250. So the melancholy work of breaking homes and splitting families goes on. The impatience of separation is too much for some, war brings with it a disregard for social restraint and we tend to adopt a pagan morality that says that every desire must be gratified. For Christian people all this constitutes a national shame...

Yours most sincerely, E.A. STONE

Council's New Housing Scheme

The Council's post-war Housing Scheme provides for 320 houses, allocated as follows: Hadstock 6, Ashdon 14, Radwinter 20, Hempstead 8, Great and Little Sampford 20, Wimbish 18, Debden 18, Little Chesterford 6, Great Chesterford 8, Littlebury 6, Elmdon 12, Chrishall 6, Wenden Lofts 2, Langley 6, Clavering (Stortford Road) 12, Clavering (Wicken Road) 14, Arkesden 18, Wendens Ambo 4, Newport 14, Widdington 6, Berden 6, Manuden 6, Birchanger 10, Stansted 30, Elsenham 12, Ugley 10, Henham 8, Quendon and Rickling 8, Wicken 6, Farnham 4, Strethall 20.

The Vicar as district councillor was involved in the post-war housing scheme. In 1943, 14 council houses had been planned to be built at Wicken Road post-war, according to this newspaper report, but these never materialised, although the Stortford Road plan proceeded and new council homes were also built on Skeins meadow at Pelham Road.

Wartime Weddings

Francis Jee from the Searchlight Camp married local girl Violet Wisby in October 1942. George Barker, Driver with the Essex Regiment, wed Ursula George while on leave in August 1941. RASC Driver Leslie Etheridge married Mary Wisby in 1944.

Seven weddings took place at Clavering Church in 1940, 6 in 1941, 3 each in 1942 and 1943, 6 in 1944 and six more by September 1945. Wartime weddings could be strange occasions, and one planned in February 1944 had to be cancelled since the bridegroom died suddenly from heart failure only days before the ceremony: Humphrey John Talbot of

The Old House, aged 60, son of the Earl of Shrewsbury, was engaged to 43-year-old widow, Marie Drummond, widow of an army captain. Of wartime weddings that did go ahead, about half the grooms were serving in the Forces - four with the Americans (see p.101). Such ceremonies, fitted into leave and limited by the prevailing austerity, inevitably acquired an inbuilt tension too, as Barbara Maine remembers of 1941 when she went to Clavering Church to marry Capt. John Halkett Baddeley of the Coldstream Guards. She recalls 'wearing the most inexpressibly awful dress, all very lonely and unhappy with the war on and not knowing what was going to happen'. Others British Forces weddings here, in addition to those pictured, were: Ernest Beckwith/ Jessie Barker; Thomas Barnwell/ Kathleen Law; Alec Wright/ Winifred Rogers; Eric Flack/ Irene Monk; Arthur Durham/ Doris Underwood; Alexander Greenfield/ Eva Barker; William Burton/ Vera Kemp. The youngest bride was the 17-year-old daughter of the Slingsbys at Danceys, Katherine who in 1940 married Capt Peter Cleasby-Thompson, 27, of her father's regiment, the Lancashire Fusiliers (see photo, also p.153).

127

Home Guard 1944

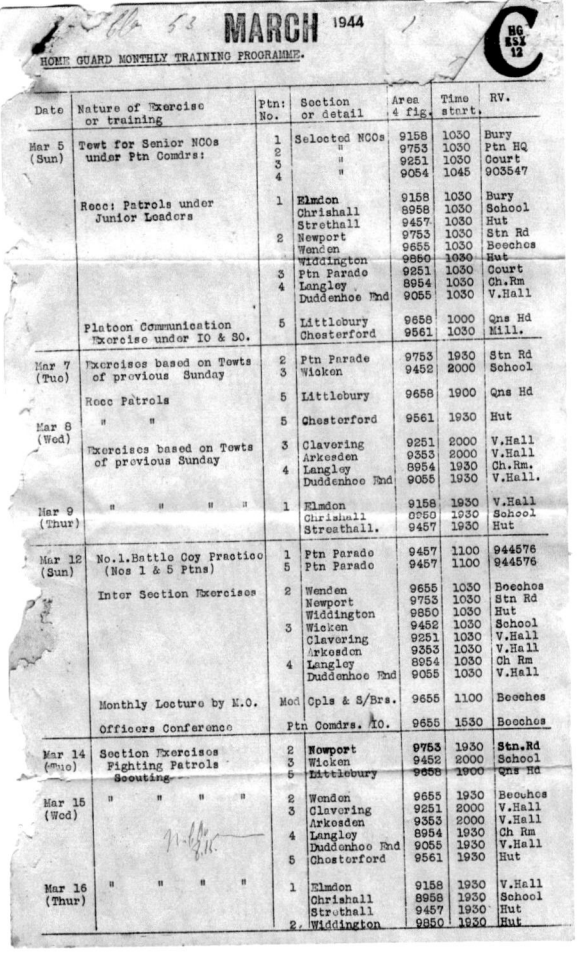

MARCH 1944

HOME GUARD MONTHLY TRAINING PROGRAMME.

Date	Nature of Exercise or training	Ptn. No.	Section or detail	Area 4 fig.	Time start	RV.
Mar 5 (Sun)	Tewt for Senior NCOs under Ptn Comdrs:	1	Selected NCOs	9158	1030	Bury
		2	"	9753	1030	Ptn HQ
		3	"	9251	1030	Court
		4	"	9054	1045	903547
	Recc: Patrols under Junior Leaders	1	Elmdon	9158	1030	Bury
			Chrishall	8958	1030	School
			Strethall	9457	1030	Hut
		2	Newport	9753	1030	Stn Rd
			Wenden	9655	1030	Beeches
			Widdington	9850	1030	Hut
		3	Ptn Parade	9251	1030	Court
		4	Langley	8954	1030	Ch.Rm
			Duddenhoe End	9055	1030	V.Hall
	Platoon Communication Exercise under IO & SO.	5	Littlebury	9658	1000	Qns Hd
			Chesterford	9561	1030	Mill.
Mar 7 (Tue)	Exercises based on Tewts of previous Sunday	2	Ptn Parade	9753	1930	Stn Rd
		3	Wicken	9452	2000	School
	Recc Patrols	5	Littlebury	9658	1900	Qns Hd
Mar 8 (Wed)	" "	5	Chesterford	9561	1930	Hut
	Exercises based on Tewts of previous Sunday	3	Clavering	9251	2000	V.Hall
			Arkesden	9353	2000	V.Hall
		4	Langley	8954	1930	Ch.Rm.
			Duddenhoe End	9055	1930	V.Hall.
Mar 9 (Thur)	" " " "	1	Elmdon	9158	1930	V.Hall
			Chrishall	8958	1930	School
			Strethall.	9457	1930	Hut
Mar 12 (Sun)	No.1.Battle Coy Practice (Nos 1 & 5 Ptns)	1	Ptn Parade	9457	1100	944576
		5	Ptn Parade	9457	1100	944576
	Inter Section Exercises	2	Wenden	9655	1030	Beeches
			Newport	9753	1030	Stn Rd
			Widdington	9850	1030	Hut
		3	Wicken	9452	1030	School
			Clavering	9251	1030	V.Hall
			Arkesden	9353	1030	V.Hall
		4	Langley	8954	1030	Ch Rm
			Duddenhoe End	9055	1030	V.Hall
	Monthly Lecture by M.O.	Mod	Cpls & S/Brs.	9655	1100	Beeches
	Officers Conference		Ptn Comdrs. 10.	9655	1530	Beeches
Mar 14 (Tue)	Section Exercises Fighting Patrols Scouting	2	Newport	9753	1930	Stn.Rd
		3	Wicken	9452	2000	School
		5	Littlebury	9658	1900	Qns Hd
Mar 15 (Wed)	" " " "	2	Wenden	9655	1930	Beeches
		3	Clavering	9251	2000	V.Hall
			Arkesden	9353	2000	V.Hall
		4	Langley	8954	1930	Ch Rm
			Duddenhoe End	9055	1930	V.Hall
		5	Chesterford	9561	1930	Hut
Mar 16 (Thur)	" " " "	1	Elmdon	9158	1930	V.Hall
			Chrishall	8958	1930	School
			Strethall	9457	1930	Hut
		2	Widdington	9850	1930	Hut

Through all these years, the 'Dad's Army' had been ready for action, and the chance survival of a few fragile documents - on cheap wartime paper, damp, torn and nibbled by mice - offers an insight into how they kept themselves up to scratch. The documents show how the Company was divided into several platoons:

- Platoon No 1 Elmdon, Chrishall & Strethall
- Platoon No 2 Newport, Widdington, Wenden
- Platoon No 3 Wicken, Clavering, Arkesden
- Platoon No 4 Langley & Duddenhoe End
- Platoon No 5 Littlebury, Chesterford.

Training exercises included recce patrols, sending messages, first aid and stretcher bearing, fighting patrols, scouting, battle drill, judging distances, care of arms, trigger pressing, inspection of arms, ammunition and kit, radio telephone & signals, grenades, musketry, bayonet fighting etc. It was a very demanding programme in addition to platoon parades and a weekend camp, while officers had to attend a monthly lecture, conference and additional training. Platoon No 3, which covered Clavering and Arkesden, met at the village hall but other sections would meet in huts, schools, pubs, houses and streets. A faded old letter with company orders dated 8th April 1944 reveals that even at this stage there was a fear of gas attack – Major Paget Crosby, Commanding Officer of C Company, warned that in forthcoming 'ops' bombs might be charged with mustard and gas spray, therefore all anti-gas equipment must be examined and repaired. There is also a note that Pte A. King was discharged from Home Guard duties as he had reached the age of 65. A torn little chit shows that in December 1944 Lt J.C. Ambrose claimed petrol expenses at sixpence a mile for driving 83 miles on Home Guard duties. Lt Ambrose lived at Thurrocks, where these documents were found over 60 years later by Stuart Abrahams during renovations - they were stuffed behind a wall and had lain there all this time. He recalls that there were a lot of others which were destroyed, but he realised the historic interest of the papers and saved them.

Emergency Medical Arrangements

Some even more fragile documents were found pasted on the inside of a grandfather clock which used to be kept at Danceys when the Slingsbys lived there during the war and now belong to their grand-daughter. Mrs Dorothy Slingsby (pictured), a former WW1 nurse, ran the Nursing Association and represented the Red Cross on the Clavering Invasion Committee, so this probably explains why the documents were kept in this safe place. This and other torn old papers appear to be instructions on arrangements in the event of invasion. Some are dated 1943, others may be earlier. The torn paper below gives the locations of Medical and ARP centres and directions for ambulances, while another identifies different markings for prioritising casualties – a mark on the forehead signified the most urgent cases.

Aussies in Clavering 1944

The Australian Chapel in Clavering Church was presented in 1950 by the Royal Australian Air Force and their relatives. It relates to hospitality they enjoyed at Clavering Court, where airmen would take a break from their stressful wartime duties. Sometimes the Oz pilots could be seen flying low over the house to mark the connection. The Court was owned by Hugo Finzel (b.1875), a tea planter in India who returned to England with his much younger wife Jean and son Richard and bought The Court in 1935, following the departure of the Bakers. The Court was a social centre – John Barwood remembers as a lad going there to play billiards: 'We had a lovely time - the person who worked there used to bring us tea or coffee and cakes, and we had a meeting in one of the big rooms.' Olive Wilson, who still lives at Stickling Green, did domestic help, while Nellie Clark was housekeeper, and Alfie Clark the gardener. When their two maids were called up, they took in evacuees (see pp.114-15). Mrs Finzel busied herself on the Home Front, organising dances, Christmas presents for the Forces, a jam-making centre, billeting, the Invasion Committee and salvage: with the help of local children, she went round in her pony and cart on Saturday mornings to collect waste paper. Ursula George ran a sewing group there, making Comforts for the Forces. It is unclear how the Australian connection came about, but a fascinating insight is offered by one of the RAAF visitors, a young pilot with 463 Squadron, Flying Officer William E. Hooper who left a diary recording a week he spent at Clavering Court in March 1944. The diary, preserved in the archives of the Australian War Memorial, reflects an outsider's view of Clavering at this time – who, one wonders, were May and Syb?

22 March 1944: 'On the way to Clavering I chatted to an Indian and at the station Mrs Finzel met us and, also a cousin of hers from India. We journeyed home for lunch and had a look see over the residence. It is very comfortable and has all modern conveniences. They have a maid and several gardeners. Mr Finzel owns quite a lot of land and so is a personage of the district. We chatted and as they have been in India we have a lot to discuss. Went for a stroll to the next hamlet.
23 March: This morning I had a chat with Clarke the gardener, and he is interesting. Then Julian and I went for a stroll with the guns. Saw two pigeons and a rabbit but didn't fire a shot. There were some fine steers in the paddock, and they are in good condition. This is grain country, oats, wheat and barley and the farmers are very busy getting the ground prepared for the crops.
24 March: A number of trees had been rooted up in the orchard and these we barrowed down to the woodheap where Mr Finzel commenced to saw them up. He is over sixty and suffers from rheumatism. After lunch I met Rev. Stone and he took me along to Langley Public School.... After school I returned to the Stones' home and when afternoon tea was over a choir practice was enjoyed. It was taken in the church built in the early sixteenth century. There has been only minor alterations and the church is in a fine state of preservation. Our next call was an A.T.C. meeting. There I met Mr. Napier and after a chat with the boys he had many questions to ask.'

'**25 March:** Mr Finzel took us for a stroll across the fields, There wheat crops, oats and barley were inspected, also a clover crop. Along the hedges willows and ash trees were pointed out and the method of draining the land was studied. Piping is laid down for this purpose and drains are made by machinery to these outlets. The soil is clayey. At one stage a huge bomb crater came across our path. There were several more in the fields. On our way back we met Mr Funston and they had a long argument over the labour problem and the increased school leaving age. These old folks fail to see why lads should interest themselves in higher education and moreover the fact of going to dances etc - it seems they enjoyed no youth -the argument was well thrashed out and no quarter given. After lunch Hugh and I played several sets of tennis and hurried home for a bath. After supper we wandered off to meet a couple of girls and had a bit of a party.

26 March: This morning we went to church and enjoyed a service on Passion Sunday. After lunch I wandered out on to the lawns and it was so grand in the sun that I lay down in the sun and had a sleep. After supper Hugh and I wandered off to meet the girls and after a few drinks ended up on a haystack. It is sticky stuff and I do not wish for another episode.

27 March: After lunch I called on Mr Stone and he took me across to the Clavering School. This is controlled by the Council – this means that its upkeep falls on this body. The teachers are chosen by a school board comprising Councillors and local people. The teacher is still paid by the Government... They knew their work but Mr Richardson has failed to develop the individuality of the pupil... In the junior school, student teachers were busy implanting knowledge and some artistic work was examined... At the Kindergarten level Miss Luff and... children were busy making a farm setting and as I chatted with them they showed intelligence. Their answers were complete and they knew what they were doing. The child is being trained here, and it is a pity it is being lost further up. As this section closed at 4 p.m. I had a chance of talking with the two students. Their courses are just the same as ours, but they have to pay for their tutoring and all expenses entailed. When told about our system they looked in amazement. On the way home I had the company of ten of the pupils and once out of school these youngsters had heaps of questions to ask. Not long after arriving home a phone came through and so an invitation from May & Syb to spend the evening with them. At 7.30 p.m. I left with Mr Napier for Saffron Walden to speak to a group of the Air Training Corps. Their O.C. Mr Chapman was a fine gentleman and on leaving received an invitation to come and visit him whenever I had an opportunity. Again the beauty of Australia was laid out before these young lads and after the lecture came lots of questions. Finally I reached Clavering at 9.30 for the party and the girls had a grand supper for us. Just as soon as Syb and I had done the dishes a fireside chat and a cuddle was enjoyed. Bed came along about 1.30.'

28 March: Mr & Mrs Finzel took us to Bishop Stortford and whilst waiting for the train I sent several cables off. Had lunch at the Victoria Street R.R.Q. and it cost me 4/2. Food is dear here and one pays for a wholesome meal. Eventually arrived back at camp at 3.45 p.m. and received a bit of a reprimand for being late.'

Clavering Court 1930s. *(Acknowledgement for diary to Australian War Memorial Archive)*

April 1944

My dear Friends
Few blessings can be desired so much just now, by the great majority of people, as the blessing of peace. Few things could make us go so wild with excitement as to know that at last peace had come... Peace doesn't just come when the order is given to cease fire, and we stop actual fighting with our bodies. Peace didn't come when the Cease Fire was sounded in 1918... you can't have peace when you are uncertain about the course of things... you can't have peace when you are deeply conscious of having done evil yourself... you can't have peace when life is empty and meaningless and there seems no object in what we do... so the message of Easter coming as it does at a time of furious struggle is Peace...
Yours most sincerely, E.A. STONE

June 1944

My dear Friends
We have come to a time in this war when on all sides we are warned of the fierce fighting that lies ahead. While we all pray that 1944 will prove a year of decision we must not blind ourselves to the fact that casualties may be heavy. It is because I feel that at this coming great hour in the history of the war our men and women in the Forces should not be without the encouragement and consolation of the Christian Faith, that I have accepted the invitation of the Chaplain of the Fleet to serve as a temporary chaplain in the Royal Navy. So for the second time during this war I shall be away from the parish for an indefinite period. I feel sure that you will readily accept any inconvenience which my absence may cause in the life of the Church and parish for the sake of those who are in the Forces. For myself I appreciate the opportunity of serving the men and women of the senior service and will hope for a happy return to the parish when victory is won.
Yours most sincerely, E.A. STONE

So the Vicar's dream came true and he managed to get back into the chaplaincy, thanks to the help of the Vicar of Berden and the Rural Dean who filled in the services – and of course his indispensable wife. And it was on the eve of achieving another ambition, the holding of a grand Empire Day Parade with all the uniformed organisations taking part (see p.134-5). It was also the time of D-Day indirectly referred to in the Vicar's July letter, and the Liberator crash, to which he did not refer. The Vicar was away when the new menace of flying bombs appeared, so his wife must have dealt with the billeting of the fresh wave of evacuees it prompted.

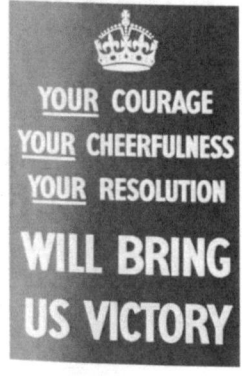

One way and another, the spring and summer of 1944 were busy times both nationally and locally in the annals of war.

Royal Navy Chaplain 1944

His first attempt to do so having come to a premature halt in 1942, Rev. Ernest Stone was delighted when a new opportunity to serve as a Forces chaplain arose in the summer of 1944. This time he became a Royal Navy Chaplain, and was then away from Clavering until after the end of the war. The Vicar continued to send news home from his troopship, writing in August 1944 that he had been 'busy getting accustomed to the life and speech of the Royal Navy... The sailor is a man like other ordinary men; but the life he lives and the characteristic conditions of his service are in many ways peculiar to the Navy.' As his parishioners in Clavering and Langley were celebrating harvest, he wrote in October: 'I found myself conducting a service at sea... The sea was not too smooth, and we had a job to keep standing at times as we sang our hymns, but still we got through very well and did our bounden duty.' He could not reveal his location, but it must have been Norway as he mentioned fjords and mountains:

'Here we are then in this outpost, like so many other groups in different parts of the world, a group of men miles and miles from any habitation, rarely seeing any civilians, just a tiny part of the great machine of war... we think a lot about home, we look and hope for letters that tell us about home. We get used to reading newspapers which are two or three weeks old and we listen to the broadcast news bulletins from time to time. We study, and I run classes and discussions on various subjects in the Dog Watches for all who are interested, and on several evenings a week we show films in our cinema. I am aware of what little details men crave to know. Life for you may often seem very quiet and ordinary and there may not seem much to write about, but yet it is the quiet everyday activities of home that mean so much... the excitement of a group of men when letters from home have arrived needs to be seen to be believed.'

True to his word, he wrote, from his floating 'vicarage', 120 letters to the 'boys and girls' in the Forces and, for the first time, like them, he would spend Christmas in a foreign land. He had leave in February 1945 but then returned and celebrated Easter 'on mess decks, in holds and in nissen huts'. Finally, the war finally came to an end and he described their service of thanksgiving for peace – they toasted VE Day with a double issue of rum. Rev. Stone wrote his next parish letter from the Vicarage, but was then called away again to spend a last few months as chaplain at a Royal Naval Air Station in Sussex – a place that was to feature greatly in his future life. While he was away, the parish was overseen by the churchwardens, notably Claude Simmonds (pictured) who often discussed church matters while out hunting with Mr George, the Langley churchwarden.

Empire Youth Sunday 1944

The Sunday nearest to Empire Day had been observed as Empire Youth Sunday since 1939, and Clavering briefly attained national fame when *The Times* printed this photograph of the Clavering church parade which took place on Sunday afternoon 21 May 1944. The service was also broadcast on the radio, as described by the Vicar in the parish magazine. Lt Ledward marshalled the procession on Hill Green, and they then marched via Blacksmiths Corner through Bury Meadow where this photo was taken, with Lt.-Col. H.W. Faure-Walker of the Coldstream Guards taking the salute – beside him out of sight is the Vicar of Clavering. Others watching were Lt Ambrose of the Home Guard, Capt A.W. Overall, Flt. Lt. M.O. Willmore, Flt. Lt. B.E. Chapman and F.O. W.J. Finch of the ATC; senior ARP Warden Edward Beamish standing next to Leading Fireman Arthur King, also there was Jimmy Clark JP, chair of Clavering Parish Council, the Guide Commissioner, E.W. Chapman, and Messrs Charles Simmonds (behind King), F. Anthony and J. Luff. The parade was led by Sgt. Vassar Rowe (Special Constabulary), followed by Saffron Walden Church Lads Brigade band, then junior Home Guard, Army Cadets, Air Training Corps, National Fire Service and Women's Land Army. It all made a wonderful spectacle.

This is how the story appeared in *The Times* issue of the following day, on the same page as overseas war news, the contrast between the two images being particularly stark.

Empire Youth Sunday. 'Our parade and service on May 21st was an unqualified success. For some years it has been a secret ambition of mine to see the members of the various organisations of our two villages parading together, and, headed by a band, make their way to a service in the Parish Church. This we have achieved and we are most grateful to all those who in various ways co-operated so excellently to make such a great success. Altogether it was a most impressive occasion. The splendid photograph taken by the Times photographer and printed in that paper on May 22nd showed well the beauty of Clavering and contrasted with the photographs of war-scarred Italy which appeared below it, made one very thankful that our life here is so undisturbed by war. I am told that a broadcast description of the parade and service was given in the General Forces Programme.'

A second photograph shows the ladders stored at ground level and on the roof in case incendiaries fell on the church. It shows Guides, Scouts and Wolf Cubs, followed by mothers and little children, entering the church. After the service the parade was addressed by Lt-Col Faure-Walker (pictured right) in the churchyard. Dick Law, who attended Clavering School at that time, thinks the smart little boy watching (pictured left) may have been 11-year-old Tommy Deeprose, an evacuee from Bermondsey who came here in 1940 and lived with his sister Maisie at Yew Tree Cottage in the Druce.

135

Liberator Crash 1944

One of the most memorable events of wartime Clavering was the crash of an American Liberator bomber at the Mills on 12th June 1944. A number of accounts survive and one of the eye-witnesses, Des Abrahams, gathered photos and documents associated with the crash. Farmworker Stewart Abrahams still collects bits of the plane from ditches today.

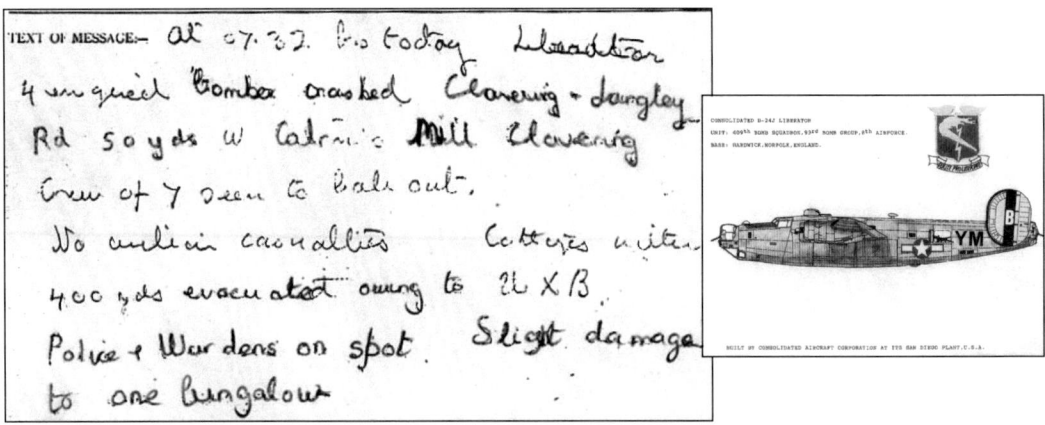

ARP message form sent 12 June 9.38 am reporting Liberator crash. Below, Mrs Dora Caton in her ruined outhouse at the Mills – a bomb hit it then rolled to the road.

Des Abrahams 'It was a bright sunny morning on 12 June 1944, when I became aware of a crashing United States fully-laden bomber on an early morning raid on Germany. Living on the farm at Sheepcote Green, my first indication was my father, out feeding the animals at 7 am, running back into the house saying, 'you better get up, there's a plane coming down and the crew have jumped out!' The bomber crashed into the ground about halfway between Clavering Farm lane and Thurrocks Farm, with no damage to human life, but some of the bombs exploded on impact. Myself and others, followed by Americans from Nuthampstead, got as near as possible to the burning plane, about 400 yards away. Together we watched the burning plane until one of the remaining bombs exploded. There was much Anglo-American partnership as we all dived to the nearest ditch, the exploding bomb scattering soil and metal uncomfortably close. One of the bombs on impact had catapulted some half-mile or so and crashed through the outhouse of the bungalow on the hill by the Mills, and ended in the road. The road was closed and the bomb defused, probably by Americans from Nuthampstead. Mrs Caton had a very lucky escape as she had recently been in the outhouse. John and Audrey Caton [pictured opposite sitting on the shell which had rolled out of Mrs. Caton's shed], must have been also lucky, having been in the bungalow at the time.'

Isobel Beckwith: 'We watched the crew come down by parachute, the plane kept circling around until it finally crashed. I thought it had hit the Church as it was so low when we last saw it. It made a terrible noise and pieces of the plane were scattered all over the village, one wheel almost into Langley. It was one of our own planes returning to Nuthampstead after one of their raids. All the crew landed safely except one with a broken ankle, another landed in a pond. But people soon went to help them and took them in.'

1944 Nancy Caton 'I was going to work at 7 o'clock and saw this plane coming across and all of a sudden they all came out of this aircraft as fast as they could. That was the one that fell up the Clavering lane where the Lakes are now. When we cut the corn during the summer we came across flying boots in the corn.'

John Barwood: 'Chubby was cycling with me at Poorbridge road that day and looked up and saw parachutes coming down and I said, 'they're bloomin' Germans'. But we carried on to work and it wasn't till night when I went down the village they were talking about it. They were Americans and the aircraft crashed up near the mills, we went up to see it. Apparently something went wrong with the works and they had to ditch it.'

Mike Preisig: 'Early one morning a bomber crashed between the Valence and Clavering Place, this was a four-engined American Liberator with a full load of bombs. One of the bombs demolished a shed on Catons Hill and lay in the road until collection. A propeller fell in Coley Lane, making a big dent which was visible for many years. The crew all landed safely at Rickling.'

Dick Law: 'There was an old wash shed which had a direct hit and the bomb rolled into the road. The bomb went down a steep bank below the bungalow. The road was closed, we were not allowed to pass it. The airmen parachuted out. The propeller fell off and landed in Coley Lane.'

USAF 93rd Bomb Group 409th Bomb Squadron report: 'One engine practically shook itself off the a/c and was about to tear itself to pieces. All landed safely. One of the 2,000 lb bombs landed in the centre of a small village and this had to be evacuated. Two of the other bombs went off when the plane crashed. Lt Fruchter [pilot} is in hospital with a broken leg.'

Rev Ernest Stone - A Merciful Deliverance: 'The parish of Clavering was mercifully delivered from what might have been a terrible catastrophe. A Liberator aeroplane from which the crew had baled out, because it was in difficulty, crashed down into a barley field scattering some 2,000 lbs bombs over the countryside. We are happy to record that there were no casualties to anyone, either in Clavering or among the crew. The Civil Defence services and the Bomb Disposal Squads did their work admirably and are to be congratulated.'

Parts of the Liberator bomber which crashed at the Mills in 1944, found by Stuart Abrahams in a ditch: left, engine with detonator rod inside; right, bomb end fragment. Above, John and Audrey Caton sitting on one of its bombs.

Troops in Clavering

On the face of it, these troops pictured at Bridge End, look like one of the many manouvres which were commonly seen here during the war, still remembered by those who were children at the time. Some were special events like the mock invasion exercise in May 1941, 'somewhere in the Eastern Counties', with over 10,000 vehicles and 75,000 men taking part. Some were more local, like the one in July 1942 directed by Lt Col Slingsby of Danceys. The biggest of all was in preparation for D-Day – one person remembers queues of vehicles in Starlings Green in readiness for the big day. But it seems unlikely that photography would have been allowed of such exercises. The context of these pictures is not known, but the participants do not look like regular English troops – the officers lounging on the bridge almost suggest it might have been staged for a film, and the Langley pictures opposite, part of the same set inherited by Ann Banks, suggest some sort of training exercise.

138

Officers in Langley

These photographs
appear to be taken on
the road between the
green and the church
at Langley Upper
Green. In some ways,
they resemble a film-
set rather than a
serious training
exercise, with
figures wearing
German, Italian
and other
officer
uniforms,
standing around
waiting for
something to
happen. Are
they holding
maps or scripts?
What is the
significance of
the flag? All a
bit of a mystery!

D-Day June 1944

Although people were used to seeing troops on the march, they noticed increased activity in the build-up to D-Day although what was actually being planned was kept a close secret. Meanwhile many villagers in uniform were also getting ready. Cpl George Barker (pictured in 1944) joined the Army five years before the war began, serving in the 1st Battalion, Essex Regiment. As an army driver, he experienced both the beginning and the end of the war. He recorded his memories of returning to France the day after D-Day and what happened afterwards.

'I drove a three-ton Ford with spare parts used for repairs. In January 1944 we moved up to Durham and then to a campsite where we were engaged in a large exercise training for the invasion. In March the Battalion went to Inveraray for ten days special training but the transport didn't go. Next move was to Christchurch where the drivers had to practice driving on and off the landing craft. In May we were at Beaulieu waiting for D-Day. The Battalion landed on D-Day, 6th June, but I went on D-Day plus one. Their duty was to capture Bayeux but they got held up so they did not get there until too late to go in. They waited until morning to make an attack on the town, but the Germans had disappeared overnight which was very lucky. The next time they went into an attack we did not have so much luck - we had a disaster. We lost lots and lots of men. It was a wooded area they went in called Vernieres Wood, but after the war they renamed it Essex Wood. I was about two miles away from the Front, and so I had an easier time in '45 than I did in '39. The only time I went up to the Front was after they had been in action, and me and Ken, another fitter, we used to grab a vehicle and go up to the Front and check the Bren-gun carriers, and ask the drivers if there was any trouble. The Sergeant in charge always wore his steel helmet, scared stiff he was. The Battalion was in many battles before we got into Holland. The Germans flooded large areas so the troops couldn't make an attack, all they could do was patrol an area... Eventually the water went down so the troops could push on and the war finally ended on 5th May 1945 and we finished up in Germany at a small place called Unna, and from there the Battalion moved to Berlin, but I was discharged from Unna in March 1946. We went back in lorries and got shipped to Dover.'

Extract from *Clavering Remembered* by George Barker (2011)

Left, memorial commemorating the disaster which the late George Barker recalled at Essex Wood on 11th June 1944. Right, George's war medals and his Essex Regiment badge, worn at the last Remembrance Day he attended before his death at the age of 96.

ESSEX WOOD

2nd ESSEX REGIMENT
"The Pompadours"

We will remember them.
11th JUNE 1944

140

July 1944

My dear Friends,

It was the day after D-Day and I was sitting at the front of a bus passing through the City of London. There were only a few passengers and the conductress at the back of the bus was speaking to someone near her about the King's broadcast of the previous evening... The invasion of Western Europe by the Allies was prefaced by King George with a simple call to prayer for God's blessing, affirming that our purpose was to put God's will first. The whole enterprise was sealed with the spirit of true religion. As the King spoke, paratroops, gliders and infantry, tanks and guns and engineers touched down on French soil, four years and a day after the completion of the evacuation from Dunkirk. The nation has felt a sense of relief at the opening of the Second Front. So far things have gone well but no feeling of false exaltation must obscure our thoughts of the grim work which awaits our sailors, soldiers and airmen. Let us await whatever the coming days have in store for us with sober confidence and freedom from unworthy excitement. 'I desire solemnly to call my people to prayer and dedication' said the King. That is the spirit in which we must approach the trials and anxieties of the coming months...

May I thank you all very much for your kind wishes in the new work I have been asked to undertake. I shall value greatly your thoughts and prayers in the special job that I shall be doing and when it is done I shall look forward to being with you all again. Almost all my seven years in Clavering and Langley have been spent either during the war or during the months of preparing for it. How strange, but yet how welcome, peace will be to us all! With every blessing on your and our dear boys and girls who are away from us just now.

 Yours most sincerely, E.A. STONE.

The end of the war was in sight but there was no let up in the demand for every spare penny to be put into national savings. In July 1944 it was the turn of Salute the Soldier Week as 'a fitting tribute to our gallant boys and girls in the front line'. This time Clavering managed to surpass its target of £7,686 and raised £8,510, opening the campaign with a village hall social where everyone gathered to buy their stamps. Fund-raising also began in anticipation of the day when villagers serving in the war would return home. A new account was opened at the Post Office Savings Bank, the Clavering Forces Fund. Of recent years', said the vicar, 'it has been our custom to send a present at Christmas to all our boys and girls in the Forces. If, as we all hope, peace may be here before Christmas, then it has been suggested that the fund may well provide home-coming gifts for those who are now away from us.' All of this was in addition to various special appeals that went on throughout the war, for instance the village fete that year provided a sum to the fund which sent parcels out to PoWs.

141

August 1944

My dear Friends

My writings in our magazine must be somewhat infrequent I fear in the months that are ahead, but as I look out of my 'vicarage' window across an expanse of water which, by its constant movement, seems to reflect the restlessness of man, it is the peace and quiet of Clavering and Langley that seem rather far away. How often have we said one to another in the parish of recent years that except for the absence of our loved ones and our care and anxiety for their welfare, 'we hardly know there is a war on'. The absence of our boys and girls is indeed hard enough to bear, but if in addition our life was lived in a city half blasted to pieces by bombs and with sirens wailing several times a day, how much harder life would be! How true it is that we are seldom very grateful for blessings which come to us so regularly and over a long period.

Yours most sincerely, E.A. STONE.

The ship's company of HMS Cumberland on which John Bowles of Clavering served during WW2. Ernest Stone wrote his vicar's letters from a Royal Navy vessel where he was chaplain in the latter part of the war.

October 1944

My dear Friends

It is natural after five years of war that we should think from time to time of what we would like to do to celebrate the announcement of the cease-fire with Germany, even though some of the ideas which come to mind may not be very practical ones. I overheard a conversation the other day among some sailors on this very matter. Suggestions were being made for rejoicings of various kinds, for a sailor has a reputation for knowing how to enjoy himself. Being cooped up in an iron box on the ocean for weeks at a time, Jack has ample opportunity of planning what to do on his next night ashore. After a number of suggestions had been put forward, one fellow said: 'Well I think chaps, that there's one thing that we ought to do, and that is go to church'. Such a proposal, so very different in character from the others put forward, one might have thought would have been met with derision, but no, it was received quite calmly and with respect... The people of Florence gathered in their churches when their city was liberated and the most moving of the scenes in Paris after its liberation was the Te Deum in the Cathedral of Notre Dame. The present war is a struggle against evil and no act could be more fitting than that we should pause soon after the cease-fire has sounded for a few minutes of thanksgiving and renewed self-dedication. I am arranging for our churches to be open day and night very shortly, so that at any time there will be an opportunity for any who wish, to spend a few quiet moments in God's House.

Yours sincerely, E.A. STONE

Evacuees again 1944

In the summer of 1944 there came a new danger – the V-1 better known as the doodlebug, a new and terrifying weapon developed by the Germans who dropped up to 150 flying bombs every day – by July they had killed 2,752 people and injured another 8,000. The planes followed a route known as doodlebug alley across Sussex, Surrey and Kent but they also reached areas to the north of London. However it was still much safer here than in London and this led to a new influx of evacuees escaping to the countryside. As before Clavering homes became a refuge, as the Vicar wrote in his August 1944 letter:

'May I commend to your care and attention the numbers of town dwellers who have recently come among you. As you know billeting has been my concern since the beginning of the war and I could fill a book with my experiences and accounts of various meetings I have attended and official instructions that I have received. As a parish we have an excellent record for hospitality in time past and the proportion of evacuated persons who have remained in our midst is second to none in the rural district of Saffron Walden. Now once again, and for some of us it will be the third or fourth time, we are asked to open our doors to homeless strangers. I do not believe all the sensational stories that one reads in the press about the refusal to billet certain families, very often the explanation is the hysterical state of some of the women who should be accommodated by themselves. At the same time the brand of shame must rest on those heartless persons who, having room, refuse shelter to a mother and her children. Those who have so little feeling for suffering humanity that they wriggle and shift and use every excuse even to downright lies, rather than take in the stranger, make us marvel at the inhumanity of man. I feel sure that there will be none in Clavering or Langley who will act in such a way... The new weapon aimed at London and Southern England has meant another influx of visitors, young and old. For many this new visitation has been a tremendous strain. In this comparatively safe and peaceful area, it is difficult for us to appreciate the sufferings and strain of your brethren in London and elsewhere. We can show our sympathy by a hearty welcome, even if it means some inconvenience. Our men and women overseas are standing so much for us, that our inconveniences must appear as luxury compared to their lot. Remembering him who said "I was a stranger and ye took me in" we will do our best.'

Registered			Name		d.o.b.			Home address	
3	7	44	Turner	Jean	4	2	34	Charles Turner	23 Glenham Rd, Nr Ilford.
3	7	44	"	Marjorie	27	1	36	"	
17	7	44	Akers	Leonard	23	12	33	Charles Akers	108 Stratford Rd, Plaistow E 13
17	7	44	"	Joan	27	2	32	"	"
18	7	44	Keam	Beryl	12	1	33	"	
20	7	44	Revonski	Philip	31	1	32	Mr. Revonski	36 Napier Rd Tottenham
31	7	44	Baker	Irene Joan	25	3	36		
31	7	44	Atkinson	John	14	5	33	Mrs Atkinson	123 Montague Jubilee Queens Crescent Street, Kentish Town NW.5
31	7	44	"	Roy	23	6	35	"	

School records of some of the London children who came to Clavering as evacuees from doodlebugs in 1944. Most returned to London by the end of the year.

In Memoriam John Newland 1944

Alfred John Newland was born in Clavering in 1920, the elder son of James and Gertrude Newland of Starlings Green. His brother Bill says that he was always known as John and, after leaving school in 1934, would cycle to work at Rayment's Brewery in Furneux Pelham, working long hours in the bottling plant on low wages of ten shillings a week. While cycling to and from work each day, John befriended a jackdaw which would perch on his shoulder while going to work and wait for him when he left for home in the evening. During the late 1930s, John played cricket regularly for Brent Pelham until called up in 1939 at the age of 19. He was with the Royal Artillery serving in France in 1940, and survived Dunkirk. Later he was sent to the Middle East and transferred to the 16th Battalion Durham Light Infantry. Having come through the whole war up to then, it was tragic that in the final months of the Italian campaign, he was seriously wounded and died from injuries on 13th September 1944, at the age of 25. This is John's gravestone at the Coriano Ridge War Cemetery in Italy.

KILLED IN ACTION.—Mr. and Mrs. James Newland, of Starlings Green. Clavering, have recently heard that their elder son, Alfred John, has been killed in Italy. Joining the Royal Artillery at the beginning of the war he served in France in 1940 and later in the Middle East. He had recently been transferred to the Durham Light Infantry.

In Memory of
Private ALFRED JOHN NEWLAND
1517940, 16th Bn., Durham Light Infantry
who died age 25 on 13 September 1944
Son of James and Gertrude E. Newland, of
Starlings Green, Essex.
Remembered with honour
CORIANO RIDGE WAR CEMETERY

Auxiliary & Civilian war service

There was virtually no unemployment during WW2, and all able-bodied adults were doing something war-related, including most women. Early in 1941 there was a need for 100,000 women to work in factories and auxiliary services. Betty Atkinson was typical of many, working in a munitions factory. At the end of that year it became compulsory for all single women to work in anti-aircraft, police, fire or other essential work and 1.7 million women were conscripted. From among the young women of Clavering, Marjorie Baker and 'Budgie' Elwell served in the Auxiliary Territorial Service (ATS – see p.43), Frances and Hilda Riley in the Navy, Army and Air Force Institute (NAAFI) and Laura Slingsby in the Voluntary Aid Detachment (VAD). Others including Vera Barnwell, Vera Kemp, Mildred Player, Violet and Margaret Wisbey, Queenie King and Joyce Revell, were named on the Vicar's list printed in the parish magazine as they were doing war-related work of various kinds.

Civilian and auxiliary workers in WW2: Queenie King, Violet Wisbey, Hilda Riley NAAFI, Laura Slingsby VAD, Betty Atkinson munitions worker, Right, Claude Simmonds, high-ranking civil servant. Below left, Wilf Carter, munitions worker, in 1940.

By 1944, compared to just over a fifth of workers in the Forces, one-third were doing paid civilian war work. Among Clavering men with important Civil Service jobs was Claude Simmonds (photo right), who lived at Piercewebbs in Pelham Road, and worked as Director of Public Relations at the Board of Trade. He was also a churchwarden and kept the church going while the vicar was away on chaplaincy duties. After the war, in 1946 he was appointed a member of a Commission set up by the Archbishop of Canterbury to advise on restoring the power of

Christianity in Britain. Most people performed humbler but no less vital roles – local builder Harold Walford did aircraft maintenance (see p.78), and village carpenter, Wilf Carter (photo left) cycled to and from Woolwich Arsenal, where he was one of 30,000 wartime employees. He was part of a team which developed projectile infantry anti-tank (PIAT) weapons, and other weapons. He enjoyed the work and used to lodge there during the week and cycle home at weekends. Cycling back to Woolwich, he would carry on his handlebars rabbits which he had ferreted at the weekend and which found a ready market in town.

December 1944
(printed in January 1945 magazine)

My dear Friends

I have just finished my self-appointed task of writing in the name of the village a letter to all our boys and girls in the Forces. I have greatly enjoyed my letter writing. I see that the number is over 120, and as you can guess that wasn't done in a few minutes. There have been times when I thought I had set myself an impossible job to write all these letters in addition to my service duties, but by sitting in my cabin, often far into the night, I have managed to write to all whose addresses have reached me. It wasn't a long letter, just two sides of a piece of notepaper; there was nothing very original, the traditional good wishes, an assurance of our thoughts and prayers and our joyful looking forward to the time for the return home... This will be the first Christmas that I have spent in a foreign land and so I can understand something of the feelings of those who have spent four or five Christmases away from their family circles. It is to men like this that letters mean so much, sometimes more than food.

Yours most sincerely,

E.A. STONE

Christmas card sent home in 1944 to his mother at Hill Green, by John Bowles, who at that time was serving with the SE Asia Command on board HMS Cumberland.

With the King's Forces 1944

By Christmas 1944 there were four names of Clavering men on the Roll of Honour, and a further 98 serving in the King's Forces – new additions below. As this issue of the magazine went to press, the Vicar congratulated one of them, Sapper Hubert Law (pictured here in 1938), serving in the Middle East, who had been mentioned in dispatches and awarded the Oak Leaf in 1944.

George Allard
Maurice Atkinson
Thomas Barnwell
William Burton
Roger Carter
Harry Defriend
Leslie Etheridge
George Frostick
William Law

Charles McMillan
Hayden Newland
Anthony Newton
Eric Poulter
Peter Teale
Arthur White
Frederick Wrenn
Leonard Wrenn

By the end of the war, nine members of the Poulter family were on the list of King's Forces. However, the family had become dispersed due to the death of their parents - Jessie in 1942 and father John in 1943. The Poulters had lived at Blackbird Cottage, Wicken Road, an unusually large family with 16 children born over a 26-year period between 1903 and 1929. John and Jessie saw most of their boys go off to war, but did not live long enough to know that all of them survived. Those mentioned on the church war memorial were Bernie (b.1916), Eric (b.1924), Kenneth (b.1923), Len (b.1918) who was in the airborne forces and took part in the Normandy landings, and Tom Poulter, which may be a nickname for one of the others. Some were too young to be called up. Eric Poulter joined up in 1935 and was in the RAF, and Bernie Poulter in the Suffolk Regiment. Bernie had joined the Army in 1934 when he was 18 and served 12 years including the war. Some of the Poulters are pictured below, left to right: Bernie, Eric, Len and their half-brother Jack Jeffery (b.1906) who was much older and served in the Royal Navy. The identity of the Royal Marine Poulter is uncertain, and the one in white sailor's uniform is Dennis Poulter, who served in the Navy after the war. A national newspaper once carried a story about the family with so many boys in uniform. It is certainly remarkable that, both before, during and after the war, the large family from Blackbird Cottage did their bit for Britain! **Some of the Poulters in uniform.**

Chapter Eight
1945: 'The magnitude of the task'

In 1945 what became known as the 'Second World War' finally came to an end. It was a fast-moving, action-packed year, with one victory after another for the Allies in Europe. But terrible news took the edge off any tendency to triumphalism: the discovery of Auschwitz, Belsen, Dachau, Buchenwald; the devastation of Dresden with all its treasures; the millions of homeless refugees. Mussolini, Himmler and Hitler were gone and Nazi war criminals rounded up, but nothing could atone for the unspeakably cruel attempt to annihilate the Jewish race. The joy which had erupted on VE Day 8th May, was repeated on VJ Day 14th August, but what a price the world had paid – an 'Iron Curtain' descending on Europe as Churchill had predicted; frightening atomic power unleashed on Hiroshima and Nagasaki; the revelation of prison camp horrors under the Japanese; and an estimated total of 55 million deaths worldwide amid unimaginable destruction. What a mess the world was in, and there was so much to do. The new Labour government promised great change, but meanwhile Britain was broke.

Even before the end of the war, the Vicar of Clavering did not mince words in stamping on the notion that the post-war world would be 'something like Heaven'. The service-men he met appreciated 'the magnitude of the task that lies ahead'. In January 1945 he pointed out how many were still dying in the war, even while others were making a fortune out of it. But the end was in sight and, there would come a time when 'the news will only tell of the weather and of the comings and goings of people in peaceable ways, planning and building a new world'. The only way to achieve this brave new world, he repeated again and again, was to maintain the wartime spirit of community, and create 'a new brotherhood'. But through much of the year, Rev. Stone was not able to be with his flock, as he was still serving as a chaplain in the Navy, taking Easter services in a 'little chapel in a nissen hut', probably in Norway and marking VE Day at sea, rather than on land in his own parish church. But Clavering celebrated the end of the war with bellringing, church services and a village hall social. The young people, in the form of the Cheerio's Concert Party (see illustration),put on a victory show to packed houses, 'Smiling Through', which like many events at the time, helped to raise money for the Clavering Homecoming Forces Fund. The Vicar was back by the time of VJ Day, expressing everyone's 'unutterable relief' that it was all over at last. His September 1945 letter (see p.162) was a succinct summary of what a close-run thing it had been, particularly in 1940, and of the challenge that lay ahead. Once again he said it was up to Christians to make a success of the peace so hard won: 'Perhaps without God you can win a war but you can't win the peace'. His Forces work was not yet over, however – he had to go and spend a few more months as a chaplain in Sussex with the RNAS, popping back to Clavering for harvest services. In the village the various wartime organisations were winding up – off went the last bundle of knitted garments for the Forces, away went the Home Guard uniforms and the ARP equipment and the phrase, 'for the first time in six years' could be spoken of events like the Remembrance Day parade – and a peaceful Christmas, with loved ones home or due to be demobbed.

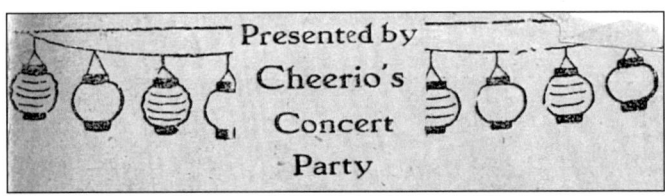

Presented by Cheerio's Concert Party

January 1945

Letter from the Vicar – OVERSEAS

A year ago many of us thought that the war might reasonably end in 1944. But nevertheless we can still look forward to the post-war world which some people seem to think will be something like Heaven.

There will come a time when we shall not bother much about the news. For the news will only tell of the weather and of the comings and goings of people in peaceable ways, planning and building a new world. Then the time will come when we shall all be together again. Our sons and daughters will return to us from the North, South, East and West. The long months of separation will be over. Letters will begin to speak of "home again." Then they will come to us.

From what I know of service men, they don't think that, and more and more they are realising something of the magnitude of the task that lies ahead. No one can pretend that burdens are equally shared. All the talk about equality of sacrifice is sheer humbug to the serving man. Some already are bearing burdens heavy enough to crush them. Some are carrying no burdens at all, but yet hundreds are still dying daily on the various war fronts, ships still fall victims to U-boats and aircraft fail to return. A few are enjoying the war, making a smashing profit out of it, piling up the money growing fat out of the agonies of others. I don't think anyone envies them – there is a hell of our own making. But there is a great need for a continuation of that sense of friendship and interdependence, that experience of belonging to a community which many have felt for the first time as members of the crew of a submarine, a tank or an aircraft... We all care desperately about our boys and girls away from us and look forward to welcoming them home into our village community.

Yours most sincerely, E.A. STONE

A wartime photograph at Mill End Dairy Farm, symbolising the old world that largely disappeared with the war. Margot Maine, two-year-old nephew Simon, Bar Maine, Mr Mossman and Mr Boyton.

Wartime Church

A major worry during wartime was whether the ancient parish church might get damaged by incendiaries. Fortunately the Government in August 1941 made the generous gesture of giving free insurance for the fabric of churches, although this did not cover all the contents, and an inventory of church goods was carried out that year. The Parochial Church Council decided to insure the church for £3,400 at a premium of £12, placing an alms box in church for donations towards this. There was a good response to this appeal, and the church spent another sum buying ladders (see 1944 photo) so that every part of the flat roof and parapet could be reached if fire did break out – buckets of sand and water were placed there in readiness.

The church was much affected in many other ways by the war. Service times had to be altered because of the blackout and double summer time, but there were more special services at this critical time when everyone needed strong support and the uniformed services paraded more frequently. The Vicar introduced Mothering Sunday services for the first time, and there were parades on Empire Day, Farm Sunday and Harvest Festival. The annual National Day of Prayer was particularly poignant, celebrating the anniversary of the Battle of Britain when, as the vicar put it, we were saved by 'a few hundred British boys in their fighting planes – those lads saved Britain and the world'. The Vicar was distressed at the ban on bellringing and the loss of these skills, and also the effect of the blackout on choir practices. Rev. Stone had worked hard to build up the church choir when he first came to Clavering so that by 1938 it was 'one of the finest of village choirs in the district'. By the end of 1940 this was no longer possible: 'Some of our men have joined the forces, some have moved from the parish, a number of our boys have left school and their voices have broken and several of our girls are now at work where it is difficult for them to be regular attenders. Besides all this there is the added difficulty in these days that we cannot hold choir practice. At one service during November for the first time for several years there was no choir at all! ... We regret that carol singing in the village this year will be impossible but

PARISH MAGAZINE

The Parish Church of
St. Mary and St. Clement, Clavering.

while the war can prevent us singing outside we can still hold our annual carol services...' He made an appeal for more young people to join, and by 1942 had a good youth choir organised - with 13 boys and girls who practised on Friday evenings at the vicarage with Mrs Stone, Mrs Luff and the Vicar. The choirmaster of Westminster Abbey special choir must have had some local connection as he conducted them now and then. The war reduced the size of the church magazine, and indeed many such newsletters disappeared in wartime due to a shortage of paper and increased production costs. But the Vicar knew it was important as a means of communication, and also as a record for posterity – up to 230 copies were sold at home and sent overseas to those serving in the Forces to help them feel closer to home. In 1946 the price went up to threepence.

In the summer of 1943 the Vicar became quite ill with jaundice but everyone rallied round, not least the devoted Mrs Stone, who chauffeured him around. By September, he was back in harness, running harvest services to celebrate the record harvest that year, with all the uniformed organisations parading and a special peal by the bellringers he had gathered together again. The war also meant that the parishes lost their vicar for two long periods, first when he went to be an RAFVR Chaplain and later as an RNVR Chaplain. His first attempt to become a chaplain had been abandoned, and the explanation about the difficulty of making arrangements reveals that Clavering clergy had a hard time.

While it is very pleasant to be back in the quiet and peace of this corner of Essex with one's own family again, yet it is, as you can imagine, a great disappointment to me to give up even for a time a work which has such vast opportunities for good among our boys and girls... this difficulty of finding an active priest to take charge of such a scattered parish is largely because of the smallness of the income available for the Vicars of Clavering and Langley. Every year when I have paid a pension to a former incumbent, a mortgage repayment for necessary improvements to Clavering Vicarage incurred by my predecessor, the dilapidations charges on two Vicarages and the rates on one of them, I have spent £300 of my income. You can imagine that there is not a great deal left on which to live and keep up a large house and garden. In fact to be your vicar and living in the simple way in which we do, has been costing me £100 a year beyond the income available, and I am wondering just how much longer I can afford to be your Vicar. I know that it all sounds very absurd and chaotic to pay a man a salary and then to take back over half of it, but there it is. It will not always be like this, the pension will one day cease and the mortgage will in a few years be repaid. There are no bonuses or higher wages for the clergy in wartime but only the added burden of increased taxation. In the Church of England we have been living too much on the endowments with which churchmen of early generations equipped the Church and those are for the most part quite inadequate to meet the altered conditions of the present day... this is a problem which sooner or later must be faced by the church as a whole.

The perennial problem of finding people to do things was exacerbated in wartime when so many people were busy with voluntary war work. So the value of those who helped the church was even higher. In those days, Mrs Kemp and Mrs Livings kept the large church clean with only the vicarage vacuum cleaner as an aid. When Miss Mary Martin gave up playing the organ in the spring of 1943, there was no one else available, so Mrs Luff who already played the organ at Wicken Church, agreed to fill in during wartime. That autumn the church also lost its excellent clerk and sexton, George Livings (pictured right) who retired through ill health, the Vicar paying warm tribute: 'In the six years he has undertaken this work George has transformed the churchyard at Clavering from its jungle-like appearance into one of the best kept churchyards, for its size, in the neighbourhood. In these days of vast destruction the creation of beauty becomes a more urgent duty than ever... thanks to the untiring efforts of our sexton coupled with the care given by relatives to individual graves we have in our midst a thing of beauty.' With grave-digging and other duties as well, it was possible to earn about £40 a year, he added, seeking a replacement sexton, but the position remained vacant.

Finally, the war came to its weary end. It was a matter of great thankfulness that none of the stray incendiaries or bombs had landed on Clavering Church, but the Bishop launched an appeal to repair the 392 churches, 222 parsonages, 67 church schools and 24 church halls in Essex damaged or destroyed by war. The Vicar wrote: 'We in our two villages have two priceless possessions in our parish churches which are fortunately undamaged by enemy action. In other parts of our County of Essex and diocese of Chelmsford serious damage has been done.'

Week of Prayer and Self Denial for work of the Church in Essex

The work of the church in Essex has been carried on under very great difficulty in recent years. Some of our churches, church halls and vicarages have been completely destroyed, and a very large number have been damaged. The parishes of Essex in common with other parts of Southern England have been called upon to suffer from the menace of the flying bomb, but the courage and devotion of clergy and people have been remarkable and the way in which work is being carried on under very difficult conditions must be an example to us all. The offerings on Sunday, October 22nd will be given to the Bishop of Chelmsford's fund.

Reconstruction of the Church in Essex

The Bishop is launching an appeal for £300,000 for the above purpose. This appears a colossal and frightening sum. Divided among the communicants of the diocese, it is about £3.10s per head. Churches, schools, halls and vicarages have suffered badly in Essex and still suffer. It is up to us all to do our bit. This is a challenge to our love for our church. In many of our villages the churches and schools were built by our ancestors. Let us show them we care as much and more than they did. Details of the scheme will be issued later. Meanwhile think about and, above all things, pray about it.

North side of Clavering Church before the war.

The Slingsbys of Danceys

In memory of
THOMAS SLINGSBY
MC · Deputy Lieutenant of Essex
Lieut.Colonel XX The Lancashire
Fusiliers · of Danceys, Clavering
for 24 years a Churchwarden
Born 1886 · Died 17 Feb^ry 1965
OMNIA AUDAX

Among memorials in Clavering Church is this one, just inside the south door, dedicated to Lt Col Thomas Slingsby, MC who lived at Danceys in Middle Street. Col Slingsby (pictured left) had experienced the Somme and after WW1 commanded the Lancashire Fusiliers in India. During Ww2 he was involved in civil defence training, until called up out of retirement to a post at the regimental HQ in Bury, Lancs. John Barwood was apprentice gardener here during the war and recalls: 'The Army commandeered Danceys barn and put a young soldier on duty at the front gates. When Col Slingsby arrived home he was stopped by the soldier, and he blasted out 'This is my home!' He said he would be reporting him to his commanding officer. The soldier winked to me because I was working nearby.' On another occasion Col Slingsby was in the drive when a bomb fall nearby – this must be the UXB at Blacksmiths Corner in 1943 (see p.122). His wife, Dorothy, a former nurse who had served abroad in WW1 on a hospital ship, also contributed a great deal to the Home Front, recalls granddaughter Philippa Thurlow: 'They were wonderful people, worked incredibly hard in very difficult circumstances. My grandmother was an unassuming and gifted person who gave a huge amount to the village through her life.' Dorothy would go out on a bike with a torch at night to shoot rabbits for the table. In the garden they kept chickens and a pig, fed with a copperfull of steaming potato mush on the Raeburn. Dorothy's older sister, Laura was with the family in India, then came home and stayed with the Barclays in Brent Pelham; during the war she served with the VAD, and postwar married Charlie Barclay. Among junior officers during their stay in India was Peter Cleasby-Thompson (pictured left on crutches c.1948) who, on the troopship coming back to England, taught the Slingsbys' 13-year-old daughter Katherine how to dance. It was the start of a great friendship and when she was only 17 they were married at Clavering Church (see p.127), and their daughters were born at Danceys during the war. Peter was one of the early parachutists, experienced Dunkirk and served in eastern Europe, north Africa and the Far East, was a member of the SAC and twice awarded the Military Cross. On one occasion when someone tried to burgle Danceys, Peter brandishing his sword chased the thief through a hedge! Their children Ariel (b.1942) and Philippa (b.1945) still have fond memories of their grandparents and parents at Danceys, of old-time dances at the village hall, using the water pump in Middle Street, cycling to Berden for first aid classes, buying rationed sweets at Kell's shop in Pelham Road and playing hide-and-seek in the big old barn which is still there today.

Home Guard Stand-down 1945

12th. BATTALION   HOME GUARD.

No. 3 PLATOON, "C" COMPANY
October 1944

Clavering Court billiard room was the meeting place of one of the Clavering groups of Home Guard, with another one meeting at the Church End clubhouse and a third in a furniture van in the Mills yard at Sheepcote Green. This photo, a memento before disbandment, was taken in October 1944 outside Clavering Court. Among local members were John Bunting, Walter Revel, Laurie Atkins, Len Matthews, Stan Newel, Peter Gowlett, Reg Claydon, Stan King, Willie Sell, Frank Talbot, Ronnie Monk, Ronnie Atkinson, Bill Gammon and Eric Chapman.

On 7th April 1945 in Clavering Village Hall the 'Stand Down' Party of No 3 Platoon 'C' Company. 12th Essex Home Guard, was an evening to remember:

'There was a large attendance of Home Guards and their guests... and representatives of the local Civil Defence Services. Douglas Luff and his band were in attendance and the entertainment included a revue by the Home Guard in 3 'spasms' entitled '1940 and all that'. The revue was written and produced by Lieuts Ashton and Ledward and was compered by the former. The performers were Lt Ashton and Ptes G. Bailey, P. Gowlett and 'Ninety' Dyer from Arkesden and Lt Ledward, L/Cpl King, L/Cpl Sampford, L/Cpl Barker and Pte Bunting from Clavering and Wicken. The ladies' parts were played by Mrs. F. Talbot and Mrs. Barker. The scenery and lighting, which were most effective, were provided by Lt Talbot and Sergt Wisbey, assisted by a highly competent stage gang consisting of Ptes Chapman, Watford, Law, Abrams and Sullivan. On the final curtain Lt Ledward expressed the hope that this was only the beginning of many shows in the Village Hall, in which it was hoped to interest everyone in the district. He then handed to Lt Talbot from the members of No 3 Platoon, an autographed book as a token of their appreciation and gratitude. The Commanding Officer, Lt. Col. Slingsby, presented the members of the platoon with their certificates of service, and a happy and memorable evening ended with 'Auld Lang Syne' and the National Anthem.'

In Memoriam Frederick Wrenn 1945

The last name to be added to Clavering war memorial was that of Sapper Frederick Wrenn, who was serving with the Port Operating Company of the Royal Engineers when he died aged 27 in Italy in the closing months of the war. The Commonwealth War Graves Commission archive shows that his wife Winnifred was at Forest Gate in Essex, but his parents Ernest and Lucy Wrenn actually lived at Blacksmiths Cottage in Middle Street. The date of Sapper Wrenn's death, 9th April 1945, was the start of the final offensive in the Italian campaign, so it seems likely that he lost his life during the attack on the German lines which began that day. (Since he is buried at Bari War Cemetery, however, it is possible that his death was connected to an explosion in Bari harbour.) The Bari War Cemetery contains 2,128 Commonwealth burials, and here Fred Wrenn's tombstone records how he lies in 'some corner of a foreign field that is forever England' – Rupert Brooke's immortal words written just before he lost his own life in this part of the world during WW1. Tragedy followed tragedy for, having lost their son, Fred's parents lived only another six years and were both buried on the same day in January 1951 in Clavering churchyard.

In Memory of
Sapper FREDERICK WRENN

2003295, 991 Port Operating Coy., Royal Engineers
who died age 27

on 09 April 1945
Son of Ernest and Lucy Wrenn;
husband of Winnifred Joan Wrenn

of Forest Gate, Essex.
Remembered with honour
BARI WAR CEMETERY

May 1945

My dear Friends

The good news from the war fronts has added to our joy in the eternal victory of the first Easter day. Here, in these parts, we have missed the English accompaniment of Easter – the spring weather and the spring flowers, and we must wait a few weeks yet before the snow will be off the mountains and the grass green once again. But Easter is the same wherever you are, and whether it was in our little chapel in a nissen hut, or in one of the ships after climbing up a 'Jacob's ladder', we were still able to join in the great family service. So, miles from home, we kept the great Christian Festival, and instead of worshipping in beautiful parish churches we gave thanks to God on mess decks, in holds and in nissen huts...

We shall need these great virtues if we are to turn this mad world into something that makes sense. We shall win the war of course, but what then? From time to time we have been warned against wishful thinking, yet there are millions who seem to believe that after the war we shall be in a brave new world. That is just blatant nonsense. Money won't do it. Bricks and mortar won't do it. Only a new spirit can do it – a new brotherhood – a new allegiance to a rule and way of life which is God's rule and God's way, not ours at all... As we look forward to happier days we shall need all the courage we can muster to follow the course we know to be right. These war years have been full of courage and heroism, shown by all ranks of the services and by many at home...

As the first disciples found, it will only be as we rely on our Saviour Christ, believing His promise, trusting not in our own strength but in the power which is from above, that we can look forward with hope.

Yours very sincerely, E.A. STONE

Returned Prisoners-of-War 1945

Returned Prisoners of War. We are thankful to be able to report that Tony Elwell, Sidney Law and Dennis Wombwell, who were until recently prisoners of war, have arrived home safely and in good health.

In the spring of 1945, Clavering welcomed back village men who had been prisoners-of-war in Europe, including Sid Law (b. 1923, photo 1944) who had joined up in 1941 and served in Germany, Africa and Italy before being taken prisoner in 1944 in North Italy, spending the last year of the war at Moosburg PoW Camp in Munich. The things he saw have never left his memory.

'Where I was at Moosburg next to Dachau concentration camp, there was a great big camp with all the German political prisoners. We used to be working on the railway in our clothes, and they were working in pyjamas and they had got no strength whatsoever, all they used to have was a bowl of soup and a glass of water... There used to be a dozen a day fall dead on the railway line when we were working. A bullock cart would come along and just pick them up. They were only bones and they would just stick in a fork and load them on the cart... We were better fed because we sometimes got two bowls of soup... I used to volunteer for work to get food and work every day seven to five... The camp next to where I worked, it was just black smoke... we did not know what was happening but discovered afterwards they were burning the people... they were making us clear the line so they could get more people down there to be burnt up. We did not know that until we were finished... Auschwitz was another big place on the Polish border. I went into lots of the places ... but I did not want to really look at them. I was a PoW only 12 months. That was the end of the war and for the last eight weeks of the war they asked for volunteers to go and dig air raid shelters and I went to Bavaria. I was digging air raid shelters up there for the Nazis until the war finished... I saw Goering and Mengele who was in charge of prisoners there. He is the one who murdered all the Jews in the camps. All the high-ranking German officers were there, hundreds and hundreds of them, then all of a sudden they had all vanished. The American Army came through where I was ... we were liberated by the 14th Armoured Division. I got released and then went to work for the Americans. We flew back to Belgium....' **Edited extracts: *Clavering Remembered* by Sid Law (2012).**

The more unfortunate PoWs in Japanese camps, were not released until after VJ Day in August. Frank Monk, who had lived at Parsonage Farm, Clavering, left his work as a woodsman to join up aged 20 in 1939, and went with the Cambridgeshire Regiment as a driver in January 1942 to Singapore, where he was sent straight into battle before he had time to unpack. After some fierce fighting defending Singapore against the Japanese, he was listed as missing in February, and then spent 3½ years as a PoW. Then came the horrors of forced labour on the building of the Burma Railway from Bangkok to Rangoon, where Frank was one of 240,000 Allied PoWs and Asian labourers working in terrible conditions – over 100,000 of them died. Frank never spoke in detail of his captivity. but he suffered appalling leg ulcers which almost resulted in amputation. By the end of the war he was working on airstrips in Thailand. But at least he came home – and lived to the age of 92 at his Berden home, one of the longest-lived survivors of the infamous Burma railway project.

Wartime Village Hall

Surely the most prescient development in Clavering was the building of a village hall in 1937, for this building became a huge asset to the Home Front when war came. It was only in peacetime use for a couple of years, and highlights included excellent play evenings put on in 1938 and early 1939 by the Saffron Walden Women's Institute – one forerunner of the emergence of Clavering Players post-war. In the first few years of the war, a lot of its success was thanks to Mr and Mrs A.E. Caton, and there was considerable dismay when they resigned as secretary and treasurer, 'on account of increasing pressure of their business' in January 1944. They had been active for nine years and their work had been so efficient that not only was there a profit for everyday needs, but a goodly sum for 'necessary improvements to the hall after the war'. This photo shows how the interior looked at this time – then just a basic one-room building, heated by two coal-burning Tortoise stoves and with Elsan toilets, but it did have a curtained stage perfect for concert parties and bands, and a good floor for dances. Up to 1937, the only meeting places had been the old clubroom in Church End and the schools, but they were unsuited to many events. Clavering needed a proper hall and in 1936 the Parish Council had paid £20 for a piece of waste ground owned by the Luckies brothers at the back of the forge opposite Hill Green. It took a huge amount of fund-raising to cover the £220 loan to build it, with whist drives, dances, raffles, cake stalls, flower shows, sports and sideshows. Lots of people contributed, and the stalwarts would go round the houses collecting pennies towards the hall. 'Rab' Butler, the local MP, declared the hall open on 18 October 1937 and presented the committee with a large electric clock to go inside.

Even before the official declaration of war, the hall had been designated by the ARP as a first-aid station, and a series of ARP lectures on first-aid organised. Here people came to collect their identity cards. Once war began, evening events could take place only if the windows were completely blacked out so that no chink of light escaped – not easy in a public hall with lots of windows. Corrugated iron was erected at the front of the hall too. When the evacuees arrived in large numbers, the hall provided temporary accommodation for a few nights while billets were sorted out, and every year a place where the little children far from home could enjoy a children's party using extra food permits supplied for the occasion, and a puppet show and games. The village hall minutes are rather sparse during the war period, but surviving snippets reflect some of the impact of the war. One of the first problems was that the village hall committee chairman, Lt Col Slingsby was called up to rejoin his regiment and had to resign his post, replaced by Vassar Rowe, the farmer of Curles. The committee decided to invest in War Bonds and later in the Clavering War Savings Group. In 1941, if the hall was to be used by troops, they decided to remove their precious crockery from the hall. Best remembered were the fortnightly dances ('sixpenny hops') when a number of bands became familiar visitors – the Mascot Band from Newport, the Delf Band run by Doug Luff and the Dansonian Dance Band run by Mike Preisig of Clavering. All this brought in plenty of income for the hall committee, who invested it in war bonds, as well as useful sums for wartime charitable causes and extra income for the band members. The dances (see p.65) formed a most important boost to morale during wartime – it is difficult to imagine where they could have taken place without the hall. Then there were the fortnightly whist drives, Boy Scout, Women's Institute and other club meetings – the whole panoply of community life opened up because of this wonderful facility, which also offered a venue for wartime needs. One example was a film show provided by the Ministry of Information in April 1941, a programme which 'dealt with various aspects of the war, the training of men and women for various branches of war work and life as it is lived in the great towns under air raid conditions. As we left the hall most of us must have been grateful that we lived in one of the safest parts of Britain', commented the vicar. Another was a free cooking demonstration by the Ministry of Food arranged by Mrs Stone, the Vicar's wife. There was no kitchen in the hall at that time, but the demonstrator used an oil stove to show how to make the best of wartime rations. The annual harvest camps, by which London schoolboys came to help with the harvest, were able to use the grounds for their tents and the village hall facilities, likewise the annual fetes which resumed once the worst war years had passed and raised money for various good causes. Socials and other meetings would be held for the big savings weeks, or just for fun and occasionally there was a special show. The best shows came at the end of the war, when the Home Guard staged a revue for their stand-down celebrations, and later the Cheerios Concert Party (see p. 164) put on shows to great acclaim from the audience which included Americans from local airbases. When the Forces came home in 1946, this is where the Homecoming events were held and the children's Victory parties – and this is where the village said goodbye to their Vicar in 1946 (see below). What a marvelous asset the hall had become – it is hard to see how the war could have been won in Clavering without it!

Clavering Village Hall **Annual Meeting**	At the end of the meeting several speakers expressed their deep appreciation of all that the Vicar had done for the village, and especially the Village Hall, and wished him well in his new work.

June 1945

OVERSEAS. My dear Friends,

It is a few days after the official ending of the war in Europe and so perhaps you would like to know something of the thoughts and the hopes of those who were away from home as this great news was proclaimed, and of our celebrations... Whenever possible, both ashore and afloat in H.M. Ships the 'lower deck was cleared' which means that the whole ship's company of officers and men met together and then we joined in a short act of thanksgiving... To men who had known the dangers of the sea and the violence of the enemy, who knew what it was to be torpedoed and mined, the words of the psalmist came with a new and greater meaning. Then a place was found for a remembrance of our brothers at the other side of the world in the battle which still goes on, and for all for whom the end of war is not the end of suffering. As far as we could, we kept VE day in the happiest way possible, even though here we are miles from any human habitation. Leave was granted until midnight, and His Majesty ordered 'Splice the Mainbrace', the signal for a double issue of rum to everyone. Home was foremost, I suppose, in most men's thoughts during the day. How many would like to have been able to share with their wives and families the rejoicing at the good news! The broadcast descriptions of celebrations in various parts of Great Britain were listened to with great interest and the BBC's efforts in this connection were greatly appreciated... We have met together in church on such a number of special occasions since the war began that I would have valued the privilege of being with you on VE day... my regret at not being with you all was tempered with gratitude at being of some small service to men who have endured far more perils, dangers and discomforts than we, who have been fortunate enough to spend most of the war in our own homes in the quiet and peace of Clavering and Langley, can ever imagine. What of the future? The cease fire in Europe does not mean that most of those in the Forces can catch the next boat home! Patrols must still go on searching for U-boats, minefields must be swept and convoys of ships must be escorted... Vast forces must still be employed on the continent and our navy and air force must hasten to help those who have been engaged in the War in the East, that there too victory may not be long delayed. To the completion then of our task must we all devote ourselves, both at home and abroad.

Yours most sincerely, E.A. STONE

The PRAMS BREAK THROUGH

Our children
are advancing
all along the line.
Advancing
into the future.
For their enemies
are scattered—
the haters and killers
are destroyed.
And the Prams
are charging forward
into the parks
into the playgrounds
on to the village greens
into the sunshine
of Peace,
and Security,
and Health,
and Education,
and happier living.
As we fought
and worked
and saved
to destroy their enemies,
let us fight
and work
and save
for our children—
for the larger victory
of Britain's future.

THANKSGIVING WEEKS

Winning the war did not mean the end of savings drives, now called Thanksgiving Weeks, with emotive advertisements like this one in the local newspapers.

VE Day Celebrations

And so the Second World War finally ended, first in Europe on 7th/8th May, then in the Far East on 14th August. The lights went on again and bells rang out once more all over England. Huge crowds celebrated in London, and every village and town joined in the two-day holiday. In Clavering for VE Day there was much joy with bonfires, parties and services.

> ## CLAVERING
>
> VE-DAY was celebrated with the ringing of the church bells at 3.30 p.m. and again before the service in the evening. The church was full and an appropriate service was conducted by the Rev. F. G. Albany, of Farnham. Bonfires were lighted after darkness fell and on Wednesday evening a Victory Social was held in the Village Hall. The morning service on Thanksgiving Sunday was attended by members of the Red Cross Detachment, Fire Service, Air Raid Wardens, A.T.C., Home Guard, and Girl Guides who carried the colours. Major M. D. Seaton (lay reader) conducted the service.

The Homecoming Forces Fund had been in operation since 1944 and was swelled with an outburst of activities throughout 1945 - village hall dances, Forces Week, concerts, the Red Revels Concert Party, the Victory show, Clavering fete and other events that memorable summer. In the autumn about 100 boys and girls had their own Victory party in the Village Hall, enjoying tea, games and entertainment by Clown Bertram. The celebrations revived in 1946, when the finally troops came home. Here are two personal memories.

'It was a time of celebration, and I remember the bonfire that was quickly built on the village green in Langley, and the feelings and emotions that people were experiencing, and it was said that one returned soldier ran through the village firing a shotgun in the air when he first heard the news! It took some time for things to come back to normal, but with people returning from the Forces, and reconstruction taking place, gradually things changed, and while it would never be quite the same as in pre-war days, a new era began to take shape.'
Douglas Savill

'We were all thankful when we heard that the War had ended, and there were parties going on all around. I still kept on working as my husband did not get demobbed until 23 January 1946 but he had leave for the Christmas which was very nice. We had a party and he dressed up as Father Christmas, my sisters were with us for Christmas Day and the children were so excited. I was out delivering meat the day he came home, and when I got back to the shop, George (the Manager) said, "There has been someone here to see you, so you will have to go home and find out". I was soon on my bicycle and home and of course it was him home at last.'
Isobel Beckwith

VJ Day - August 1945

(published in September magazine)

My dear Friends,

The news last week of the unconditional surrender of Japan has brought unutterable relief to all of us. For ten years there has been war in the world and we ourselves for almost six years have been at total war. For much of these six years Britain was placed in the front line of the battle, for agonising months we were in imminent peril of invasion. At any moment we might have lost not only our freedom, but everything that makes life decently and genuinely human. We were spared that horror... War leaves the world worse off spiritually no less than materially... We have all read the flood of letters and articles in the press regarding the latest triumph of human genius, the atomic bomb...

Yours most sincerely, E.A. STONE

CLAVERING

VICTORY CELEBRATIONS.—A Victory Peal rung on the Church bells in the middle of the day marked the first day of the Victory holiday in Clavering. In the evening there was a large congregation for a service of thanksgiving in the Parish Church, which was conducted by the Vicar (Rev. E. A. Stone, R.N.V.R.), who was home on leave. The bell-ringers again rang a peal before and after this service. On Thursday evening the Village Hall was lent back to the village by the Harvest Campers, who were using it during August, and a very large number joined in a Victory party. There were games and competitions for all ages, and dancing. Miss Joyce Baker proved a competent pianist.

Royal Navy Leading Signalman John Bowles was serving in the Far East on HMS Cumberland, when the atomic bomb was dropped. He still has this 1945 postcard showing scenes from the Japanese surrender.

162

October 1945

My dear Friends

For these last few months of my time in H.M. Forces I am chaplain to a Royal Naval Air Station in Sussex... In my talks with people just now it seems that there is creeping on a subtle mood of disillusionment rather akin to that feeling that we must have had as children as we watched a precious building in the sand on which we had worked so hard, gradually disappear before the tide. There is an impatience about things today resulting in a feeling of frustration in our young folk. A great war has been won which required our every effort and now in the rush to settle down to a more normal way of life, hindrances and restrictions seem to obstruct us. The change from war to peace may at times be a weary journey and there may be stumbles and painful halts, but we must keep on. We must still hold on to our dream of better things even if they seem a long time coming true...

Yours sincerely, E.A. STONE

December 1945

Very soon now we shall be keeping the festival of Christmas " for the first time for six years " in a world that is not at war. Christmas in these last few years has been spent in some strange places by some of us. Sometimes in barracks with comrades all round or perhaps in isolated posts with only two or three to share the meal. Others have been on the high seas and some in hospitals and sick bays. But wherever it has been we have thought of those from whom we were separated. I remember last Christmas Eve, when with inches of snow on the ground, our " nissen-hut-church " was full of men who had come to join in the midnight celebration of Holy Communion. " It came upon the midnight clear " we sang, and I have been at few more inspiring services.

What of Christmas in this year 1945? Despite the continuance of wartime conditions and all the suffering and hardship there is to be found, and despite the grim possibilities of atomic energy, we shall all have again the same expression on our lips, " A happy Christmas." In a number of homes it will be a case of " four feet on the fender " again after a lapse of years, as someone once defined a home. Fathers and brothers, many of them at least will be back at home, even if it is only for Christmas leave, and the ancient toast of " wives and sweethearts " will not have to be given so many hundreds of miles away. But wherever we shall be, let us thank God for our homes on Christmas Day. It doesn't take so very much to make a home, not a great big house, nor a lot of money, nor a car. It takes a bit of faith and a bit of patience, rather a lot of trust and unselfishness (more than some people think), and all the love that we have in us. We have to do our share and God does His share and then we've got that wonderful thing we call home.

The Cheerios

At the end of the war, everyone was having parties, and the spirit of the times was nowhere better expressed than in the jolly japes of the Cheerio's Concert Party, who gave several shows in the village hall in 1945-46, including a Christmas pantomime, *Aladdin*. Joan Trower (nee Jackson) was then aged about 20, and remembers how the younger people of the village, led by Doug Luff and Biddy Glasscock, were organised by Frank Talbot with rehearsals at Clatterbury House. The illustration below shows the programme for the spring 1946 Homecoming show, still recalled by Joan: 'I remember the sketch, 'Cycling Through' in this programme - Freddie Sampford and I were on the stage on two bicycles with fixed wheels and I was Freddie's girlfriend, being brought to Clavering.' Below is a local newspaper report on the summer 1945 Victory show when Joan was also on stage.

' The young people of Clavering and district gave their Victory Show, 'Smiling Through' to two packed houses in the Village Hall on June 29th and on July 14th. The production was by Douglas Luff and consisted of choruses, songs, duets (pianoforte and vocal), cross-talk, a cowboy scene and a farce entitled 'Hang it'. The members of the cast were Olive Bowles, Joyce Baker, Joyce Buckley, Faith Goodwin, Biddy Glasscock, Joy Hubbard, Joan Jackson, Joan Ward, John Barltrop, Gordon Bridges, John Caton, Charlie Evans, Douglas Luff, Peter Law, Stanley Rushant and Donald Saggers. The audience on both evenings was most appreciative and there seems to be a demand for further performances in other villages. The company are much indebted to Messrs E Abrahams, Eric Chapman, R Law, F. Walford as scene shifters, D. Sullivan as curtain steward, Mrs. F. Talbot and Mr. E. King as dressers, Messrs Cook, Glasscock, J. Luff and E. Martin as stewards; and to Messrs A. Darby, F. Talbot and H. Wisbey who were responsible for the excellent lighting effects. financially too, the shows were a great success, £31 having been raised for the Clavering Forces Fund and £26 for the Essex War Relief Fund.'

Part I	PROGRAMME	Part 2
1 . . OPENING CHORUS - - - - Company		1 . . CAN CAN - - John, Peter, Doug, Stan, Freddie
2 . . THE TEN LITTLE NIGGERS - - Boys' Chorus		2 . . SONG - - - - - - - Olive
3 . . THE WAITER - John, Joan, Bid, Faith, Freddie, Stan, Peter		3 . . ONE GOOD TURN - - Bid, Stan, Joan, Peter
4 . . SONG OF SONGS - - - Bid and Doug		4 . . SONG - - - - - - Doug
5 . . CYCLING THROUGH - - Joan and Freddie		5 . . SNOW WHITE SELECTION - Boys' and Girls' Chorus
6 . . 50 STORIES IN 5 MINUTES - John, Freddie, Peter, Stan		6 . . MACNAMARAS' BAND - - John, Joan, Bid, Doug
7 . . CHICKERY CHICK - - - Girls' Chorus		7 . . HOTEL SERVICE - - Freddie, Stan, Joy, Peter, Olive
8 . . SONG - - - - - Freddie		8 . . LET THE PEOPLE SING - - - - Albert
9 . . FARMYARD CAPERS - - - - Company		9 . . FINALE - - - - - Company

'THANK YOU' to all who have helped with the Show in any way

Children's Christmas Parties

Almost every year throughout the war, Clavering provided a wonderful party for its evacuees, with financial help from London County Council. The first was in December 1939 when somehow 150 children and 50 foster parents squeezed into the Village Hall, 'a great day for the children of Clavering.... made possible by the generosity of several local residents and a gift from the borough of Tottenham. After games the evacuated children presented two plays and the party concluded with an excellent conjuring performance by Mr J.W. Humphries of Saffron Walden.' They went one better at the 1942 party and engaged Mrs Nancy Henry, one of the most famous puppeteers of her day, who thrilled everyone with a puppet show. It was a great disappointment when she was too in ill to come in 1943, but 80 children enjoyed a tea which 'presented a prewar appearance' with cakes and jellies (see newscutting above). The 1944 party was postponed into early 1945 but the Vicar was missing as he was away on chaplaincy duties – the children were delighted when Mrs Stone gave out a gift of chocolate from him. There was an ample tea prepared by Mrs Morgan and her helpers and lots of games. A special guest was Alan Rhodes, who had been headmaster of Clavering School in the early 1930s and was now Deputy Education Officer for Essex, who 'spoke to the children and recalled the days in which he had taught their fathers and mothers and older brothers and sisters'. They also this time had a return visit from puppeteer, Mrs Nancy Henry, whom the children welcomed as an old friend and 'the puppets expressed the wish of everybody – that 1945 will bring us peace'. And so it proved. After six years of war, the final children's party went ahead for the village children in December 1945, even though all the evacuees had by then returned home, so no extra money or food permits were available from London County Council.

The tradition of children's parties resumed later organised by the Clavering British Legion. Many of these children would have been born during the war, and this photo taken in 1951 at the Village Hall must reflect a similar scene to those wartime events.

Chapter Nine
Post-war: 'The circle of the community'

The year after the war finished was a strange time, as people slowly re-adjusted to the longed-for peace, but in a country impoverished by the effort of winning the war. Once again, the Vicar reflected the changing moods, writing in January about how tired some people were, 'tired of waiting, tired of hoping, almost tired of trying'. Others realised how much they had to be thankful for. Many were still waiting for demob including the Vicar himself, but he wrote about the mixed feelings everyone would have, and how the villages needed to find a new sense of community: 'Unless in a village we do live as a true community supporting one another in efforts for the good of the whole village, what hope is there that the world can become a community of nations!' And he observed:

> I passed by this afternoon the building in London where the Conference of the United Nations is meeting. As I gazed up at the array of flags, one for each nation repre-sented, which adorned the outside, I could not help thinking of the tremendous problems facing those who would establish peace on a sure and firm foundation. What need there is for prayer that all who are engaged in these giant tasks may be guided by the true light!

JANUARY 1946: My Dear Friends

We know what sort of welcome is awaiting our men who have been away from us for such a long time – a rapturous and thankful welcome at being once again safe in the family circle. But this will be only the immediate reaction and the time comes when the first flush of enthusiasm dies down, when the everyday round of domestic life has to be resumed and the returning man or woman has to fit himself again both into his home life, and into a civilian life which is so different from the one he has been living for years past. The family are all much older than they were before the break-up; those who have been away, as a result of seeing the world and taking part in great adventures, have gained experiences not shared by those at home. But the stay-at-home members of the family have endured too in a way which it is difficult for others to understand. It is going to be a testing time for that family before they find again a mutual understanding, sympathy, and respect, upon which to build a happy home...We have to bring back during this coming year our returning men and women into the circle of the community...

Yours most sincerely, E.A. STONE

Clavering rose to the challenge, and there was a revival of enthusiasm for bellringing, church choir and sport, with the resumption of both cricket and football. Ever since she came to the parish in 1937, the Vicar's wife, Mrs Doris Stone had been the local Earl Haig Poppy Day organiser, and now ex-servicemen took up this work. A Clavering & District branch of the British Legion, with 40 ex-servicemen was formed in November 1946, covering four villages. Claude Simmonds was chairman and Lt Col Thomas Slingsby president. The founding members included Jack Livings, still a Legion stalwart today. The branch was popular, rapidly rising to 150 members. These photos (see opposite) show a Legion parade down Pelham Road and the first branch dinner in the village hall in 1946, with local men who had served their country in time of war.

Another event in the Livings family in 1946 was the resignation of Nurse Blodwen Livings (pictured left) who had been District Nurse for 14 years and looked after everyone through the war: 'She has always been a welcome visitor to our homes. Countless babies must have come into the world by her aid and Clavering, Arkesden and Langley who have shared her services will be sorry at her resignation', commented the Vicar, while Dr Browne and Dr Salaman spoke of her 'unfailing cheerfulness which helped to cure a patient quite as much as her practical ministrations'. A few years after the war, however, tragedy befell Nurse Livings when she died of tetanus after being scratched by barbed wire.

There were other events that first year after the war, including another show from the Cheerios, a pantomime which raised another sum towards the Clavering Homecoming Forces Fund, which was shortly wound up at £688 with a final list of recipients published (see Appendix 1). Mrs. Luff wrote out a roll of honour which was framed and put up in church, and a gift of six guineas with a certificate designed by artist Allen Mold was given to each one at a special event in the village hall (see p.171). The official day for Victory celebrations was not until 8th June 1946, and Clavering Parish Council raised a special rate to pay for a busy programme of children's sports, a social with games, dancing and a talent competition, ending with a bonfire on Hill Green. Wet weather hit the outdoor sports, but the younger children had their own victory party in November. No photos of these momentous events have come to light, but in 1995 Clavering commemorated the 50th anniversary of VJ Day on Hill Green (pictured below), and later in the village hall, the same places where celebrations had taken place in 1945.

Villagers gathered in front of the Methodist Chapel on Hill Green in August 1995 to celebrate the 50th anniversary of VJ Day.

And so, slowly, life got back to normal - although years of austerity lay ahead, the farming cycle had to keep going, and very soon the Vicar's 1939 prediction about combine harvesters would come true: 'that mechanical monster which in passing through the cornfields converts the standing corn into threshed grain and straw. No sheaves to be set up in the field, no pitching into wagons, no building of ricks, no threshing later in the autumn, all is achieved at one single stroke. The expense of such machines I understand is at present too high for them to be very common but who knows what changes may come in the next ten years!' In fact, it took slightly less than his predicted ten years – this Massey-Harris was in use at Sheepcote Green Farm by 1948, one of the first of the 'mechanical monsters' that would continue the wartime transformation of farming.

Clavering Welcomes Ex-Servicemen

Social and Presentation in Village Hall

On Monday evening, in the Village Hall, Clavering people gave their official welcome home to the men and women of the village who had served in the Forces. A large number of the hundred men and women in the Services were able to be present with their friends.

The proceedings opened with the singing of the National Anthem and this was followed by a minute's silence in memory of the five men from the village who were killed in action.

Everybody enjoyed a very good meal and the opportunity it gave of renewing acquaintance with a number who had been away for several years.

Following the meal the Cheerio Concert Party presented their "Cheeri Show," produced by Douglas Luff.

In the interval Mr. H. T. Cook (chairman of the Welcome Home Fund), supported by Miss B. Glasscock and Mr. D. Luff (hon. secretaries) and the Vicar (hon. treasurer), welcomed those present.

One by one the men and women went to the platform to receive an envelope containing six guineas, together with a suitably engraved card designed by Mr. Mold and portraying a view of the village, with a suitable message of appreciation.

The Chairman briefly referred to the various efforts that had been undertaken in the past few years to raise the money for a suitable welcome home, and the eagerness of everyone to help the funds.

Mr. D. Luff referred to the willing help and co-operation he had always had.

Comradeship of the Services

The Vicar (Rev. E. A. Stone, R.N.V.R.), in a brief speech, said that he belonged, as it were, to both sides of the footlights, for he was both treasurer of the fund and a returning Serviceman. He had never known such a generous response to any fund as there had been to the Welcome Home Fund, which had reached a total of nearly £700. He reminded those present that in all the strange and unfamiliar places they had been during the war years, it was always the thought of home and their families that made their life worth while. It was a great day to be officially welcomed home: Could they, he asked, bring back that experience of comradeship they had all found in the Services, for if so, village life would be greatly enriched.

Mr. Jack Livings thanked, on behalf of the recipients, all who had in any way helped towards making the evening such a memorable occasion and this was heartily endorsed with rousing cheers.

Members of the Concert Party then continued their show, which was received with great applause, and at the end Mr. Cook thanked all who had taken part in the concert and congratulated the young people on their performance.

The cast of the Cheeri Show were: Olive Bowles, Beddy Glasscock, Faith Goodwin, Joy Hubbard, Joan Jackson, Joan Ward, John Bunting, Peter Gowlett, Douglas Luff, Stanley Rushant, Fred. Sampford.

Girls' Chorus: Sylvia Barnard, Rosy Bowles, Ruby Bowles, Dorothy Foster, Connie Gibbs, Betty Law, Audrey Monk, Joyce Monk, Doreen Rogers. Boys' Chorus: Brian Atkinson, Gordon Atkinson, George Evans, Derek Frostick, Brian Kemp, Hugh Law, Michael Livings, Clive Matthews, Malcolm Smither, Philip Wootton.

THE
CHEERIOS
CONCERT PARTY

present

CHEERI SHOW

Produced by Douglas Luff

Friday - 24 May - 1946
Saturday, 25 May 1946

Local newspaper report on the exciting event on Monday 27th May 1946 when Clavering welcomed home the villagers who had served in the Forces and entertained them with the Cheeri Show (see p.164) which had already been performed the previous weekend. All the recipients of the Clavering Homecoming Forces Fund (see Appendix 1) were invited to receive a gift of six guineas and a copy of Allen Mold's welcome home card (see p.171).

Some of the Clavering people in the Kings Forces WW2.

Welcome Home 1946

On your return home from serving in H.M. Forces in the Second World War of 1939 to 1945, the residents of Clavering wish to mark by this card and the accompanying gift, their appreciation that you left the comfort of your home in the village in the service of your King and Country.

CLAVERING · ESSEX

Professional artist Allan Mold designed this special card which was given to all the homecoming Forces members along with a cash gift from the village when they returned to Clavering in 1946. Allan was one of those who came to Clavering to escape the Blitz, and never left. He lived with his mother and sister at Sticklings Green, and their cottage became a refuge for other London evacuees. His sister Rosamund worked on the land during the war. Allan was a distinguished artist, a member of several art societies and exhibited at the Royal Academy. When he died aged only 46 in 1952, there were warm tributes to his great abilities and personality.

Departure of the Vicar

The Vicar was demobbed in 1946 and came back to Clavering, but decided his work was done and it was time to move on, telling a local newspaper reporter: 'There is a tendency for country clergy, particular the younger ones, to remain too long in one spot'. Wife Doris had just given birth to a second daughter, Clare, and they were off to Clymping in Sussex where he would both run a parish and also continue as civilian Chaplain in the Fleet Air Arm. He announced this in May 1946 and left in October. Rev Ernest Stone would return to Clavering 40 years later by invitation to lecture about his years in wartime Clavering. But he remained in Sussex until his death at the age of 94 in 2004, his wife having died many years earlier. A final letter to his parishioners modestly summarises an incumbency of huge challenge and achievement.

> Looking back over these nine years and thinking of the momentous happenings that have taken place in the world during that time one is grateful for the opportunity of being of some small help to you during these most difficult years. The war with its problems made life very complicated for us all, I hope I was able to solve some of the difficulties you brought to me.

My dear Friends,
It is nearly nine years since I became your vicar and how much has happened during that time! The war, and preparing for the war, seem to have occupied most of the time. In spiritual things it is terribly easy to settle down and the parson in a village tends to become an 'institution' almost part of the fabric of the place, after some years. It is because I feel this temptation so strongly that I have decided that it is right for you and for me, that there should be a change... I remember the Bishop inviting me to come and be Vicar of Clavering with Langley, he was not quite sure whether it was right for a young man to come to a country parish. I was then only 28 years old but he regarded me as somewhat of an experiment... My wife and I came among you at the end of our honeymoon and set up our home at the Vicarage. We shall always carry with us the memory of the warmth of your welcome and the help and kindly interest that you have always shown towards us. We found plenty to do in those early years in the beautifying of our churches and fortunately shortages and coupons were unheard of then... I remember my wife spending many months over ecclesiastical embroidery and the almsbags, pulpit frontals and veils and burses are mostly her work... And so I take my leave of you... May God's blessing be upon you and your families and upon your work.
Yours most sincerely, E.A. STONE

The Vicar's new living was accompanied by a continuation of his wartime chaplaincy work, at HMS Peregrine. Civilian chaplains were a new idea and Rev. Stone had to get special permission from Whitehall. One of his final duties here was to chair the annual meeting of Clavering Village Hall, when those present 'expressed their deep appreciation of all that the Vicar had done for the village and wished him well in his new work'. Here are the memories of a child, June Holland (nee Riley), who experienced their kindness.

'Reverend Stone was very parish orientated. When my stepfather died, Mr Stone came to our house in the Druce and said that he had a call from Addenbrookes and he was very seriously ill. He said he would take my mother to the hospital. He waited all night and brought her back in the morning. I liked Reverend Stone very much. As a child I liked anyone who would give me the time of day and say a few words to me because I never got any in my house. He liked children. Mrs Stone was a tall lady, very kind, very caring. She organised all the choir gowns, very good at sewing, cleaned the brass, organised the children's corner – the Guides went camping with Mrs Stone, and she organized a first aid group, Junior Red Cross.'

A later tribute to Doris Stone, at her funeral in 1990, described her brilliance as a teacher, a deep interest in botany, her sensitive mothering, thrift and skills at needlework, cookery and gardening, the hospitality of the vicarage and her deep faith. By all accounts, therefore, Clavering and Langley were exceedingly fortunate to have this remarkable couple at the helm during this critical time.

Photographs lent by Judith Bridger (nee Stone), born in 1938, with her father Ernest in the vicarage garden in 1941 and outside Clavering Church with her mother Doris in 1942. Most of the Vicar's nine-year incumbency was spent helping the villages prepare and get through the war, and sort out its aftermath.

Then the Stone family packed up and departed from the Vicarage and it really was the end of an era, a unique and extraordinary time in the history of Clavering – and a period of which we would know very little but for the record kept by the Vicar in the parish magazine, copies of which he later donated. Through this book, *Clavering at War*, the author hopes that the legacy of Ernest and Doris Stone and those with whom they shared the journey, on the Home Front in the village community and among the Kings' Forces, auxiliary services and civilian work in the wider war-torn world, can finally be given the recognition it deserves.

Postscript – Village War Memorials

The names of those who died in the war were afterwards inscribed on three village war memorials – in stone outside the Congregational Church (top), on wood inside the Parish Church (centre) and on a brass plaque (bottom photo) which used to be in the former Methodist Chapel. Only the first one has all six names and the plaques exhibit a variety of spellings, but the sentiment is the same: '*To the Glory of God... Greater Love Hath No Man Than This... They gave their lives for their friends*'.

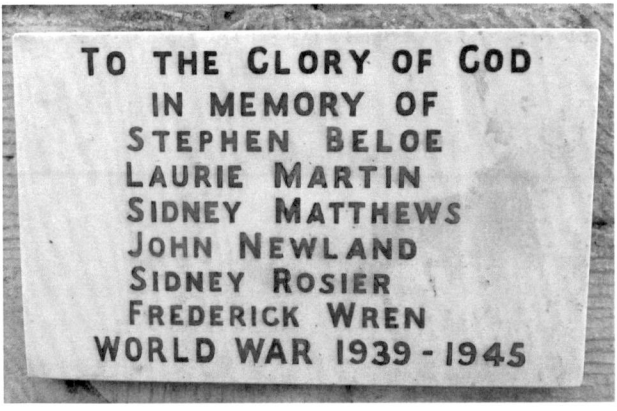

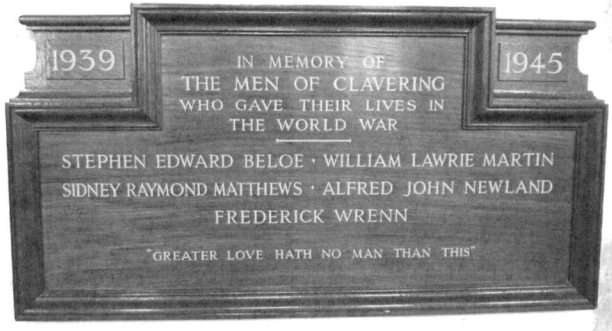

Appendix 1: Clavering Homecoming Forces Fund

In March 1946 a special committee, set up to administer the Homecoming Forces Fund, published a 'list of those who in the opinion of the committee and in accordance with the terms of the charity are the rightful recipients'. There were 101 names on the list, 89 men and 12 women, plus relatives of five of the six Clavering men who lost their lives. Quite a lot of names are missing, even though they had served in the Kings Forces, since they had to fit a certain criteria to have 'lived in the village three months before they joined up, or in the case of single men or women living away, that their parents lived in the village.' All of those on the list were given a cash present and certificate to mark their contribution to the war effort through service in the King's Forces.

Clavering Homecoming Forces Fund. We print below the list of those who in the opinion of the committee and in accordance with the terms of the charity are the rightful recipients.

Fred. Atkinson, Joseph Atkinson, Maurice Atkinson, Peter Atkinson, William Atkinson, William Bailes, Frank Baker, Reginald Baker, George Barker, Hubert Barker, Phillip Barker, Sidney Barker, Dennis Barnard, Leslie Barnard, Reginald Barnard, Walter Barnard, John Bowles, Peter Bowles, Sidney Bowles, Albert Buckley, Percy Burgess, Roger Carter, Norman Caton, William Caton, Anthony Creighton, Anthony Elwell, Cyril Elwell, Donald Elwell, Duncan Elwell, George Frostick, Fred. Gilbey, Bob Glasscock, Bert Hill, Jim Jackson, Percy Kemp, Reginald Kemp, Percy King, Stanley King, Richard Kybird, Fred. Law, Hubert Law, Kenneth Law, Leslie Law, Robert Law, Sidney Law, William Law, Dennis Ledward, George Livings, Jack Livings, Percy Livings, Ernest Matthews, Fred. Monk, Leonard Monk, Hayden Newland, Anthony Newton, Kenneth Newland, Reuben Newland, Jack Peacock, Eric Peel, Bernard Poulter, Eric Poulter, Kenneth Poulter, Leonard Poulter, Tom Poulter, Fred. Revell, John Riley, Ralph Rogers, Charles Seabrook, Claude Simmonds, Thomas Slingsby, Alfred Smither, Ernest Stone, Cecil Stone, Joseph Sweeting, Frank Tant, Peter Teale, Charles Turner, Eric Turner, Gordon Turner, Leslie Turner, Fred. Whyman, Derrick Wilson, Eric Wilson, Maurice Wombwell, Norman Wombwell, Leslie Woods, William Woods, Leonard Wrenn, Marjorie Baker, Jean Cooper, Irene Craig, Francis Davis, Olive Nicholson, Joyce Revell, Hilda Riley, Marie Riley, Joan Simmonds, Laura Slingsby, Joan Teale, Dorothy Whyman and the relatives of Stephen Beloe, Laurie Martin, Sidney Matthews, John Newland, Frederick Wrenn.

Appendix 3
Clavering
Residents 1940
(Source: *Harts Yearbook* 1940)

Abrahams, C. W., Farmer, Sheepcote Green
Ambrose, C., Stortford Road
Anderson, Gen., Further Ford End
Andrews, C., The Town
Anthony, F., Lyndhurst, Pelham Road
Archer, F., Home Farm
Archer, H. F., Bell View, Stortford Road
Atkinson, C. H., Sandy View
Atkinson, E. Baker, Wicken Road
Atkinson, F. K., Council House

Atkinson, L. J., The Manse
Atkinson, M., Arkesden Road
Atkinson, R., Middle Street
Atkinson, S. D., Princess of Wales
Atkinson, S. P., Hill Green
Atkinson, W., The Druce
Bailey, L., Arkesden Road
Bailey, Mrs. Stortford Road
Baker, F. W., Wicken Road
Baker, H. G., Middle Street
Baker, Mrs. W. Arkesden Rd.
Baker, W., The Town
Barker, A., Police Constable, Wicken Road

Barker, E., Hall Cottages
Barker, J., Hall Cottages
Barker, S. J., "Waggon & Horses"
Barker, T., Court Cottage
Barltrop, T., Arkesden Road
Barnard, A., Bird Green
Barnard, H., Mill Lane
Barnard, H., Sticklings Green
Barnard, W., Middle Street
Barnes, F. W., Hill Green
Barnes, Miss H. B., 5, Church End
Beamish, E. V., Fairbank. Stortford Road
Beloe Mrs. E. A.. Hill Green
Blackborow, A. E., Oakdene, Stortford Road
Blakesley, D. F., Lantern Thatch
Bowles, S., Hill Green
Boyton, S., Sheepcote Green
Brant, A. G., Lower Ford End Farm
Bristow, C., Starlings Green
Burgess, Mrs. F. G., Arkesden Road
Butcher, E., Starlings Green
Burgess, J., Middle Street
Byford, R., Middle Street
Cakebread, A., Sticklings Green
Cakebread, W., Hill Green
Carter, E., Pelham Road
Caton, A. E., Windy Ridge
Caton. Mrs. D., The Bungalow
Caton, E. W., General Stores, The Mill
Chapman, P. W., Clavering
Chapman, Mrs. S., Starlings Green
Chesham, H., Hill Green
Cheshire, G. A., Starlings Green
Choat, G. T., Pelham Road
Clark, A. L., Sticklings Green
Clarke, Mrs M., Sticklings Green

Clarke, A., Hill Green
Clarke, J., Boot Repairer, The Town
Claydon, F. J., Wicken Road
Claydon, W., Mill Cottage
Cole, J., The Druce
Cole, J. P., Arkesden Road
Cook, G. A., Wicken Road
Cook, H. T., Chestnuts, Arkesden Road
Cooper, E. B., Farm Bailiff, Thurrocks Farm
Copeland, B. F., Chequers Cott.
Copeland, F., Brocking Farm
Copeland, L. A., Bird Green
Creighton, Mrs, Middle Street
Custerson, Mrs F. A., Farmer, Ford End
Davis, A. H., Church End
Deards, E., Wayside, Pe'ham Rd
Ellis, T.. Deers Green
Elwell, R. S., Hill Green
Emmett, Mrs. E., Hillside, Hill Green
Estall, Mrs. C.. Arkesden Rd.
Fawley, Miss R., Kells, Stortford Road
Finzell, H. C. The Court
Foster, A.. Yew Tree Farm
Foster, C. D., Yew Tree Farm
Foster, H., Deers Green
Foster, G., Yew Tree Farm
French, F., Church End
French, W., Church End
Frostick, H., Greenscroft
Funston, E., Farmer, Clavering Place
Gammon, P. W., Clavering
Gayler, E. H., Wicken Road
George, E., Sticklings Green
Glasscock, Mrs. M. Post Office
Glasscock, Mrs E. Hill Green
Glasscock, T. C., Pelham Road
Godfrey, G. K., Brocking
Hanly, A., Middle Street

Harding, Mrs S. K., Bank View
Hawkes, J. F.. "White Horse", Starlings Green
Hill, Miss F. E., The Cottage, Hill Green
Hill, T. Wicken Road
Hogg, Mrs. C. E., Rottingdean
Howard, J., Greenlands, Wicken Road
Jackson, Mrs. D., The Druce
James, Mrs. A., The Oak
Jeffrey, C., Sticklings Green
Jeffrey, N., Hill Green
Jones, E.. Sheepcote Green
Joslin, J., Builder, Ware Pond
Kell, C. A., Farmer, Pelham Road
Kemp, D. Middle Street
Kemp, F., Farmer, Moat Farm
Kemp. F. G., Moat Farm
Kemp, H. W., Middle St
Kemp, L. P., Deers Green
King, A.. The Swan
King, A. D., Brooklands
King, H., Near Mills
Kybird, E.. The Stores
Larkins, — Ruttells
Law, B., The Town
Law, Mrs. E., Middle Street
Law, F., Middle Street
Law, G., Yew Tree Farm
Law, Joseph, Wicken Road
Law, R., Sticklings Green
Law, W., Council House
Lewis, A. P. 4, Church End
Lincoln, Miss A. C., Sheepcote Green
Lincoln Miss C., 5, Council Cotts.
Lindsay, P., Ponds Manor
Livings, C., Church End
Livings, G.. Middle Street
Livings, Miss O.. Church End
Livings, P. J., Hill Green
Livings, W. R., Stortford Rd

Lloyd, Miss E. C., Bungalow, Chapel Meadow
Luckock, R. H., The Old House
Luff, J. R., The Willows
Maguire, Miss J., Sheepcote Green
Martin, C. E., Builder and Undertaker, Hill Green
Martin, J. H., Pelham Road
Martin, The Misses, Home Farm
Matthews, A., Starlings Green
Matthews, E., Ponds Cottages
Matthews, H. C.. Sticklings Green
Matthews, J., Ponds Cottages
Matthews, L., Arkesden Rd
Matthews, W. J., Deers Green
Maynard, Miss R.. 5 Council Cottages
Monk, Albert, Bird Green
Monk, Arthur, Bird Green
Monk, L. 6 Council Cottages
Monk, T. W., Church End
Monk, W., Rounds Road
Monk, W.. Bird Green
Monk, W.. The Druce
Monk, W.. Sticklings Green
Morgan, D., Pleasant View, Hill Green
Morris, Miss E.. The Nook, Stortford Road
Mossman, Mrs M. Pelham Rd
Mynott. A., Drucecroft
Napier, J. C., Appletree Cott.
Neville, Mrs, Arkesden Road
Newland, A. W., Sheepcote Green
Newland, C., Council Cottages
Newland, J., Ponds Cottages
Newland, J., Pelham Gates
Newland, L., Inn., Pelham Gates
Newland, R., Starlings Green
Newman, Mrs M. A., Middle Street
Newton, T., Sticklings Green
Nickolson, Miss O., North View, Pelham Road

Noble, F., Parsonage Farm
Nunn, Miss H., Church End
Parish, H., Starlings Green
Peacock, J., Wicken Road
Peacock, W. W., Butcher, Arkesden Road
Piggott, R., Sticklings Green
Popham, A. D., Fox and Hounds
Poulter, J., Wicken Road
Prime, Miss M., Stortford Rd.
Read, A. G., Mill Lane
Reed, Mrs. E., Arkesden Rd.
Revell, S., Farm Bailiff, Hill Green
Revell, W., Hill Green
Reynolds, A. E., Hill Green
Richardson, A. J., School-master, Pelham Road
Rogers, D., Sticklings Green
Rogers, O., Middle Street
Rogers, R. S., Sheepcote Green
Rogers, W. J., Elmstead Cottage
Rolfe, P., The Bury
Rowe, P. V. H., Farmer, The Hall
Rowe, V. H., Farmer, Curls Farm
Rust, E., Stort Cottage
Rust, F., Wicken Road
Sandwith, Mrs, Thatched Cottage, Hill Gren
Sear, Mrs. E., Wicken Road
Sell, C., Arkesden Road
Sheldon, C. W., Home Farm Cottage
Simmonds, C. J., Piercewebbs Cottage
Skinner, Misses, Hill Cottage
Slingsby, Lt.-Col. T., Danceys
Smith, Mrs. G., Starlings Green
Smith, J., Danson, Stortford Green
Smith, W. & A., Farmers, Roast Farm

Smither, A. W., Stortford Rd
Sonneborn, A. E. H., Mill End Farm
Stevens, Miss E., Sheepcote Green
Stickland, J. J., Yew Tree Cottage, The Druce
Stock, S. J., Baker and Grocer, Sheepcote Green
Stone, A., Stortford Road
Stone, Rev. E. A., The Vicarage
Swannell, W., Starlings Green
Talks, R., Starlings Green
Teale, H. E., Valence Manor
Tebbs, T., The Bungalow
Trustrum, F. T., 1 Church End
Turner, C. G., Pelham Gate
Walford, F. E., Wicken Road
Walford, J. E., Hill Green
Walford, J. F., Hill Green
Walker, F. J., Curls Farm
Waters, G., Mill Lane
Webling, G. C., Church End
Wheeler, F., Ford End
White, C., Wicken Road
White, H. G., Hill Green
Whyman, J. N., Hill Green
Whyman, H., The Druce
Whyman, P. A., Mill Lane
Whyman, W., Deers Green
Williams, H., The Bower
Wilson, E., Bird Green
Wilson, E., Sticklings Green
Wilson, H. & Son, Newsagents
Wisbey, Mrs K., Middle St
Wolsey, F. G., Arkesden Road
Wombwell, B., Arkesden Rd.
Wombwell, N., Hill Green
Wombwell, W. G., Chapel Cottage
Woodham, Mrs. S. J., Wicken Road
Wright, H., Church End

Appendix 3: Clavering Chronology 1937-1946

1937: Rev. Ernest Stone appointed Vicar of Clavering and Langley.

1938: ARP classes started.

1939: <u>Feb</u> - census of evacuee accommodation taken. <u>May</u> – ARP wardens appointed, Red Cross branch set up. <u>June</u> - first local men called up for national service; evacuee arrangements in place. <u>July</u> – ARP exercise in garden of Old House. <u>Aug</u> - Blackout exercise. <u>Sept</u> – war broke out; evacuees from Tottenham arrived; school opening delayed. <u>Oct</u> - evensong moved to 3.30pm; 100 extra pupils in Clavering school; Danceys first-aid post set up. <u>Nov</u> - sewing parties started; wastepaper collection began. <u>Dec</u> – 200 evacuee & local children enjoyed Christmas party in village hall. Searchlight camp set up 1939-40.

1940: <u>Feb</u> -appeal for wastepaper. <u>March</u> - Walden Minstrel Troop performance; allotments offered for dig for victory. <u>May</u> – HE near the Mills; Searchlight camp appeal; War savings group set up. <u>June</u> – Sidney Rosier killed; Dunkirk survivors home; salvage meeting Bury Meadow; scrap-iron dumps set up; salvage controllers appointed. <u>July</u> – LDV formed; bellringing banned. <u>Aug</u> – first air raid warnings; cricket matches suspended except ladies' team; Bobby Jeff RAF killed. <u>Sept</u> – national day of prayer; HE at the Mills; Parsonage Farm destroyed by incendiaries; good harvest; sewing parties completed 1,000 garments in first year; Spitfire savings appeal. <u>Oct</u> – Blitz heard in Clavering; more evacuees arrived. <u>Nov</u> - complaint re Home Guard Sunday parades. <u>Dec</u> – HE in Clavering. War Resisters Farm set up 1940-41.

1941: <u>Feb</u> -evacuee parties. <u>March</u> – War Weapons Week; Ministry of Information film show. <u>April</u> – Stephen Beloe killed; Fire Watchers three groups every night; War Weapons savings campaign. <u>May</u> - nursing training course; Home Guard parades banned during Sunday services; jam-making scheme; Laurie Martin killed. <u>June</u> –evacuee survey; jam centre set up. <u>July</u> - youth club meeting; salvage drive; Pig Club formed. <u>Aug</u> – Invasion Committee set up; Church insured for £400 contents; Brownie Pack formed; schoolboys harvest camp. <u>Sept</u> - lorryload of old iron sent off. Searchlight camp moved to new site next to Clavering Hall farm in 1941. National Fire Service in 1941.

1942: <u>Jan</u> – Vicar became RAFVR Chaplain; ATC set up. <u>Feb</u> – Sidney Matthews killed. <u>April</u> - Warship Week savings campaign; night watching by Fire Guard discontinued. <u>May</u> – waste-paper salvage taken over by District Council. <u>July</u> - ATC flight set up. <u>Aug</u> - Vicar back in parish; schoolboys harvest camp. <u>Oct</u> - opening Village Youth Centre; Americans hospitality scheme started. <u>Nov</u> - postal order for 12s to all enlisted Clavering residents; Debdenairs concert in aid of RAF Benevolent Fund; no ringers 15th Nov victory of Battle of Egypt. <u>Dec</u> - church bells at Christmas.

1943: <u>Feb</u> – new minister Rev. W Morley Congregational church. <u>May</u> – bellringing permitted again. <u>June</u> - fresh vegetables sent by WVS to seamen; Army Cadets started; Wings for Victory savings campaign; book drive. <u>July</u> – Cubs & Scouts set up. <u>Aug</u> – schoolboys' harvest camp; Farm Sunday church parade; Fete village hall grounds. <u>Sept</u> - Langley Vicarage became Women's Land Army hostel. <u>Nov</u> – UXBs at Blacksmiths Corner. <u>Dec</u> – Guide Company formed.

1944: <u>Feb</u>- Vicar in council housing survey for District Council. <u>May</u> - Empire Youth Sunday service featured in *The Times*. <u>June</u> - American Liberator crash at the Mills. <u>Aug</u> - Vicar now Royal Navy chaplain; more evacuees; schoolboys harvest camp; Salute the Soldier savings campaign. <u>Sept</u> – John Newland killed. <u>Nov</u> - Invasion Committee disbanded.

1945: <u>April</u>- stand-down party Home Guard; Frederick Wrenn killed. <u>May</u> – VE Day celebrations; prisoners-of-war returned. <u>July</u> - National Fire Service party. <u>Aug</u> - Cheerios Concert party; VJ Day. <u>Oct</u> - vicar RNAS Chaplain; sewing parties wound up; Clavering Forces list drawn up.

1946: Clavering Forces Fund wound up; homecoming card designed by Allen Mold; Welcome Home party; cricket and football clubs restarting; Victory celebrations; homecoming show; roll of honour erected in church porch; children's victory party; departure of Rev. Ernest Stone after nine years as Vicar of Clavering & Langley.

Appendix 4: Wartime Clavering Walk

Distance: 4½ miles. Names in bold refer to relevant articles in the text – see index for page numbers. The full description can be found as Walk 9 in *History Walks in Clavering*, **by the author of this book. See Frontispiece map.**

Beginning at the **Village Hall**, this walk goes round the village centre and passes many places which have wartime associations. Walk across the Jubilee Field past the playground, then to the <u>right</u> of the tennis courts. At the bottom, turn <u>right</u> over a stile and along the Kingswater stream, crossing a footbridge at the end onto the road opposite **Clavering Court**. Turn <u>left</u> along the road past **Coley Lane**, through **Stickling Green** past Place Farm and veer <u>left</u> up to **Clavering Mills**. Turn <u>left</u> down the Mills hill, then where the road bends, turn <u>right</u> at the bottom along the back lane. After a short distance, turn <u>left</u> over a footbridge to the **Dam meadows**, through the kissing-gate to the **Parish Churchyard**. **Bury Meadow** is to the east of the churchyard. An empty yard beside the north churchyard is site of the former **Clavering Lower School**. The church tower houses the **Church bells**. The **Parish Church** has many reminders of the war. From the church go up through the gate to **Church End**, past the **Guildhall** and **The Old House**. Opposite Church End is Saville Close formerly site of the **Upper School**. Turn <u>right</u> along Pelham Road past **Piercewebbs** and the Old **Vicarage**. The field on the right was one of many ploughed up from pasture in WW2. Veer <u>left</u> up the hill, past **Curles Farm**, then turn <u>left</u> along a byway, Parsonage Lane. Just past **Parsonage Farm**, turn <u>left</u> along a waymarked footpath through the fields. Turn <u>left</u> across a waymarked footbridge, and along field-edges towards the road. Turn <u>left</u> past the **Pillbox** on the bank – the field just crossed once housed the Army Searchlight Camp. Over to the right is **Clavering Hall Farm**. Go down to the **Stortford Road** verge and turn left along the verge into the village – this passes **Clavering Shop**, Fairfield (where the Senior ARP Warden lived), the **Allotments**, the **School, Appletree Cottage** and the former Congregational Church (now Christian Centre) with its **War Memorial** in front. Turn <u>right</u> down the main road, passing **Danceys** on the other side of the road, **Blacksmiths Corner** (pictured below), past **Brooklands Farm** and over the **Bridges**. After passing the *Fox & Hounds*, follow the **High Street** past the former **Swan** pub down to **Hill Green** and so back to the Village Hall.

Blacksmiths Corner as it once looked - but road signs were removed during the war,

Appendix 5: Tips for Housewives

Wartime housewives were expected to make do and mend in all things, and the parish magazine each month offered readers' tips, a selection of which wartime hints and economies make quaint reading – potatoes had many uses!

- A raw peeled potato placed inside new tight fitting shoes and left overnight will result in comfortable fitting shoes next morning.
- Grate a raw potato and leave to soak for several hours in a little water. Dip a cloth in the liquid and use it to clean soiled coat collars.
- To keep your hands nice and soft and white, rub them over occasionally with a cold boiled potato.
- When baby first tries to walk, rub the soles of his shoes with raw potato. This prevents them from slipping.
- *Warts*: apply water, in which potatoes have been boiled, several times a day.
- *Cramp at night*: Take a dozen plain corks, tie loosely in butter muslin, and place at foot of bed between sheets. The corks absorb moisture and relax contracted muscles.
- *Headaches*: get a cabbage leaf, boil, squeeze out water, put on back of neck, repeat 2-3 times.
- *Chilblains:* mix together lard and dry mustard, a speedy cure.
- *Lumbago and sciatica*: mix well-beaten new laid egg white (or olive oil) with 1 tablespoonful of turpentine, sprinkle on flannel and apply to seat of pain.
- *Sleeplessness:* before going to bed eat a thin sandwich of bread and butter with a sprinkling of cayenne pepper between the slices.
- Slit Swan Vestas down the middle with a sharp knife = two matches instead of one.
- Living in 3rd floor flat, to hear baby crying in pram downstairs, hang microphone over pram.
- To keep baby safe make big wooden sugar box with castors and pull along as mother works in different rooms etc.
- *Corns:* scoop out hole in top of swede and fill with salt until liquid formed – bottle this and rub on corn night and morning for few days, then withdraw corn.
- *Hiccups:* old Chinese remedy, moisten small piece of newspaper with tongue and place in centre of forehead, forget all about it and you will find in a short time the hiccups have disappeared.

> A SUGGESTION FOR AIR-RAID LECTURES.—A flannelette blanket will become air-tight if dipped in this solution : $\frac{1}{4}$ lb. of sugar of lead and $\frac{1}{4}$ lb. of alum ; dissolve each separately in $2\frac{1}{2}$ gallons of water. Mix the two together, then soak the blanket in it for 12 hours. Dry. The same solution will make coats waterproof. (Mrs. F. GREENSTED.)

- When mattresses get hard and bunchy, rip them, take the hair out, pull it thoroughly by hand, let it lie a day or two to air, wash the tick, lay it in as light and even as possible, and catch it down as before. Thus prepared, they will be as good as new.
- If there is a loose tile in the hearth, stick it down with condensed milk or mustard.
- A child's sixpenny cricket bat, well padded, makes an excellent sleeve board for ironing.
- Save as many stones as you can from prunes, dates, plums etc they can be washed, well dried and wound with material to match frocks etc and used as novel buttons.
- Vests which have shrunk can be made into panties thereby saving three coupons.
- We must try to prolong the life of our shoes now that a woman has to give up five coupons and a man seven – put in trees as soon as taken off, give shoes a rest on alternate days.
- Our boys in the Services prefer machine made socks to hand knitted ones because of the way the stitches run as soon as the socks begin to wear, a good way to prevent this is to darn heels and toes on inside with some matching floss.

General Index

Index of Surnames (in text)